THE MULE MEN

A History of Stock Packing in the Sierra Nevada

LOUISE A. JACKSON

2004
Mountain Press Publishing Company
Missoula, Montana

Third Printing, April 2014

COVER PHOTO
"A string of mules on the high country trail."
—Crowley Family Collection

Maps by Tony Moore, Moore Creative Designs

Library of Congress Cataloging-in-Publication Data

Jackson, Louise a.
    The mule men : a history of stock packing in the Sierra Nevada /
Louise A. Jackson.
        p.   cm.
    Includes bibliographical references and index.
    ISBN 0-87842-499-7 (pbk.   :   alk. paper)
    1. Frontier and pioneer life—Sierra Nevada (Calif. and Nev.) 2. Shipment
of goods—Sierra Nevada (Calif. and Nev.)—History. 3. Outfitting
industry—Sierra Nevada (Calif. and Nev.)—History. 4. Sierra Nevada
(Calif. and Nev.)—Commerce—History.   I. Title.
    F868.S5J33 2004
    979.4'4—dc22
                                            2004013671

PRINTED IN THE UNITED STATES

MP Mountain Press
PUBLISHING COMPANY
P.O. Box 2399 • Missoula, MT 59806 • 406-728-1900
800-234-5308 • info@mtnpress.com
www.mountain-press.com

*To all the mule men and women who
dare to dream and persevere.*

High Sierra pack train, 1947. Sketch by packer Ed Thistlethwaite.
—Livermore Family Collection

We are packers three of the M.K.P.
The outfit to which we are bound.
In all the length of the Sierras,
Our betters cannot be found.
Be it lumber or tourists or powder or rock
We can handle it equally well.
With a diamond hitch on the son of a bitch
We'll pack it from here to hell.
When it comes to mules we're nobody's fools
For we savvy their various ways.
We pack them right and we cinch them tight
And hope to hell it stays.
And with horses, too, our skill comes through
For we love that animal bold.
And the well-deserved pride in the stock we ride
We never attempt to hold.
With the women folks we are no slow-pokes
For we're handsome and dark and tall.
We know it's real, that sex-appeal,
And not a trick at all.
But our morals, they shall forever be
The pride of the outfit's name.
We would gladly die for the M.K.P.
In the glory of her fame.
Then it's three times three for the M.K.P.,
The outfit to which we are bound.
To hell with the bosses and up with the three
That bring the trade around.
And we love to boast as we drink our toast
And fill up our cups once again,
That we are the three that accomplish the most
The "Young and Experienced Men."

—ED YEOMANS,
"Packers Three of the MKP," unpublished song, 1929
(Livermore Family Collection)

Contents

THE SIERRA NEVADA

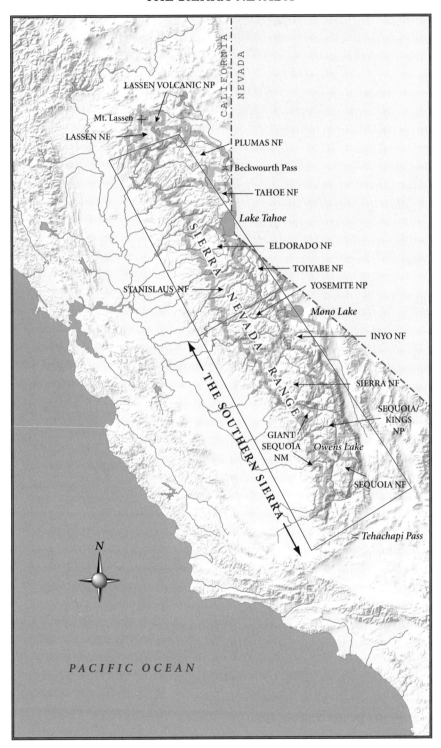

LASSEN VOLCANIC NP

Mt. Lassen

LASSEN NF

CALIFORNIA

NEVADA

PLUMAS NF

Beckwourth Pass

TAHOE NF

Lake Tahoe

SIERRA

ELDORADO NF

TOIYABE NF

STANISLAUS NF

YOSEMITE NP

Mono Lake

NEVADA

INYO NF

THE SOUTHERN SIERRA

RANGE

SIERRA NF

SEQUOIA/ KINGS NP

GIANT SEQUOIA NM

Owens Lake

SEQUOIA NF

Tehachapi Pass

N

PACIFIC OCEAN

THE SOUTHERN SIERRA NEVADA

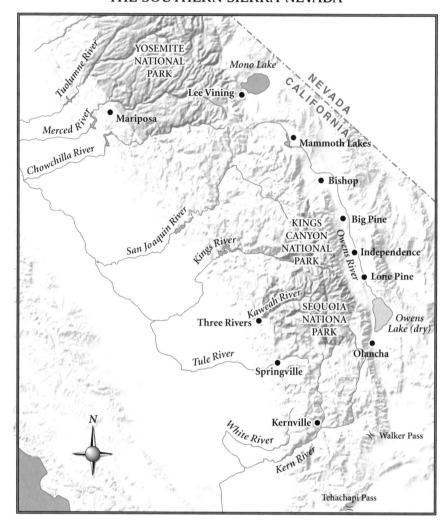

MAJOR HISTORIC STOCK TRAILS

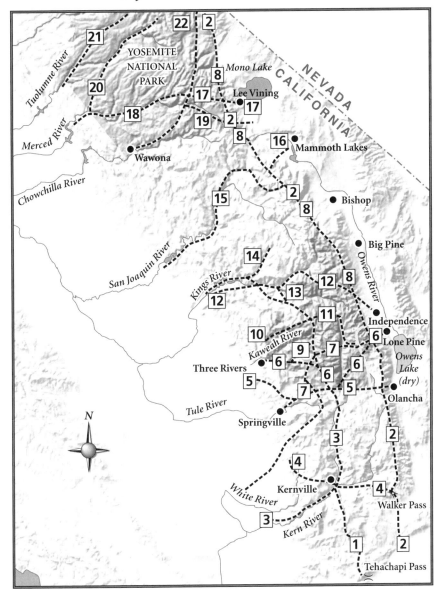

1 Tehachapi Pass: 1776 (prehistoric origins)
2 Pacific Crest: 1960s-1980s
3 Kern River: 1770s (prehistoric origins)
4 Walker Pass: 1834 (prehistoric origins)
5 Dennison/Jordan: 1861-1862 (prehistoric origins)
6 Hockett: 1862 (prehistoric origins)
7 Poison Meadows Cutoff: 1896
8 John Muir: 1915-1933
9 Farewell Gap: 1874 (prehistoric origins)
10 Giant Forest: 1870s (prehistoric origins)
11 High Sierra (Elizabeth Pass): 1928-1932

12 Kearsage Pass: 1860s (prehistoric origins)
13 Copper Creek: 1870s
14 Tehipite Valley: 1870s
15 Mono Creek Pass: 1860s (prehistoric origins)
16 Mammoth Crest: 1860s (prehistoric origins)
17 Mono Lake/Tioga Pass: 1874 (prehistoric origins)
18 Merced River: 1850s (prehistoric origins)
19 Mono Pass: 1850s (prehistoric origins)
20 Aspen Valley: 1870s
21 Tuolumne River: 1860s (prehistoric origins)
22 Virginia Canyon: 1860s (prehistoric origins)

MAJOR HISTORIC PACK STATION SITES

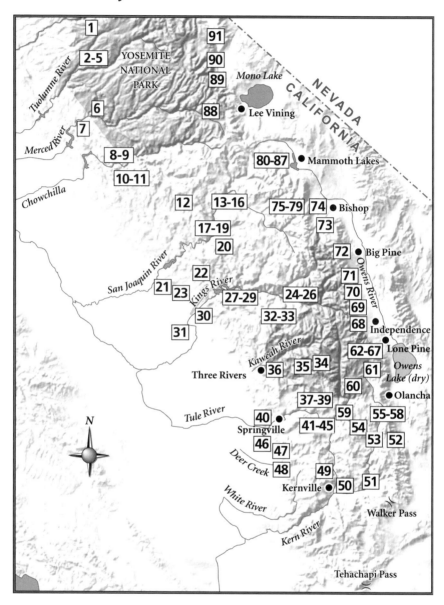

KEY TO MAJOR HISTORIC PACK STATION SITES

1 Hardin Lake	31 Dunlap	62 Cottonwood Lakes
2 Mather	32 Wolverton	63 Carroll Creek
3 White Wolf	33 Giant Forest	64 Lone Pine Canyon
4 Big Meadows	34 Mineral King	65 Whitney Portal
5 Aspen Valley	35 Silver City	66 Manzanar
6 Yosemite Valley	36 Three Rivers	67 Symmes Creek
7 Mariposa	37 Dillon's Mill (Dillonwood)	68 Onion Valley
8 Wawona	38 Mountain Home (Balch Park)	69 Oak Creek
9 Fish Camp	39 Camp Wishon	70 Aberdeem
10 Beasore Meadows	40 Springville	71 Taboose Creek
11 Bass Lake	41 Camp Nelson	72 Big Pine Creek
12 Jackass Meadows	42 Quaking Aspen	73 South Fork Bishop Cr.
13 Edison Lake	43 Road's End	74 North Fork Bishop Cr.
14 Mono Hot springs	44 Belleview	75 Pine Creek
15 Florence Lake	45 Fairview	76 Rock Creek
16 Blayney Meadows	46 Tule River	77 Hilton Lakes
17 Huntington Lake	47 California Hot springs	78 McGee Creek
18 Big Creek	48 Posey	79 Convict Lake
19 Shaver Lake	49 Greenhorn Pass (Summit)	80 Lake Mary (Mammoth Lakes)
20 Dinkey Creek	50 Kernville	81 Mammoth
21 Academy	51 Weldon	82 Red's Meadow
22 Coolidge Meadows	52 Little Lake	83 PUmice Flat (Devil's Postpile)
23 Balch Camp	53 Kennedy Meadows	84 Agnew Meadows
24 Crown Valley	54 Monache Meadows	85 Deadman Creek
25 Cedar Grive	55 Haiwee	86 Shawhawk (Minaret Summit)
26 Horse Corral Meadow	56 Sage Flat	87 June/Silver Lakes
27 Ten Mile Creek (Barton's)	57 The Oaks	88 Tuolomne Meadows
28 Hume Lake	58 Olancha	89 Virginia Lakes
29 Grant Grove	59 Jordan Hot Springs	90 Green Lakes
30 Thomas Mill (Millwood)	60 Tunnel Meadows	91 Twin Lakes
	61 Cottonwood Creek	

Preface

Stock packing was one of the most significant industries of early California. Without pack trains the exploration, settlement, and recreational development of our western lands would have been virtually impossible. Nevertheless, there has been very little written on the subject. Most writings on the Sierra Nevada give little to the importance of packing. Even less is heard from the packers themselves.

For the mule men, day-to-day chores and outdoor work are all-consuming, leaving little time for keeping diaries, taking pictures, or creating concrete records of the unique activities that fill their lives. "For most, life is a personal thing and their own affairs don't leave time to waste on memories of the past," pack operator Sam Lewis wrote toward the end of his life.*

With only a few small published histories, magazine articles, and personal memoirs to reference, putting this book together has involved gathering hundreds of letters, memorandums, government reports, and notes. In addition, and more important than any written sources, are the packers' oral histories. Personal interviews and storytelling sessions have provided the meat of this packing history.

The book basically covers only two hundred years, from the 1750s to the 1950s. The physical area is the southern Sierra Nevada, the backcountry containing most of California's wilderness and national park lands. From Yosemite to the Tehachapis, the Tuolumne River to the Kern, these lands above and beyond any major roadways are the wild areas where the majority of the modern Sierra packers have plied their trade.

_____

*Sam Lewis, unpublished memoirs, 1968, Eastern California Museum.

I have included annotated notes to cite references and expand information. A glossary of packing terminology is also included to help the general reader understand some of the packing industry's special lingo. The appendices list historic pack outfits and backcountry camps, to jog the memories of those who have packed in the past.

The story itself stands alone, written to preserve the unique flavor and identity of a way of life that is passing.

INTRODUCTION

OF MEN, MULES, AND MOUNTAINS

THE MEN

Descendants of the pioneer, the mountain man, the cowboy, and the teamster, High Sierra packers are a breed of their own. They are men and women who have chosen to forgo the comforts of civilization and embrace the simplicity of the wilderness. As modern purveyors of one of the most ancient of mankind's developments, the taming and usage of animals, they carry on a method of transportation that began over five thousand years ago.

Historically, most pack-outfit operators and their workers were nonconformists by nature, which sometimes put them at odds with the government agencies running the national parks and forests in which they worked. It wasn't easy satisfying everyone. Sustaining long hours of hard physical work in rough terrain, early packers dealt with danger, disaster, and recalcitrant animals, all while trying to adhere to government regulations and catering to city-bred clients, often for small or nonexistent profits.

Although their individual stories may differ, packers of the southern Sierra Nevada have had two traits in common: an unquenchable thirst for the high-country wilderness and a love for the business itself. The packing game, with all its difficulties, has always offered its practitioners a rich variety of daily experiences and enabled them to forge special friendships with customers, other packers, and the animals.

THE MULES

When man learned wild animals could be tamed, he stopped being his own pack animal. By 3000 B.C. it had been discovered that horses and asses could be bred to each other, thus creating man's favorite pack animal, the mule.

Usually sterile, the mule is the offspring of a male donkey and a female horse. Its smaller counterpart, the result of mating a male horse with a female donkey, is called a hinny.

A friendly pair. —Charles Morgan Collection

A mule resembles a horse in height, appetite, uniformity of coat, and the shape of its neck and rump, but it has the short, wide head, thick mane, long ears, thin legs, and small hoofs of a donkey.

Like their mothers, mules can be trained through voice command, can read and act on a rider's or packer's emotions, and have a good sense of direction, even at night. But, like their fathers, they will refuse to do anything that might hurt them or their loads. "He guards the load entrusted to him with intelligence and faithfulness," Oscar Lewis extolled in his memoirs, "being careful not to knock it against the trunks of trees, stooping low to let it pass under an overhanging limb, planting his feet firmly in dangerous places, eyeing the rocks that jut out over the trail round the mountain side, lest in an evil moment his pack striking one, he be thrown from the narrow path, and hurled into the abyss below. The moment the pack is loose or anything drops from it he stops."[1]

Mules are more patient, sure-footed, hardy, and long-lived than horses and they are considered less obstinate, faster, and more intelligent than donkeys. Wrote wrangler John Crowley, "There are good mules and bad mules, but no dumb mules that I have ever known."[2]

A mule always knows what he is going to land on before he steps. "If you overload them they will just lay down on you," wrote Yosemite area pack operator Johnny Jones. "You can push a horse across dangerous ground, but you have a time getting a mule to go where he shouldn't. They sense everything, a fracture, a bad place, a cave-in. They just won't go."[3]

Thoughtful consideration of dangers can make a mule fearful and obstinate, but it also makes them excellent bear detectors. While stopped at a campsite during his 1875 trip through the southern Sierra, John Muir noted that his mule, Brownie, was listening and looking around cautiously as if doubting the safety of the place. "All mules have the fear of bears before their eyes and are marvelously acute in detecting them, either by night or day," Muir wrote of the experience. "No dog can scent a bear farther and as long; therefore, as your mule rests quietly in a bear region, you need have no fears of their approach. But when bears do come into camp, mules tethered by rope too strong to break are not infrequently killed in trying to run away."[4]

Intelligent, individualistic, and often stubborn, mules have as much personality as the men who work with them. In his trip journals from 1930 through 1939, Ike Livermore always listed the names of the mules along with the names of the human members of each party. Barney, Tobe, Sam, Slim, Bogus, Tommy, and Baby were as important as any of the paying customers.

"It is true that mules are often slow, ornery, mean, lazy, dirty, noisy, bothersome, peripatetic and stubborn," Livermore wrote. "And yet they are comical, friendly, dependable, smart, uncomplaining, hard working, sure footed, easy keeping and long lived."[5] In short, mules possess all the traits that are perfect for pack-train travel in the mountains.

THE MOUNTAINS

The Sierra Nevada is a difficult mountain range to travel, especially in the south. It rises as a tilted, four-hundred-mile-long block of the earth's crust, unbroken by any river or valley across its forty- to eighty-mile width. Its high country is one of the most inaccessible areas in the United States. For 180 miles, deep canyons, rushing rivers, precipitous slopes, immense glacial cirques, granite outcroppings, and over five hundred peaks that rise twelve thousand to fourteen thousand feet above its base create an almost impassable barrier. Only four fully paved roads cross the range between Tehachapi and Sonora Passes, and all but the lowest, Walker Pass, are closed in winter. Above the snow line, most of the High Sierra region is uninhabited for over half the year and its wilderness trails are open to pack travel only four to five months a year.

The Sierra Nevada that we know today had its origins 600 million to 100 million years ago in the Pacific Ocean, where two giant slabs of the earth's crust met, with the Pacific Plate sinking under the North American Continental Plate and pushing up portions of the continent's margin. Metamorphosed ocean crust sediments that once filled large trenches along the coastline now lie exposed in the Sierra. Other rocks derive from volcanic magmas that changed with heat and pressure into various new forms, including gold-bearing quartz.

From around 220 million to 80 million years ago, massive amounts of the earth's crust melted into magma and erupted as volcanoes or solidified below the earth's surface. The trapped magmas became a huge expanse of granite that replaced most of the earlier rocks to become the Sierra's core. Since the formation of the granite, the entire Sierra Nevada region has experienced repeated episodes of uplift and erosion. The modern Sierra rose from gentle, folded coastal hills into a range that today stands as high as fourteen thousand feet above its origins and approximately 120 to 160 miles inland from the present California coastline.

The Sierra Nevada's massive bulk influences the entire state of California, including its weather, natural history, water distribution, and agriculture, commerce, and transportation patterns. It encompasses portions of two states, eighteen counties, nine national forests, three national parks, two national monuments, several state and county parks, and more than three million acres of wilderness that include as many as thirteen life zones: from foothill oak savannahs and tangled slopes of chaparral, rising up to dense fir, pine, cedar and giant sequoia forests, across glacially carved cirques, lake basins, and alpine tundras, to barren, windblown peaks.

The Sierra Nevada is a land of tremendous diversity. Over thirty-five hundred of its native species make up more than half of California's plants. Two hundred of those are rare species, and more than four hundred grow only in the Sierra. This diversity supports approximately four hundred species of mammals, birds, reptiles, and amphibians. Still, it is a quiet land, its wild creatures generally shy and hidden. Mammals

An early-season trip ascending Forester Pass, 1932. —Sequoia National Park Archives

7

most often seen are mule deer, coyotes, squirrels, chickarees, and an occasional bear, fox, bobcat, or cougar. A variety of smaller birds, jays, hawks, and crows are common, with rare sightings of eagles. Fish include the native golden trout and several planted varieties of trout. An assorted number of insects seem less shy to visitors than the animals.

The southern Sierra wilderness, where most commercial packers operate, is not an easy land for people to visit. The weather can be harsh, with heavy rains and snowfall on the western slopes and wild thunderstorms at all elevations. Streams and rivers can be unpredictable, trail crossings and bridges are often washed out, windfall and wildfires leave large areas inaccessible, and each year brings avalanche and rockslide damage. Even the topography is hazardous—every pass from west to east lies at high (over eleven thousand feet) elevation.

Despite the obstacles, the range's vast resources and diverse natural beauty have brought people into its wilderness. For the past two centuries, the exploration, mining, stock grazing, lumbering, hydroelectric development, and recreation of the Sierra Nevada have all been dependent on mule men willing to ply its rugged trails.

THE PACKING BUSINESS

CRISIS

Word arrived at three o'clock on a Sunday afternoon in July 1940. A thirty-five-year-old member of a Sierra Club High Trip had suffered a heart attack thirty-seven miles into the back-country wilderness. Ray Buckman, owner of the Mineral King pack station in Sequoia National Forest, cursed at the news. One man on the trip had already died, and Ray's partner, Ike Livermore, had left the party to pack the body out to Owens Valley. But this new victim of high altitude was still alive, and it fell to Ray to try to save him.

Within an hour Ray had sent his corral boss, Jack Alltucker, in a truck with a respirator and two oxygen tanks up the narrow, winding, twenty-five-mile road to the pack station. In the meantime, Ray dispatched one of his wranglers to round up a pair of the outfit's strongest mules while he prepared for an all-night ride.

Ray Buckman, Mineral King Pack Outfit. —Barbara Hansen Collection

Threat of high water on the trail down Rattlesnake Creek.
—Crowley Family Collection

But complications intervened. On meeting a car on a blind
curve, Alltucker ran his truck off the road. One lone manzani-
ta bush kept the vehicle from rolling down the steep canyon,
but there was no way to get the truck back on the road. Without hesitation, Jack and the other driver hauled the equipment up to the man's car, and within another hour it was
safely delivered to the station, where Ray was waiting with
the mules.

At 6:30 P.M., Ray and one of his wranglers left the pack
station with two of their best riding horses. They rode up
to the twelve-thousand-foot-high Franklin Pass, down the difficult Rattlesnake Creek Trail to the Kern River, then up to
Rock Creek. Normally the trip takes a good eighteen hours
in daylight, but that night Ray and his wrangler made it in
twelve, with one hour's rest for the stock. When they arrived
at the Sierra Club's camp, Ray had a long red scratch across
his forehead, marking where a tree limb had struck him in

the dark. But all his efforts had been for naught, for the next morning the man died, and Ray packed the body out.

Such was the life of a High Sierra packer in the nineteenth and twentieth centuries.

THE WORKERS

Adventure, danger, daring, and hardship were all part of owning a pack outfit. But far more basic was the day-to-day hard work and eternal handling of logistics. Most of an operator's time was spent organizing trips, hustling up business, hiring and overseeing workers, paying bills, dealing with regulations, and enduring hours of paperwork.

The owners of a pack outfit usually were its operators. Most often, in the early days especially, the owners not only managed the business and ran the pack station, but they led the trips, too. On large trips, however, one person could not do it all, so outfit owners hired wranglers to pack and care for the animals. The wrangler's duties required an astounding array of skills. They often acted as guides or cooks on wilderness trips and helped out around the station by feeding, shoeing, loading, handling, and doctoring the mules. Most important, they had to know how to survive in the backcountry and how to keep the customers happy.

Pay for the job was not high. Wranglers' wages in Yosemite around World War I varied from forty to seventy dollars per month, depending on duties. Some were paid by the day, ranging from one to three dollars. The extra responsibility of dealing with the food and kitchen equipment dictated that a cook be paid more than a general packer, usually a dollar a day extra. Tips and special jobs could add to the base pay. One packer in the 1930s earned five dollars a day extra carrying a one-year-old child in a gunnysack on his back.[6]

At the Mineral King pack station in the early 1940s, Ray Buckman paid wranglers one dollar a day plus room and board when they were at the station, but five dollars a day on the trail. On a trip, the cost of the packers' food was included in the fee the customer paid, and Buckman knew that the expense of feeding a growing boy could far exceed the extra wages.

During and after the two world wars, professional wranglers were difficult to find. Many outfits hired "stub" packers, boys and girls still in high school, and almost all depended on college students. If a large pack train had one or two seasoned packers, it was doing well. Many of the trail wrecks and problems with government agencies were the result of workers' inexperience.

A packer's life was not easy. Much of his work was hard physical labor. Besides training and packing the strong and often stubborn animals, he had to maneuver them through rough mountain terrain, make and break camp, and, back at headquarters, clean and repair corrals and other facilities. In the early days, packers also spent much time repairing trails and often worked with Park and Forest Service crews to open new ones. On such backcountry assignments, a wrangler might have to live for days on "poordo"—which was nothing more than potatoes, onions, and bacon boiled together—to sustain him in his grueling work.

A string of mules on the high country trail. —Crowley Family Collection

Perhaps harder than all the physical demands was being away from home. Occasionally a wrangler was assigned a week or more alone to tend grazing stock, and he might be out on backcountry trips for weeks or even months at a time. Earl McKee had to leave his sweetheart to pack out for almost three months. "I always thought they were trying to keep me away from this girl that I was going with. But I fooled them. I married her the next December and we're still here."[7]

In addition to their regular work, packers were sometimes called upon to help with firefighting in the national parks and forests. According to the terms of a packing permit, whole pack operations could be pressed into service supplying fire crews and even helping fight the fires. These assignments could mean losing customers, and government pay for the work was low. Still, it was one regulation the packers couldn't complain about. After all, without the forest, there would be no packing business.

EQUIPMENT

Packing equipment changed little through the years. The mainstay of packing in the 1800s was the Mexican aparejo packsaddle. Believed to be of Arabian origin, it dates back to the first employment of horses and mules as beasts of burden. It was introduced in Spain by the Moors in the eighth century and carried to America by the Spaniards in the early sixteenth century. The aparejo continued to be used through the 1930s to carry the heavy loads of large backcountry trips, which might include iron stoves, boats, tables, lumber, injured people, and even outhouses.

The aparejo had a stiff leather covering molded to the animal's back. It was made of two envelopes joined at the top, stuffed with grass or straw six inches thick to cushion the ribcage of the animal and evenly distribute the weight of the load across its back. A platform of boards was often placed on top to carry a heavy or bulky item. For lighter loads a sling hitch was used. The pack was secured with cinches around the animal's belly and rear, often using a strap called a britchen positioned under the tail to keep the load from shifting forward. Finally, a tarp was lashed down over the entire load.

PACK-MULE EQUIPMENT

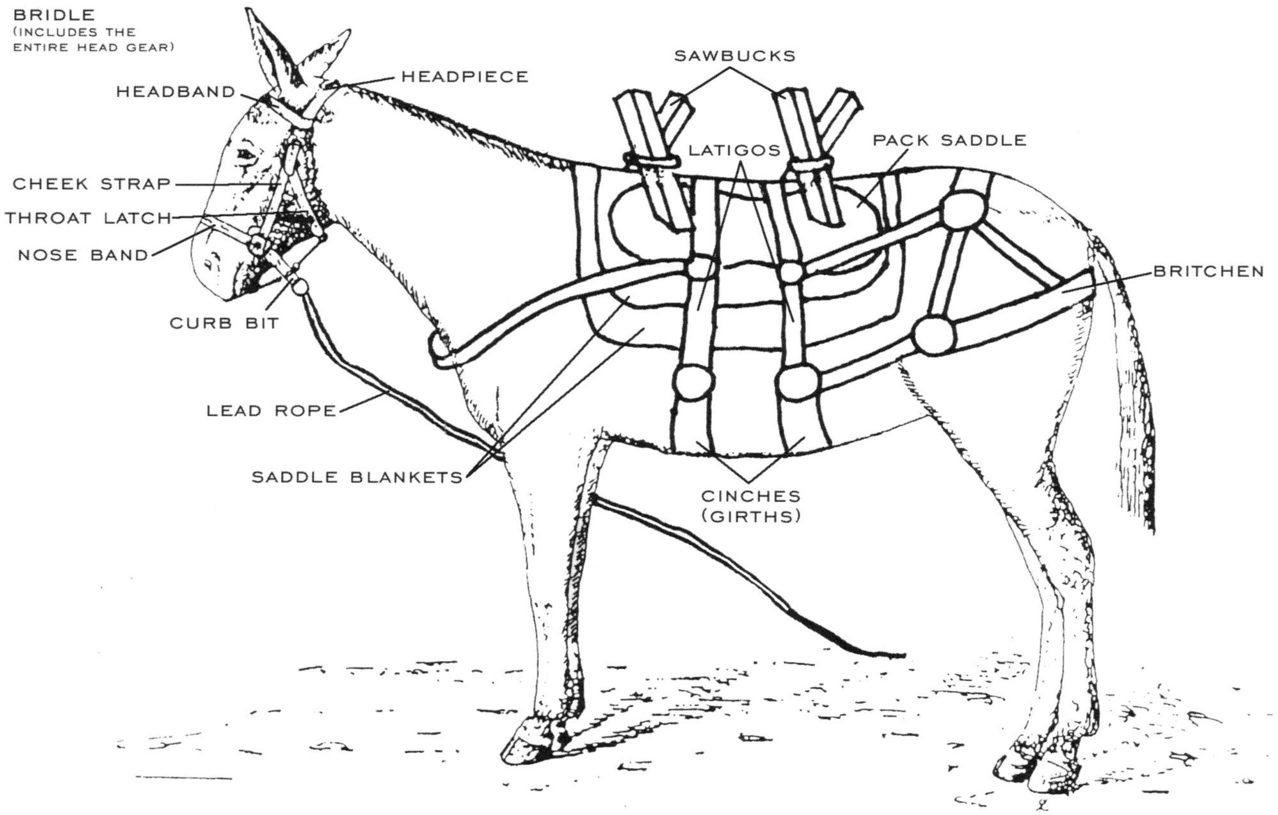

BRITCHEN

PACK SADDLE

SAWBUCKS

LATIGOS

CINCHES
(GIRTHS)

HEADPIECE

BRIDLE
(INCLUDES THE
ENTIRE HEAD GEAR)

HEADBAND

CHEEK STRAP

THROAT LATCH

NOSE BAND

CURB BIT

LEAD ROPE

SADDLE BLANKETS

While the aparejo is still used occasionally, it is outdated for nearly all packing purposes. Restrictions require lighter loads for pack animals, and helicopters can now be used for heavy loads and rescues. Lightweight sawbuck packs have become the norm on Sierra trails.[8]

The sawbuck is a wooden sawhorse frame set across the animal's back on a cushioned pad or blankets. Kyacks, stiff bags of heavy leather or leather-reinforced canvas with rigid box or frame interiors, are hung from each side of the sawbuck. Instead of kyacks, large metal or wooden boxes or leather-ends (frameless kyacks) are sometimes used. Simple slings often carry soft items such as duffel bags.

In the 1800s and early 1900s, bridles, saddles, and kyacks were often handmade. "We'd cut out our leather and rawhide string," Springville's Murat Brunnette recalled. "We used to

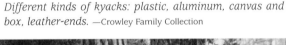

Different kinds of kyacks: plastic, aluminum, canvas and box, leather-ends. —Crowley Family Collection

RIDING-MULE EQUIPMENT

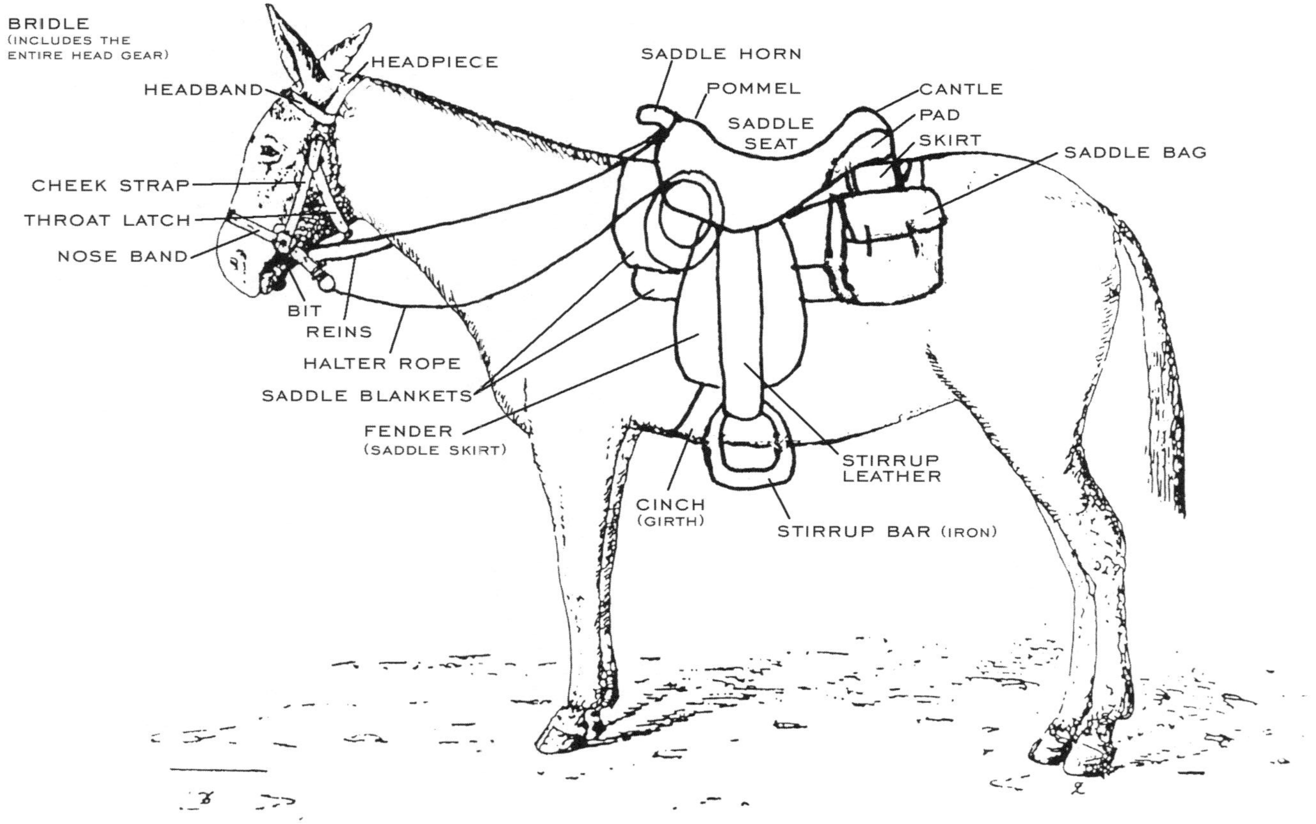

SADDLE BAG

CANTLE
PAD
SKIRT

SADDLE HORN

POMMEL

SADDLE SEAT

STIRRUP LEATHER

STIRRUP BAR (IRON)

CINCH (GIRTH)

HEADPIECE

BRIDLE
(INCLUDES THE ENTIRE HEAD GEAR)

HEADBAND

CHEEK STRAP

THROAT LATCH

NOSE BAND

BIT

REINS

HALTER ROPE

SADDLE BLANKETS

FENDER
(SADDLE SKIRT)

take those wooden boxes that they shipped the coal oil in and stretch cowhides over them. First, of course, we'd soak the cowhides in water. Those boxes were just the right size for a kiak. We'd lace the ends with rawhide string, and when we took the cowhide off the wooden box, it was real stiff. It made an ideal kiak."[9]

Special equipment had to be made to accommodate difficult items. Packsaddles were sometimes fitted with swivels to allow animals carrying long loads to make turns on the trail. Tandem rigs were connected with swiveling bars to hang heavy loads between two mules. To carry stacks of angle iron, steel posts, barbed wire, and other objects that might gouge the animal's ribs, special lipped kyacks were fashioned.

Most riding saddles were military or cowboy saddles with a horn, but sometimes customers required other kinds. There were tandem saddles designed to transport two children on one horse, and in the early days of packing, women rode sidesaddles. The sidesaddles often had a special horn and/or a special stirrup called a surcingle to give the rider greater stability on rough trails.

Caring for the equipment was an endless task. Tack had to be fitted to each animal; saddles repaired and oiled with tallow, bear grease, or other lubricants; canvas manties, saddle pads, and blankets sewn; and cinches, straps, pack bags, and slings repaired. In Yosemite, much of the equipment continued to be handmade well into the 1990s.

ANIMALS AND THEIR CARE

Good riding horses and pack mules were vital to meeting customers' needs. Packers always were looking for good western horses and mules that were sure-footed, steady, even-tempered, adaptable, quick learners, and good foragers. Ideal animals were of medium size, strong, and short-coupled, with wide foreheads and bright, steady eyes. Preferably they were low in the withers so that the saddle would not be apt to gall them. The best animals would follow without a lead rope and were not inclined to stray at night.

At the end of a season, when most new riding and pack animals were acquired, packers bought and traded stock and rounded up wild ones to fill out their remuda. If they were very lucky, they found new horses and mules that were already trail experienced. But most newly acquired animals had to be trained to tolerate being bridled, saddled, shod, and packed and to stay in line, to cross streams, to step over logs, and to walk on rocks. The operators who used wild stock, such as Barney Sears and Ed Sargent, had to break them every spring.

Handling mules took more than training—it required making friends with them and understanding that they would treat you as well or poorly as you treated them. Wranglers learned the mules' individual personalities and knew which ones were friends with one another and which ones were enemies. Some animals would fight for dominance, while others were content to be followers.

After a winter of low-elevation pasturage, all the stock needed to be conditioned and shod. The Yosemite stables employed a full-time blacksmith to forge "hot shoes" of exact specifications for each animal. However, most pack stations used "cold shoes," which wranglers formed with a sledge-hammer on an anvil without heating the metal. In a large outfit of a hundred or more animals, shoeing could take two or three weeks. After that, every four to six weeks the stock's hooves had to be trimmed and rasped (filed) and their shoes refitted.[10]

Shoeing mules and horses meant bending for hours at a forty-five-degree angle, holding up what seemed like a ton of animal bulk, enduring kicks and bites, nails in the thigh, and smashed fingers. "If I were the only blacksmith in the world I would charge fifty dollars for shoeing a horse," Steward Edward White wrote in 1906. "It is the most back-breaking, tiresome job I know of. We carried the malleable 'Goodenough' shoe which could be fashioned cold; but even with that advantage each animal seemed to develop enough feet to furnish out a centipede."[11]

In later years, outfitters also immunized their stock against tetanus, influenza, and equine herpes, and they wormed the animals as necesary. They also checked the teeth of older animals to see if they needed to be "floated," or filed down. There were occasional outbreaks of anthrax and distemper, and mules could even have heart attacks. Each packer had his own remedy for different conditions.

Feeding the animals was another big job, requiring knowledge and planning. Packers had to make sure the stock had adequate pasture in the summer and a supply of hay in the corrals during the winter. In the fall, after the season was over, the hard-worked mules and horses were let out to graze, usually on Forest Service land. The weather had to be watched carefully and the herd brought in before the first heavy snowfall. Throughout the years, a number of packers miscalculated and lost some of their stock.

During the grazing season, it was important to rotate the feeding areas to keep both the animals and the pastures healthy. As heavy usage began to deplete the grasses, packers were forced to keep their stock in the corrals for longer periods, which meant not only the expense of buying more hay and supplements, but also more frequent cleaning and more attention to health concerns arising from animals in close quarters.

In addition to caring for the animals themselves, packers maintained the corrals. They had to clean out the manure regularly, haul feed, and keep everything in good repair. At the beginning of each season, the water system was hooked up, winter damage to buildings repaired, and fencing rebuilt. Once the base camps were ready, the wranglers drove the pack stock back in from winter pastures in the lowlands. From Mariposa, Toll House, Auberry, Pinehurst, Three Rivers, Springville, the Kernville area, Olancha, Little Lake, and all along the Owens Valley, wranglers drove horses up the mountain roads and along foothill trails each spring. Dozens and sometimes over a hundred horses were driven by "point," "swing," and "drag" riders enacting the old western trail-drive scenario.[12] Some of the stock drives lasted into the 1980s.

Often the route passed by ranches and houses, and the stock would inevitably veer off the road to munch well-tended grass and flowers, much to the consternation of the owners. Automobiles were a problem, too. The wranglers would warn drivers to pull to the side of the road to let the stock go by. Most were very cooperative, but occasionally a driver would be impatient and spook the stock. One year, on the narrow Mineral King road, a driver insisted on driving through the herd. When the car crowded one of the mules, the animal kicked in the car's rear fender. The wranglers never learned whether the man's insurance policy covered that kind of damage.[13]

TRIP PREPARATION

Planning trips varied according to the type. There was the all-expense trip in which everything—saddle and pack animals, wranglers, guides, cook, food, and all equipment—was provided. On a long-term trip, the cook and riding stock remained with the party at a backcountry camp, while the pack stock returned to the pack station until needed. On a traveling all-expense trip, the stock and crew stayed with the customer, traveling from camp to camp.

For more experienced campers, there was the spot trip, in which the party was packed in with provisions and equipment and left to be picked up on a designated date. On a walking or burro trip, stock was rented to the customers with full care of the animals relegated to them.[14]

Getting enough animals for a large trip could be difficult. On some Sierra Club High Trips other outfitters, such as Pete and Henry Olivas, occasionally helped the Mount Whitney Pack Trains outfit. Injuries and sickness sometimes put animals out of commission, and replacements might have to be found on short notice. Packers also had to make certain each riding horse or mule was paired with a rider who could handle it, matching size and weight, temperament, and riding ability. To complicate matters, returning customers often requested a specific horse or mule they had become fond of.

Before any trip, supplies had to be carefully planned, stocked, and checked. Among the necessary items was a repair kit for emergency shoeing, including a rasp, a hammer, a nipper or puller, and nails. Also recommended were extra cinches and plenty of rope for tying, leading, and picketing stock, and for lashing packs. First-aid kits for both stock and people were essential. Both animals and humans were given aspirin for pain, fever, and inflammation. Alum prevented proud flesh from growing on a leg wound, and calomel was used for horse thrush and other infections. Horse liniment was included for sore muscles, and baby powder for minor saddle sores. Petroleum jelly salved minor scrapes and sores and was especially good for soothing patches where an

*Ray Buckman
working on a
packing logistics
chart.* —Barbara
Hansen Collection

animal's hair had been rubbed off. Tincture of iodine treated cuts and sore feet of both man and mule. Epsom salt was used to soak sore feet and puncture wounds. Also in the kits were suture gear and bandages.

Supplying the meals for trips took even more preparation. In 1903 George W. Stewart described the mess outfit, not including the food, carried by one "kitchen mule" for a party of six. Among the items on the list were a large coffee pot, three frying pans, two or three kettles, two water buckets, tin cups, dishes of assorted sizes, knives, forks, tablespoons, salt and pepper cans, a sugar cup, a milk pitcher, a syrup jug, two good butcher knives, a ladle, two large iron spoons, one long fork, a strainer, a can opener, a dish pan, two milk pans, a Dutch oven, a short shovel, an ax, a hatchet, a lantern and a package of matches, four bars of borax soap, five bars of Savon, two bars of sand soap, twenty-five cents' worth of candles, three asbestos mats, five hundred paper napkins, oiled paper, an oil tablecloth, and dish towels.[15]

Packing companies often included suggested commissary lists in their brochures. The Eastern Unit of the High Sierra Packers Association's "grub list" for a party of four for ten days included a myriad of canned goods, three pounds of sugar, five pounds of coffee, two boxes of Hershey bars, twelve loaves of bread, six pounds of sliced bacon, twenty pounds of potatoes, five pounds each of onions and cookies, and "fresh vegetables and meat as desired."[16]

Feeding the wranglers required even more food. On one trip, Allie Robinson provided sixteen packers for ten days with one hind quarter of beef, two hams, two sides of bacon, a case of eggs, ten pounds of canned butter, twelve bags of spaghetti, twenty pounds of dry beans, ten pounds of hard candy, twelve large cans of pork and beans, twenty-four cans of milk, and various other goods, including five cans each of sauerkraut and hominy.[17]

PACKING THE LOADS

Packing a mule was practically an art form—turning the clean side of a pack blanket to the mule's hide so the sweat wouldn't rub sores; making certain there were no folds or wrinkles under the pack; cinching the saddle without the mule blowing up its belly to keep it loose. The heaviest items needed to be on the inside and bottom, yet the packer tried to make sure the items next to the animal's hide were as soft as possible.

The mules were unloaded each evening and reloaded each morning. The packer had to ensure that the loads were balanced, that each dunnage bag weighed no more than twenty-five or thirty pounds, and that each kyack, pannier, or sling was under seventy pounds. Lifting heavy kyacks was a struggle, especially when the mule was tall or mean. Top packs of shovels, rakes, fishing rods, bedding, chairs, tables, stoves, large Dutch ovens, and other awkward items were kept under thirty-five pounds and loaded so as not to sit too high. Packers tried to keep the total load under 150 pounds for the average mule, and never over 175 pounds.

Oscar Burkhardt and Horace Elder packing a mule, circa 1910s.
—Rob Collection, Eastern California Museum

Weighing the load, Mineral King Pack Station. —Barbara Hansen Collection

Some items required special packing. Photographic plates of the early days were protected in strong wooden boxes. Survey gear was also delicate, and prized possessions needed careful treatment. The commissary load always took special handling, with each potato, tomato, apple, orange, and onion individually wrapped in newspaper to protect it from bruising. Cans and jars were wrapped in newspaper too, so they wouldn't rattle or break. Eggs were packed carefully in boxes of dry oatmeal or barley, or secured in double wrapping.

Once the animals were packed, lining up the string could also be tricky. The mules were placed nose to tail, and the spacing between them had to be just right—short enough so they wouldn't get tangled in the lead ropes yet long enough

Mineral King pack train heading out, ca. 1940s —Buckman Family Collection

to allow them to lower their heads to drink and graze. To keep them moving, the packer had to know how to dally the lead rope around his saddlehorn with just the right amount of tension.

Veteran wranglers also knew to take the animals' personalities into account when arranging their strings. The wrong mix could produce fights, distractions, balking, and competitions for position. Mules known to be recalcitrant were placed where the wrangler could reach them, so he could slap their rear ends when they balked.

ON THE TRAIL

The most demanding work began when the party hit the trail. Packers were expected to ensure the safety, health, and comfort of both humans and animals while traveling and camping in the backcountry. One of the first considerations was finding where to camp. Camping spots were chosen ahead of time whenever possible, but in new country where locations of good campsites were unknown, or when unexpected situations derailed plans, packers had to know how to find suitable spots on the trail.

The welfare of the stock came first. Campsites were chosen according to the amount of forage available, preferably about half an acre per animal. The animals required at least six to eight hours of free grazing, more in the sparse, short grasses at high altitude.[18] And the sites needed to be within ten to fifteen miles of each other, even closer on extremely rough trails, because going too far with a loaded mule was guaranteed to create cinch galls, sores, and back problems.

"One truth you must accept, believe as a tenet of your faith and act upon always. It is that your entire welfare depends on the condition of your horses," Steward Edward White advised in 1904. "Consequently you think last of your own comfort. In casting about for a place to spend the night, you look out for good feed. That assured, all else is of slight importance; you make the best of whatever camping facilities may happen to be attached."[19]

Nevertheless, on commercial trips, human comfort was also a serious consideration. Packers looked for level campsites with good water and firewood. A packer also knew to avoid

Fallen Moon Meadow, Kings Canyon National Park, 1940. A healthy meadow for grazing stock was an important consideration in choosing a campsite. —Sequoia National Park Archives

bogs and to camp above meadows, where there wouldn't be too many mosquitoes.

Choosing campsites was only one of the many challenges of packing in the backcountry. Traveling on the trail demanded astonishing knowledge and skill. Packers monitored each mule, ready to shift loads, tighten cinches, and sometimes wedge rocks under the packs to balance loads that had started to slip. If that didn't work, they had to repack the mule, preferably with the animal standing crosswise on a downhill slope. On a steep downgrade, the wrangler had to make sure the mules didn't try to knock off their forward-shifting loads on rocks or trees. To keep the animals comfortable, most packers stopped at streams to let them water and allowed them time for an occasional browse.

High Sierra trails needed to be watched constantly for hazards. The wrangler's true skills were tested in maneuvering around slick areas of wet rock or mounds of glassy granite; skirting sun-softened snowfields where the animals could break through; and struggling through ankle-twisting rocks, tree falls, protruding branches, and overgrown shrubs. At stream crossings, wranglers had to decide when it was safe to lead the stock across with a rope and when it was necessary take the packs off and carry the loads across. Savvy packers also knew to send only one animal at a time across a plank-covered bridge so the noise wouldn't panic the others.

Slowing down at these obstacles, the packer observed each mule as it made its way through. At any time, the packer might have to stop to doctor a mule that had been cut by a rock or limb, or to fit a new shoe by pounding it into shape on a trailside rock or on a miniature trail anvil. Occasionally the party had to stop to haul a fallen mule from a canyon.

The hazards could be just as threatening to humans. Quite a few people died in the backcountry. Some in river crossings, others in climbing accidents, even a few by lightning. Packers often were called off their trips to find lost campers, to participate in rescue parties, and to pack out the bodies of people killed.

Ailments were constant among both customers and wranglers. Sunburn, sore muscles, mosquito bites, yellow jacket stings, and saddle sores were the major complaints. Altitude sickness and intestinal problems were common, too. There were occasional bruises and broken bones from falling off horses or being kicked by angry mules. Packers also had to keep an eye out for poisonous plants, hornets, snakes, and other threats. Experienced mulers learned to read the animals' signals that told when danger lay ahead.

Weather, too, could cause discomfort and pose difficulties for humans and animals on the trail. Windstorms sometimes caused "widow-maker" branches to break and fall. In the spring after big thunderstorms, flash floods could wash out trails in minutes and make river crossings extremely dangerous. All packers had tales of losing stock in streams, of slippery bridges and driftwood jams they had to cross and of unexpected swims. In dry weather, when riding behind another pack string, packers could be engulfed in clouds of dust and have to cover their mouths and noses with kerchiefs and pull their hats low over their eyes. In storms, they sometimes had to find a clump of trees to take refuge under, or to rig a quick shelter out of pack canvases.

Fording a swift river. Broken Bar Pack Outfit, Mono Creek, circa 1930s. —Frasher Collection, Eastern California Museum

After a long day on the trail and having found a campsite, the packers' work was far from over. First they unpacked the animals and turned them loose for a roll in the dirt. Then they strung rope corrals or picket lines for loading the mules in the morning. Setting up camp included building a campfire, digging "biffies" (latrines), and helping the guests with their gear. Each packer also checked his string for burrs, sores, cuts, bruises, and damaged shoes. The stock was salted and fed the evening ration of grain, and a bell mare was hobbled near camp to encourage the mules not to stray during the night. Equipment was checked and mended, and leather items were hung off the ground to prevent them from being chewed by rodents. Often the wranglers worked until after dark, only then finding time to wash up.

In the morning the packers rose at least half an hour before sunup to check on the grazing stock. Going out in the bitter dawn, the wranglers sometimes found that some of

The dusty trail, Mammoth Lakes, California. In late season, the trail dirt often turns to powder. —Frasher Collection, Eastern California Museum

Mules unpacked at the end of a day and tied to a picket line, the Kern River camp, circa 1950. —Crowley Family Collection

the animals had "lit out for home" or wandered up a distant canyon. It could take hours to retrieve the stragglers and pack them, then try to catch up with the rest of the party. Meanwhile at the camp, the other packers had to fill in the biffies, shovel out manure around the camp, and burn the trash or gather it to carry out. Repacking the stock was done on dry ground, where the animals' pawing and trampling wouldn't destroy the vegetation.

Of prime importance on backcountry trips was food. Usually the cook was among the first to rise to start the fire and get coffee going. "You could hear that old hot-cake batter going 'put, put, put, put, put,' and that would wake people up," Earl McKee recalled. Food had to be stored carefully on trips to keep out rodents and insects. The McKee cook, Archie McDowell, slept in the "kitchen" at night to keep wild animals

Twenty-one Inch camp, Kern River. Tending the fire is just one job of the packers. —Crowley Family Collection

32

A mule packed for carrying out a deer carcass on a hunting trip. —Law Collection, Eastern California Museum

away.[20] The packers' own animals were known to rummage, but bears were the biggest threat, for a hungry bear could claw open cans, break jars, and rip open packages, ruining an entire trip.

In addition to the commissary, hunting was a mainstay source of food for long trips before the parks and forests restricted it. In the early days parties almost always carried a rifle, and hunting stories were a favorite campfire entertainment. Even more popular was trout fishing, which continues to be a main attraction for most packing parties in the backcountry. Often customers would arrive at the base camp with poles in hand, and the first night out they would rush to a nearby stream to catch a nice trout dinner. The next morning guests would be out fishing for breakfast while the wranglers were rounding up the stock. Leftover cold fish would be served for lunch, and perhaps there would be fish chowder for dinner.

By the end of a week, the fishing would slack off a bit and talk would turn to the best steak houses in San Francisco. By the time the party returned to headquarters, the customers were ready to go back to "civilized" eating. Then a new party would come in, limbering up their poles, and the next day the packers were back to eating fish. "After having four or five of these trips in a row during the summer, you really don't care to look trout in the eye again," packer Bruce Jackson remembered.[21]

Still, no matter how they felt, the packers played all the roles expected of them, for their jobs depended on it. To this day, successful packers are known for keeping their sense of humor while putting up with inevitable complaints, blame, and criticism. Sympathizing, reassuring, and answering interminable questions, they make sure the "pilgrims" feel confident that they have put themselves in good hands.

PART I

A HISTORY OF SIERRA PACKING

ONE

The Spanish in California

1769-1806

Throughout its human prehistory, North America had no mules, horses, asses, camels, elephants, llamas, nor any other large animal suited to taming and harnessing. According to historian Charles F. Lummis, "The Spanish introduction of the horse, mule, burro and ox to America marked the longest stride so many people, in so short a time, have ever taken in the arts of transportation."[22]

The mule arrived on this continent in 1519 with the Spanish explorer Hernando Cortez, and it played a key logistical role in the conquest of Mexico, providing the means to carry supplies and munitions to inland territories. After Cortez came Coronado, Rivera, Portola, Father Junipero Serra, and other Spanish explorers and missionaries, who also brought in pack animals on their North American land expeditions. In California, on the first land expedition from lower California to San Diego in 1769, diarist Juan Crespi listed the following as his company: Captain Fernando Rivera y Moncada, twenty-five "leather-jacket" soldiers, fifty-two mission Indian neophytes and servants, Father Crespi, a herd of two hundred cattle, and three muleteers.[23] By that time Baja California already had several Jesuit missions where horses, mules, and cattle had been introduced.

The continuing exploration of California and the development of new communities were almost totally dependent on the movements of pack trains. Where a pack train could not go easily, settlement was doubtful. "I have understood that Captain Don Juan Bautista de Anza has the plan and intention . . . to come out at San Francisco," a former mission priest wrote in January of 1775. "This, if they attempt it in the way stated . . . I fear that they may find themselves very badly disappointed . . . because of the many quagmires of the country which make it impossible to travel, particularly for pack trains as I have experienced."[24]

Despite the warning, the Anza colonization expedition proceeded with thirty families to San Francisco from a presidio at Orcasitos in Spanish New Mexico. The convoy of 240 people included twenty muleteers leading three pack trains. The 140 mules were loaded with provisions, munitions, and "equipments," which included gifts for any natives they might encounter. The expedition resulted in the settlement of secular communities at several new missions, as well as at San Francisco Bay.[25]

Probably the first domesticated pack animals in the area were those accompanying Father Francisco Garces in 1776.

The region of Francisco Garces's explorations. In 1776 Father Garces explored the Sierra foothills of central California. —Tulare County Library

Although Garces was not the first European to reach the southern Sierra Nevada foothills, he was the first to record his findings and to open a primitive trail for future pack trains.

In 1774 Garces set out from Tubac in what is now Arizona for southern California. The entrada consisted of thirty-four persons, including a score of volunteers, a Pima interpreter, and two servants; the group took 35 pack loads of provisions, 65 head of cattle, and 140 horses and acquired some "stacks-of-bones" mules along the way. After several mules and some horses died, Garces took the strongest horses and the ten best mules to the Spanish Mission San Gabriel in southern California.

A year later Garces accompanied Anza's San Francisco expedition as far as the Colorado River. There, he and another friar, Tomás Eisarc, remained "to try the temper of the natives for the catechism and vassalage of the King."[26] Eisarc stayed to perform the appointed duties, but Garces, ever a restless wanderer, decided to embark on what he considered to be a more important undertaking. He was determined to open a more direct route from the lower Spanish provinces to San Luis Obispo "or further upward, in order that thus might be facilitated the communication as the most excellent señor viceroy desires of the provinces of Sonora and Moqui with Monte-Rey."[27]

Taking a few pack animals, Garces set out with three Colorado River Indians and another Indian guide. The small group created a new trail across the Mojave River and desert to join Anza's established route to the San Gabriel Mission. On his arrival at the mission, Garces asked for mules, provisions, and an escort to help him explore the tulares of the central valley plains and to try find a shorter route to the Mission San Luis Obispo.

With a lesser outfit than he had hoped for, in April of 1776 Garces set out again to explore the interior of California. His party crossed the Tehachapi Range and headed east to the lower Kern River. His companions refused to go farther, so Garces went ahead by himself with just one mule. Finding whatever local Indian guides he could as he progressed northward, he followed native trails through the Sierra foothills as far north as White River.

Spanish military escorts for missionaries exploring the inland valleys utilized extensive pack trains. The largest of these expeditions was under the command of Ensign Gabriel Moraga. In 1806 he reached the southern Sierra foothills near Mariposa and continued across the Merced, Kings, and Kaweah Rivers to the Kern.

During these early Spanish and Mexican explorations of the late 1700s and early 1800s, pack trains were the most common means of long-distance transportation in California. Mulecraft was an honored art, muleteering a viable and respected profession. That tradition continued into the days of the American fur trade.

TWO

Early American Mulers

1827-1847

By 1832 trading trails had begun to crisscross the West, extending from the old Spanish missionary trails out of Mexico and the American Southwest to California. Along them wound the pack trains of trappers, explorers, traders, and emigrants. Before long, horses, mules, and donkeys were common couriers in the foothills and valleys of California.[28]

American mountain men were the first to take pack stock into the mountains. Young Jedediah Smith, in his 1827 trip through the eastern San Joaquin Valley, used a pack train while trapping all the lower southern Sierra streams for beaver and otter. He undoubtedly rode with what had become the trapper's standard equipage: "strong, gaunt horses . . . equipped with Spanish bits and rude Mexican saddles, to which wooden stirrups were attached, with a buffalo robe rolled up behind the saddle, a bundle of beaver traps slung at the pommel, rifles, knives, powder-horns and bullet pouches, flint and steel and a tin cup."[29]

Heading north in April with fur-laden pack animals, Smith's party tried to cross the Sierra, first up the Kings River, then over the American. Failing in their attempts, they retreated to the San Joaquin Valley. "I found the snow so deep on Mt. Joseph [the Sierra Nevada] that I could not cross my horses, five of which starved to death. I was compelled therefore to return to the valley which I had left," Smith wrote. "There, leaving my party, I started with two men, seven horses and two mules which I loaded with hay for the horses and provisions for ourselves, and started on the 20th of May."

Finally crossing over the Stanislaus River drainage, Smith and his trappers forced their way through the snow, "and succeeded in crossing in eight days, having lost only two horses and one mule." It was the first known stock crossing of the Sierra Nevada.[30]

It was seven more years before a pack train crossed the southern Sierra, far to the south of its crest. Joseph Reddeford Walker had struggled across the central Sierra from east to west in October of 1833, taking the worn remnants of his party's pack outfits through snows that trip diarist Zenas Leonard described in his journal as extending nearly halfway down the side of the mountain. On the return spring trip, with guidance from resident Californios and local Indians along the route, Walker led 52 men, 315 horses, 47 head of cattle, and 30 dogs from San Juan Batista into the Kern River Valley and over or near what is now called Walker Pass.

The primitive trails of these early forays brought in settlers. Soon small communities developed and supplies began to flow. Aparejo, or packsaddle, trains carried almost all the merchandise that inland California received. The inaccessibility of many of these settlements made stock packing a major industry.

As settlements spread through the coastal valleys of Alta California, the livestock that had accompanied them became feral and proliferated. In 1841 John Bidwell reported that the San Joaquin Valley had countless thousands of wild horses roaming through it.[31] In the 1843 *Emigrants' Guide to Oregon and California,* Lansford W. Hastings wrote, "So numerous are [the horses], that they have frequently been killed by thousands in order to preserve the vegetation for cattle, which are considered much the most valuable."[32] The first horses and mules to live in the Sierra Nevada came from that wild stock.

With the decline of the fur trade, trappers began to act as guides for emigrant parties and to deal in the horse and mule trade. Often they captured wild animals or even stole private stock to augment their income. In April 1840 Joseph Walker drove one hundred mares worth two dollars each and an unspecified number of mules worth twelve dollars each from California to Santa Fe.[33]

Pack outfits continued to cross the Sierra even as wagon trains gained a foothold. Mules traversed the increasing number of trails in conjunction with the wagon parties or as separate supply convoys. And sometimes wagon trains were forced to become pack trains. Such was the case with the Chiles-Walker party of 1843.

When the California-bound group was unable to procure supplies in Salt Lake City, they decided to split the party. Joe Chiles took twelve men with several pack animals to Sutter's Fort, hoping to resupply there quickly and reunite with the rest of the party. Guide Joseph Walker took the wagons, a few men, the women and children, and most of the food south to Walker Pass.

The Walker contingent waited for the Chiles party for ten days in the Humboldt Sink in what is now Nevada. Finally, with provisions running low and Chiles's company nowhere in sight, Walker decided to move on. By the time Walker's group reached the Owens Valley at the eastern base of the Sierra Nevada, it was November. Winter was approaching, their supplies were dwindling, and their energies were sapped. Walker directed the group to abandon their wagons and reorganize as a pack train.

The train crossed Walker Pass in early December and moved north through the San Joaquin Valley. When they finally found Chiles, they learned that by the time his group reached Sutter's Fort, early winter snows had blocked all possible central passes over the Sierra, preventing the rendezvous.

By the mid-1840s the American military was making its presence known on the roads and pack trails of California. The first American military expedition to enter California was led by Captain John C. Fremont of the United States Topographical Corps of Engineers. In December 1845 and January 1846, two separate components of his overland expedition arrived on California soil.

Ostensibly, Fremont's was a mapping and scientific expedition. However, believing they had a government sanction for unrestricted exploration, Fremont and his sixty armed adventurers, frontiersmen, and Indians wandered the roads and trails of California. For three months they defied the orders of the Mexican government to leave the province and became a driving force behind the American conquest of California.

Pack animals were crucial in this conquest. Both the Mexican and American armies depended totally on mule trains for their campaigns. The ability to acquire fresh mules and horses, as well as water and forage for them, was paramount in determining the route of a march. The Army of the West under General Stephen Watts Kearny amassed over four thousand mules in its campaign to conquer Mexican territories in New Mexico and California. On their desert journey, Kearny's troops survived by killing some of their mules for food.

With the end of hostilities in California, pack trains lost some of their importance. Supplies continued to be carried by mules from the end of wagon roads to outlying areas, but there were not many roadless settlements to service. As more emigrants arrived, more wagon roads were built for their convenience. The importance of pack trains would have continued to diminish but for a new event that propelled them to even greater importance—the discovery of gold.

THREE

Packers in Gold Country

1848–1870s

Without pack trains to supply mining camps, the California gold rush would have been nearly impossible. In 1848, the year gold was discovered at Sutter's Mill, there were few wagon roads or even trails over the Sierra Nevada passes, and even fewer into the gold-bearing canyons of its rivers. The ones that did exist were rough at best and often impassable for wagons during the winter. Thus gold seekers and those who supplied them depended on pack mules to get through.

Before 1846, almost all goods not locally produced were transported to California by ship. Dry goods from England and the United States made the long journey around South America's Cape Horn to ports in San Diego, Los Angeles, Monterey, and San Francisco, while most produce was imported from Hawaii.

The gold rush changed the entire transportation system of California. With foothill camps of hundreds of miners urgently needing food and supplies, the old Spanish carreta (cart) roadways, wagon traces, and rough trails were far too primitive to satisfy the demand. During the latter half of 1849, boats of every kind were pressed into service on the navigable portions of the Sacramento and San Joaquin Rivers. In the fall of 1849, three steamboats were disassembled on the East Coast and shipped to San Francisco to be reassembled and launched in September. In October, larger steamers were sent around Cape Horn to add to California's river trade.

The wharves of San Francisco became piled with goods for shipment to outlying areas. Most of the material was shipped by the river steamers to the largest inland commercial ports:

Yuba City and Sacramento City on the Sacramento River, Marysville on the Feather, and Stockton on the San Joaquin River to the south. From these ports, tents, mining equipment, boots, blankets, mail, flour, oranges, cheeses, vegetables, even marble for tombs and headstones were loaded onto wagons or pack trains for delivery. Mail from the eastern states arrived via the same shipping lines that carried goods and passengers. Sometimes, as California-bound emigrants began using overland trails, wagon trains carried mail. Mexican muleteers then delivered it to outlying camps.

All over California, roadways were widened and improved, bridges were built, and trails were upgraded to service the increasing traffic. However, roads could not be built to each new bonanza camp, and mules continued to be a common purveyance.

Historian J. S. Holliday tells of the pack train's importance in "getting the barrels of flour, kegs of pork and liquor, bags of beans, bales, sacks and boxes from the river ports up to the mining camps and towns. . . . In country too steep for wagons, long trains of pack mules followed trails that climbed high along narrow ridges and descended sharply to remote collections of miner' tents and shanties."[34]

Intrepid muleteers often won admiration among the miners. In the mining camp of Downieville, "The name of one [packer] has come down to us, celebrated then in song and story, Daniel Dancer of Downieville, whose pack trains threaded the canyons and the ridges of the North Yuba from Marysville to Downieville, . . . packing everything from a sack of flour to a grand piano over the perilous grades and fords without ever losing a single load."[35]

These trips could be treacherous, especially in bad weather. "Even sure footed mules, 'clipper ships of the mountains,' were often delayed by storms, mountain slides, or deep snowdrifts which made packing hazardous and sometimes impossible," Holliday notes.[36]

In winter, reported Felix Wierzbicki, an 1849 immigrant doctor, "the whole region becomes a mire—the soil is so loose and saturated with water."[37] The military learned quickly not to attempt land expeditions in the winter, for hauling with wagons became a near impossibility as "the ground was so soft that it was impossible to get them out, and they [the oxen or mules] had to be left to die or to be shot." Even the military headquarters at Monterey had to schedule its examination of the Indian territories before the commencement of the rainy season.[38]

Unlike wagons, pack trains could work all year long. Plodding through the sticky clays and soggy wet lands of the Sierra foothills, muleteers and their trains guided greenhorn miners to the goldfields and carried precious commodities to the mining camps—at highly inflated prices. As Holliday observes, "Great profits could be made in this trade, with packers charging as much as 75 cents per pound."[39]

At first, the larger, "nationwide" express companies of the 1850s didn't even try to penetrate the foothill mining regions. They stopped their services at offices set up in valley base towns such as Stockton, Sacramento, and Visalia. From there it was up to smaller express companies, often called "pack mule expresses," to carry mail, provisions, and supplies to the

Bald Mountain Mine on the White River. Most mining camps were far from main roads and were serviced by "pack mule express."
—Tulare County Library Archives

makeshift mining camps. It wasn't long before these smaller companies proliferated. The pack-mule express flourished for perhaps ten years after the discovery of gold.[40]

In the southern Sierra, transportation was slow to change. The Kern River, Greenhorn Mountain, and White River diggings had only primitive trails to service them in the early 1850s. Pack trains wound their way from the wagon-road trailheads into mining communities along both sides of the Sierra. Supplies to Petersburg on the Kern River were packed eighty miles from Visalia over the rocky Greenhorn or Bull Road Trails. A man named Thomas Heston shipped supplies up to the mines beyond Keyesville all the way from Stockton. It wasn't until 1864 that a true wagon road was completed across the southern Sierra—the McFarlane toll road over the Greenhorn Mountains.

In addition to their service delivering merchandise and mail, mules were important in transporting the gold seekers themselves—but only to cross the mountains. On the emigrant trails, oxen were the laboring animals of choice. There were several reasons for this, the cost of mules being one. In 1849 at Independence, Missouri, a yoke of oxen cost forty to fifty dollars while mules cost fifty to seventy dollars each.

However, the cheaper mules were wild. Often Mexicans were hired to break them, which wasn't easy. "A wild, unbroken mule is the most desperate animal," wrote emigrant Kimball Webster in 1849. "They kick, bite and strike with their forefeet, making it very dangerous to go about them."[41]

Emigrant Isaac J. Wistar described the process in his biography: "They were lassoed, thrown, harnessed, and dragged into place by sheer and simple force. . . . Each animal had a rope with a choking noose around his neck, at the other end of which was a mad and excited individual who walked, ran, jumped, fell, swore and was dragged."[42]

Though faster than oxen-pulled wagons, riding with a pack train was difficult. There was little room for mining equipment or household goods. If a man became sick or exhausted on the way, there was no way he could be carried. In addition, the renowned stubbornness of the mules, the tediousness of repacking them every day, their proclivity to straying, and Indian interest in stealing them were all factors against them.

But for thousands of Mexicans, there was no choice. The long trails across the southwestern deserts were little suited to wagon conveyance. With the rush from their own mining frontier of Sonora to the California goldfields, Mexicans led long caravans of pack mules into the valleys and foothills of the Sierra Nevada.

Upon arrival at the goldfields, many of these pack animals were turned out to graze and become wild again. Others were put to domestic use or were sold to entrepreneurs who took them back to Independence to resell. Some of the animals were rounded up by disaffected miners who figured they'd do better muleteering than grubbing in the ground for gold. Even with the threat of larcenous Indians and bandits, running a pack operation was a tempting alternative.

Indeed, these independent packers—often Mexicans—became the saviors of the mining camps. Before their arrival the costs of commodities were so exorbitant that few miners could afford to do much more than live off the meager provisions of the foothill lands. "Traders expect to make each a hundred percent profit upon the original price they paid," emigrant doctor Felix Wierzbicki warned miners in 1849. "In this way it happens that in the remotest points . . . [the miner] will have to pay three or even four hundred percent."[43]

But thanks to mules the Mexicans brought in from lower California and Sonora, "the price of a pack mule in some parts of the mining district a few months ago was about $500, whereas they can now be purchased for less than $150. . . . This [drop] has reduced the prices of provisions in the placers one and two hundred percent," California governor Bennet Riley reported in 1849.[44]

The greater competition ushered in the heyday of pack trains. Convoys of twenty to thirty mules were commonplace, with many consisting of fifty to sixty. Mexican mules were favored over American, as they had been raised and trained in mountainous country, whereas most American mules had been used only for pulling wagons for farming and construction.

Tougher and stronger than American mules, the Mexican stock worked well with little food and only one drink of water a day, even in the hottest weather. They could carry a person forty miles a day for ten or twelve consecutive days over a mountainous trail, and the steady regularity of their steps made them easier to ride than American mules. James Hutchings asserted in *California Magazine* in 1856, "The Mexican mule can travel farther and endure more without food than any other quadruped."[45]

Still, the mules were often overloaded. "There are many Mexicans here with pack mules . . . some of them with three hundred pounds on them," miner William Swain wrote in a letter from the goldfields.[46] Another observer in 1857 recalled, "In packing them for a trip to the mountains, the Mexicans load them unmercifully. . . . I have seen them, after going a little way, fall from exhaustion and the weight of their load."[47]

One mule that James Hutchings saw was forced to carry an iron safe weighing 352 pounds for thirty-eight miles over a rough mountain trail. It did so without accident, but after the load was taken off, the mule lay down and died. Another mule carried the main portion of a printing press to Yreka. The load "exceeded four hundred and thirty pounds. . . . On descending the Scott Mountain, this splendid animal slipped a little, when the pack over-balanced and threw him down the steep bank, killing him instantly."[48] Probably the heaviest load recorded was a six-hundred-pound millstone, transported from Shasta to Weaverville.

But these were extraordinary examples. Most muleteers were extremely careful with their animals, as the well-being of the stock was their livelihood. They fed them well, treated them gently, and loaded them appropriately. They watched them vigilantly on the mountainous trails, their loud "hippah" and "mulah" cries of encouragement ringing through the forest stillness.

"There is something very pleasing and picturesque in the sight of a large pack train of mules quietly descending a hill, as each one intelligently examines the trail and moves carefully, step by step on the steep and dangerous declivity, as though he suspected danger to himself or injury to the pack committed to his care," James Hutchings wrote.[49]

For the miners, "the arrival of a pack train is an event of some importance and men gather around it with as much apparent interest as though they expected to see some dear old friend stowed away somewhere among the packs."[50]

The protocol of operating a pack train was almost inviolate, the schedules of each day firmly set. On the trail around nine in the morning, the muleteer traveled until sunset, unpacked the cargo upon reaching a suitable campsite, then turned the mules loose to graze all night. He ate and slept beside the stack of goods for which he was responsible, no matter what the conditions. Rising early, he rounded up the stock, repacked them, and set off again.

"In the morning, when the train of loose mules is driven up to camp to receive their packs, each one walks carefully up to

Ten-stamp mill on the White River. All heavy machinery was carried by mule train to outlying mining camps. —Crowley Family Collection

his own aparajoe and blanket, which he evidently knows as well as does the packer," Hutchings observed.[51]

Some pack trains were led by a horse with a bell attached to its neck. A woman traveler in 1857 described one such train. "He is designated the bell-horse; and these mules have such affection for him that they will follow him anywhere he goes."[52]

Mule trains by the hundreds coursed the California foothills from 1848 through the 1850s. According to *Hutchings' California Magazine* in 1856, the Sierra and Plumas County pack outfits employed three hundred to four hundred men and used about twenty-five hundred mules. The quantity of freight packed on mules from the main supply town of Stockton to the central and southern counties of the Sierra Nevada was recorded at about two hundred tons weekly during the early gold-rush period.[53]

But the heyday wasn't to last. Roads and rails were built at a feverish pace, and by the mid-1860s only the most remote mining camps continued to depend on mule convoys. Still, the days of the packer were not over. Mule trains had their own role to play in the road- and rail-building explosions, supplying the survey and construction crews.

When gold was first discovered, the only roads and trails to the mines were circuitous routes around the highest portion of the mountains. In the 1850s, both federal and local governments initiated intensive survey operations to find more-direct routes. In 1855 the towns of Stockton and Murphys worked to extend the roads that serviced the Calaveras Big Trees. Murphys hired O. B. Powers to find a route over the Sierra crest to Carson Valley on the east side. The Powers survey explored the ridges and valleys between the Stanislaus and Mokelumne Rivers, resulting in the Big Trees route. This road was used heavily in 1856 and 1857, but its high altitude proved it to be impractical from early winter until late summer. It quickly fell into disuse and was finally abandoned.

In addition to government efforts, private interests invested in road development in the Sierra Nevada. The central and southern High Sierra areas, where wagon roads were considered impossible, were surveyed for packing trails. In the late 1850s, after gold and silver were discovered in the deserts east of the Sierra, entrepreneurs on the west side who wished to supply the isolated east side had only two trails to choose from. The Dennison Trail was a rough, winding affair that linked nearly every mining camp, stock range, and sheep camp south of the Kings River. Though far from perfect, it was preferred over the other trail, which was far to the south, up the lower Kern River and over Walker Pass. Then, in 1857, merchant Tom McGee, following an ancient Indian path, blazed the Mono Trail from Tuolumne Meadows, around the Kuna Crest, over Mono Pass, and down Bloody Canyon to the eastern desert.

Commercial companies also built toll roads from supply bases to the bigger mining communities. In the early 1860s two toll trails began construction in the wilderness area of the Kaweah and Tule Rivers. For four consecutive summers, pack trains carried supplies to crews building the Jordan and Hockett Trails. The Jordan Toll Trail, which extended almost one hundred miles, was built in 1861 and 1862. The Hockett Trail, completed in 1864, was one of many roads and trails built during the gold rush that were used by the military during the Civil War and throughout the western Indian campaigns.

During this period of road building, the search for potential routes for a railroad across the Sierra was also in full swing. Efforts concentrated mostly on the extreme northern and southern portions of the range, where the terrain and grades for a rail line were most practical. In 1853 Lt. Robert Stockton Williamson of the Corps of Topographical Engineers scouted the Walker Pass and Tehachapi Pass areas, but concluded they were impractical for a rail line. The following year, Williamson was to explore a possible route at or near the source of the Carson River, but before it began, a different route was chosen.[54]

The same year Williamson explored Walker Pass, John Ebbetts led a survey into the High Sierra region. The San Francisco–based Atlantic & Pacific Company recruited Ebbetts to look for possible wagon and railroad routes between San Francisco and southern Utah. Ebbetts was instructed to go toward the head of the Stanislaus River and return, if possible, by way of the headwaters of the Tuolumne.

With a string of mules, Ebbetts and his party started up the established Sonora route, a route so difficult that abandoned wagons and dead livestock marked the way. The party went over Emigrant Pass and down the east side of the Sierra to the West Walker River. Ten years later, a road was built over what became Ebbetts Pass. For years, it and the Carson and Sonora Passes were the only wagon routes over the Sierra Nevada to the central valley communities south of Sacramento City.

Amid the flurry of development, the territorial boundaries of California were still in question. In the days of Spanish and Mexican rule, almost all of California was considered a wilderness of vast plains, marshlands, and immense mountains. The Indians who lived in small villages along the major streams were the only inhabitants. Beyond the coastal mountains almost nothing had been surveyed.

A few immense Spanish land grants existed in the interior of California, but in the southern valleys, ownership boundaries were indefinite, thus easily breached and disputed. As more and more Americans arrived, they began to settle on the open, unoccupied land. Ruled completely by the Spanish, then the Mexican government, their property rights were always tenuous.

After the Mexican-American War, the U.S. acquisition of California gave rise to a need for confirmation of property lines. Surveyors were sent throughout the interior of California, riding with pack trains. When gold was discovered in 1848, Colonel R. B. Mason, the military governor of California, suggested that the gold region be laid off in numbered lots with marked boundaries. On June 22, 1849, W. M. Eddy was appointed a land surveyor in the district of San Joaquin, launching a concerted government effort to explore, map, and set boundaries in California.[55]

Seven surveys were conducted between 1852 and 1893 to determine the exact boundaries of the new state. In 1872 and 1873, A. W. Von Schmidt set the eastern boundary of California, considered official for twenty years until it was discovered to be inaccurate. Later, in the 1890s, the United States Coast and Geodetic Survey ran a detailed survey that placed the boundary between California and Nevada that we know today.[56]

In addition, in 1860 the legislature of California mandated a series of geological field surveys of the Sierra Nevada to map the area and catalog its resources. Professor Josiah Dwight Whitney, who had conducted several geological surveys in the eastern United States, was selected to head the project. Whitney's team conducted the field work for fourteen years, beginning in December 1860.

Few of the surveyors had experience traveling with pack trains, so for longer expeditions they hired hunters, cooks, and mule drivers. Perhaps typical of the parties that composed the early field trips was that of Whitney's first expedition out of Los Angeles in 1862. The company consisted of Whitney, botanist William H. Brewer, and assistants William Ashburner and Chester Averell. Accompanying them was Guirado, hired as a hunter, "a good fellow, just the one to ride a wild mule and to shoot our game, yet by far the least valuable of our crew." They also hired Mike, "a jolly young Irishman," as cook. And "last but by no means least, Pete [John Peter Gabriel], our jolly mule driver—a capital fellow in his line—young, game, posted as to mules, can tell a story, sing a song, shoot rabbits (and dress, cook and eat them)—a most valuable man."[57]

The field workers stayed in the lowland coastal ranges of California for the first two years, then in April 1863, the survey began explorations of the Sierra Nevada. Brewer and paleontologist William More Gabb rode horses on the two-month field trip along the southern foothills, from Fresno City south to the Kern River, over Walker Pass into the desert, then back over to the Kern and up the foothills to Hornitas, below Yosemite. Due to an extremely dry winter that provided little forage that year, they had no extra pack animals and carried only "a few most indispensable articles, such as blank books, paper, extra shirt and socks, packed in our saddlebags; a few instruments, a blanket and oilcloth rolled up and carried behind our saddles."[58]

In June 1863 Whitney, Brewer, and engineer Charles Hoffmann conducted an extensive survey of Yosemite Valley, Tuolumne Meadows, and the high regions around Mono Pass. They hired a man named John to accompany them with two pack mules for their provisions. In September, two young graduates of Yale, Clarence King and James T. Gardner, joined the survey, and wherever they went that year, John, the mule man, went with them. By the end of 1863, Brewer estimated he had traveled a total of 9,264 miles, 3,981 of them on muleback.

The next year another field party began extensive explorations of the highest portions of the Sierra. Those explorations, begun in May 1864, lasted into October. Brewer, Hoffmann, and Gardner made up the field team that explored the wilderness regions of the Kern, Kaweah, Kings, and San Joaquin headwaters. Dick Cotter, a miner, rancher, carpenter, and jack-of-all-trades, joined the surveyors as packer. Brewer called him "a very good fellow, but most unfortunately [he] knows nothing about packing, so we have to teach him and I think he will do well. Packing is an intricate art. To put a load of baggage on a mule and make it stay there, and at the same time not hurt the mule is a great art."[59]

Road, rail, and mapping surveys of the Sierra Nevada continued into the twentieth century, many of them sponsored by the military. During the Civil War, throughout the Indian Wars, and later in the administration of the newly created national parks, the army was compelled to build ever more, ever better trails and roads. Assisting in these endeavors were, inevitably, mulers and their teams.

FOUR

Mules and the Military

1850s-1914

In the late 1850s and early 1860s, the military used horse, mule, and even camel trains in their western Indian campaigns. Pack trains were also used in building and supplying camps and forts such as Fort Tejon in southern California, Fort Miller in central California, and Fort Independence in Owens Valley.

With the outbreak of the Civil War, military concerns dominated development in the West. As it had during the Mexican War and early Indian wars, the U.S. Army enlisted westerners—including mule packers—to help in the war effort.

In California, the Union needed a quick and direct route across the Sierra to protect its interests in the Coso mines and to facilitate the movement of troops and supplies between Camp Babbitt in Visalia and Fort Independence in Owens Valley. In 1863 a new trail was begun by John Hockett and Union soldiers were dispatched to help with its construction. For two summers weekly pack trains wound up the finished portions of the trail to supply the crews as the work progressed. Portions of the older Jordan Trail were incorporated into the route, so other trains had to use the more northern Mono Pass during the construction. The Hockett Toll Trail was completed in the summer of 1864 and remained the principal trail route across the southern Sierra for the next forty years.

Throughout the West after the Civil War, the army employed civilian pack trains equipped with aparejos rather than using wagon convoys on campaigns against transitory Indians. Their mobility and speed were proven to be so successful in operations against the Paiutes, Shoshones, and Bannocks that

General George Crook convinced the government it should purchase three of the trains he had used in the campaigns. Thus started the pack service of the United States Army.

Techniques developed by the U.S. War Department during these Indian campaigns became the standards for the entire packing industry. Most of the techniques were borrowed from the expertise of the Mexican arrieros, or packers. White bell horses or mules brought night-grazing stock back to camp each morning, where the practice of feeding the pack stock at their individual rigging sites during loading and unloading brought the animals unerringly to their own packs.

Wranglers were in charge of their own assigned pack animals, usually a group of five. They rode behind or beside their mules, loose-herding them, for the mules worked far more efficiently, more safely, and faster when they were not in a roped string.[60] Each wrangler made certain the aparejos were loaded correctly and would not rub sores or raise "body bunches," swollen, calloused flesh. If body bunches did form, the wrangler had to cut out the "steadfasts," bunches that had become so hard they looked like dried beef.

According to the *Army Manual of Pack Transportation*, the packer was required to clean each aparejo occasionally with castile soap and warm water and apply a little neat's-foot oil when the leather became hard and dry. He was expected to groom the animals in his care every day and to exercise them daily on layovers. Each mule was to be kept in such condition that it could carry a load of 250 pounds for twenty to twenty-five miles each day at a rate of four and a half to five miles per hour, without grain or hay. In rough and mountainous country, such as the Sierra Nevada, the travel distance was allowed to drop to between ten and fifteen miles a day.[61]

Working in pairs on travel days, the packers were expected to be ready to ride out in one hour and fifteen minutes. They were allowed twenty minutes for breaking camp and saddling the riding animals; fifteen minutes for breakfast; twenty minutes for putting the aparejos and all rigging on ten mules; and twenty minutes to load the cargo. A well-organized crew could be ready to march in under one hour.

On the trail, the wrangler was expected to know how to spot an animal with a sloppy or uneven pack or with any walking problem, to cut it out of the line without alarming the

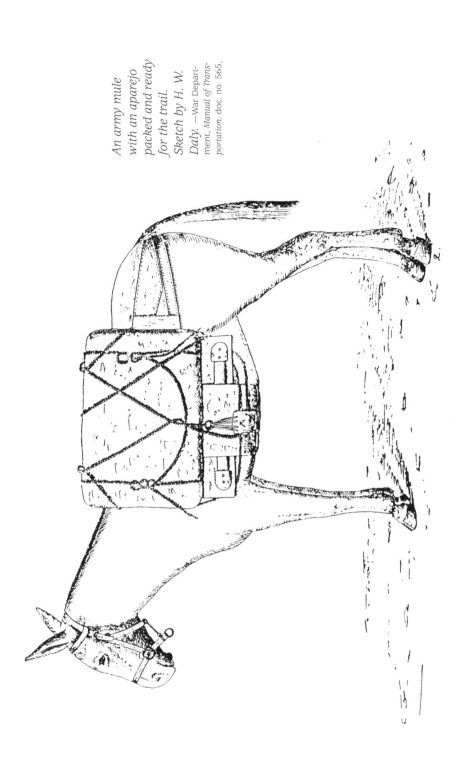

An army mule with an aparejo packed and ready for the trail. Sketch by H. W. Daly. —War Department, *Manual of Transportation.* doc. no. 565.

other stock, and to make whatever adjustments were necessary quickly so the animal would not become unmanageable in its urgency to get back into its place in the train. He had to watch carefully for the hand signals of the pack master at the head of the train so the entire outfit could obey orders instantly. A hand raised above the shoulders with fingers extended meant the gait was to be slackened. A raised hat was the signal to increase the gait. Waving the hat from side to side meant the pack master wanted the first two packers in the line to assist him. Waving a hat in a circular motion above his head required all packers but the one in the rear to come to his assistance. The extension of both arms sideways or leading the bell animal to one side of the trail brought the entire train to a halt.

Most military pack trains contained one bell horse, fourteen riding mules, and fifty pack mules. The company consisted of one pack master, in charge of the train; one cargador, in charge of the cargo; one cook; and one packer for every five animals. Regulations, chain of command, and protocol were strictly followed.

The chief packer was required to keep a daily memorandum book, noting the general descriptions of the country and climate, how the country was watered and grassed, and any incidents of interest. He also updated the roster of packers and animals and kept the train in readiness to move out at any time. Inspections to determine gear condition and stock health were routine.

The army packer was expected to know everything about packing: knot tying, herding, animal feeding and grooming, veterinary methods, and aparejo construction and repair. In addition, he was required to "be quick to note weaknesses in animals and conditions of the country that may endanger the life of the animal . . . be watchful that none may go astray . . . be kind in his treatment of animals . . . be prompt to obey all proper orders . . . always be ready for duty in all conditions of country and climate. . . be honest and honorable in all his dealings with his fellow men."[62]

Rules for a packer's conduct were also extensive. He could not tie mules in front of saloons or indulge in the use of intoxicants "to the prejudice of good order and discipline in the pack train."[63] He could not be absent from the train without permission from the pack master, be insubordinate, or read while on duty. In bivouac, he was never to use the saddle blankets for bedding or the aparejo as a seat.

The influx of government packing work in the Sierra began in the 1880s, serving military projects. One of the first, the 1881 Langley and Army Signal Corps scientific expedition to Mount Whitney, engaged a pack outfit to carry the group's astronomical instruments and supplies from Lone Pine to a base camp at Guitar Lake below the summit.

The expedition's pack train was delayed from the start, and the final climb up the Devil's Ladder boulder field to the summit had to be maneuvered on foot. Supplies included campfire wood "worth $140 a cord in that market; for it cost the troop $35 to get one-quarter of a cord to the summit."[64]

From 1891, with the creation of Yosemite, Sequoia, and General Grant National Parks, the army was appointed to manage the new parks in absence of adequate personnel and funding sources. Pack trains were the main mode of transportation in the parks, and cavalry deployments were some of the largest pack outfitters both inside and outside park boundaries.

With military packing needs increasing, local ranchers were often called upon to provide pack animals and act as guides. Other civilians with packing and backcountry experience also worked with the cavalry. Gabriel Sovulewski of Yosemite was one such important civilian. He had mustered out of the cavalry a few years earlier to become a pack instructor at San Francisco's presidio. In 1899, he was paid sixty dollars per month as packer and guide for military excursions out of Yosemite.[65]

The army's main job in protecting park resources was to rid the parks of illegal sheep and cattle herds that continued to graze the highlands. The soldiers found a few well-marked mule trails made by trains taking in supplies once a month to the herders. There were also "sheep walks," wide swaths of hoof-trampled terrain occasionally marked with piles of stones. More often, the cavalrymen ventured into areas where there were no trails of any kind.

"Officers with detachments set out on patrols that would keep them away from our base of supplies for thirty days at a time," Gabriel Sovulewski wrote. "Many times rations were short and sixteen to twenty hours of action per day covering sixty miles in the saddle was not unusual."[66]

In 1894 Lieutenant Nathaniel F. McClure led a seventeen-day backcountry assignment from Tuolumne Meadows into Virginia, Matterhorn, Kerrick, Return, and Jack Main's Canyons. With a detachment of twelve men and five pack mules and with rations for twelve days, they set out to scout for trespassing sheepherders reportedly in the area. Following the trails of sheepherder's pack trains, he and his men arrested four sheepherders and confiscated four pack mules.

In addition to expelling illegal stock grazers and poachers from High Sierra wilderness areas, the army also surveyed, mapped, and built roads and trails. In the late 1800s there were no official maps of the Sierra backcountry, only crude, inaccurate ones made by early explorers and local residents. Yosemite's first superintendent, Captain Abraham Epperson Wood, sent troopers into the Yosemite highlands on unimproved trails or traces to scout the uncharted areas and create their own maps.

Packing operations in the mountain wilderness were often difficult for the early military park superintendents and soldiers. The men relied on the well-established procedures of army protocol to provide a modicum of order and security. Even so, Captain Joseph H. Dorst, the first acting superintendent of Sequoia and General Grant National Parks, had no idea what a chore preparing a pack train would be. Sent to the mountains from the presidio of San Francisco, Dorst and his city-trained men had little experience in mule packing.

When the company arrived in Three Rivers in mid-May, the mountains were still clogged with snow, but Dorst soon learned that the weeks he would have to wait to begin backcountry patrols would not be wasted. Every bit of the spare time was necessary to get the command and the animals into working condition. Dorst described the process of preparing the mules in great detail:

> A number of mules, 20 in all, ten team mules and ten pack mules selected indiscriminately from team mules at the Presidio were turned over to me on the day I left. From these twenty mules I had to make up two teams, selected from mules that had never worked together. . . . Out of all of these team

Captain Joseph Dorst, first superintendent of Sequoia National Park. Military units guarded backcountry grazing ranges in the early years of the parks and forest reserves. —Sequoia National Park Archives

mules, unfitted by size, conformation and previous work, I had to make pack mules.

I also had to put together the aparejoes and fit them to the mules as well as pack saddles could be made to fit mules that were by nature adapted to other work. This was no small affair. There had to be a great deal of sewing of canvas and leather by the saddler, straight willow sticks of uniform size and length had to be cut and prepared to stiffen the sides of the aparejo like a frame work and grass of a certain kind without joints—so that it would not break—had to be found and cut to pad the sides of the aparejo with, after being cured so that the aparejo was padded like a hair mattress. Then the whole thing had to be soaked for a day and then girthed tight on the mule for another day so as to shape itself to fit him.

The mules had to be trained to carry packs to get the insides of the back hard and the skin tough so that the back would not get sore. The weights must be light at first and the journeys short so as not to tire nor chafe the mules. Some mules tried were found unsuitable and for some time frequent exchanges had to be made with those in the teams and the aparejos refitted and the mules rebroken.[67]

Cavalry units maintained control of summer operations in Yosemite, Sequoia, and General Grant National Parks until 1914, when the Department of Interior took over the management with civilian superintendents and employees. By that time, with the sheep and cattle grazing problems resolved, new trails could be constructed and maintained for easier recreational use. Soon recreation became the primary focus of the Sierra's national parks.

FIVE

The Birth of Recreational Outfitting

1870s–1890s

Even before there were good trails, the 1870s and 1880s saw growing recreational use of the High Sierras. Whole families escaping the summer heat and unhealthy conditions of the central valley headed into the highlands to camp at old mining and lumbering "resorts." From these bases they adventured farther into the backcountry on pack trains, usually using the stock of nearby ranchers. Riding parties explored the old sheep, cattle, mining, and Indian trails from Owens Valley communities on the east side; Kernville on the south; and Springville, Mountain Home, Dillon's Mill, Thomas Mill, Sweet's Mill, Atwell Mill, Mineral King, Converse Basin, and Tuolumne on the west side.

With the first ascents of Mount Langley and Mount Whitney in 1871 through 1873, mountaineering parties began to take packing expeditions across the Dennison, Jordan, and Hockett Trails, as well as other rough mule trails. Soon adventurers, hunters, fishermen, and nature enthusiasts also started packing into the alpine regions. For the first time, ranchers hired out their horses and mules and acted as guides for those recreationists. It was the beginning of the modern packing industry.

By 1868, on the west side, Frank Dusy was offering his professional services, packing and guiding parties into the Kings and Kaweah backcountry. On the east side, in the 1880s and 1890s, the Robinson and Olivas families had diversified their commercial mining operations to include summer pack trips into the Sierra. By the 1890s, Tim Carlin was leasing horses

*Independence pack train, 1871. The earliest pack trains origi-
nated from ranches or small towns where stock was available for
loan, rent, or purchase.* —Moor Collection, Eastern California Museum

and mules to the cavalry and to visitors who came to his cow
camp near Yosemite's old Tioga road.[68]

It wasn't just the backcountry that required pack animals.
Before 1874 the only way into Yosemite was by primitive
wagon roads that stopped miles short of the valley. In 1871
F. A. Brightman was guiding pack trains into the Yosemite
Valley from Tamarack Flat, and naturalist John Muir observed
wealthy Yosemite Valley tourists clinging to their mounts like
"overgrown toads."

Yet even Muir himself, an intrepid walker, used pack mules,
if reluctantly. In July 1875, with George Bayley, Charles Washburn, and "Buckskin Bill" as mule master, "all well mounted
on tough, obstinate mules," Muir explored the Kings and
Kaweah high country. Even when walking alone from Yosemite to the Tule River in August of that year, Muir took a pack
mule named Brownie. He wrote:

My mountaineering has heretofore been almost wholly accomplished on foot, carrying a minimum of every necessary, and lying down by any streamside whenever overtaken by weariness and night. But on this occasion I have been prevailed upon to take a tough, brown mule to carry a pair of blankets and saddlebags; and many a time while the little hybrid was wedged fast in the rocks, or was struggling out of sight in a wilderness of thorny bushes I have wished myself once more wholly free, notwithstanding the hungry days and cold nights that would follow.[69]

Few people dared to explore the high country without pack animals. "On account of the very considerable distance to be covered and the total absence of any kind of habitation or supply stations, a pack train is almost a necessity, though some times a most troublesome one," University of California geology professor and Sierra backcountry traveler Joseph N. Le Conte wrote in 1907. "Generally the best mountain raised mules or burros should be used. Saddle horses are, of course, useless and merely serve to increase trouble and anxiety." Le Conte noted that with all the impediments to pack train travel, "the jagged talus slopes that fill the bottoms of all the lower canyons, the wild torrents and precipitous divides," it was more practical to rely on knapsacks for higher districts, but almost no one heeded his advice.[70]

The first expedition to Mount Whitney that included women, the Porterville group of 1878, involved over two weeks of mule and horse packing from Dillon's Mill to Mount Whitney and back. In 1886 young Emma Crowley wrote to her newlywed husband in Los Angeles that she was going on an expedition from Mineral King to Mount Whitney with friends. "You see, we have it all set up," she exulted. "We are going to ride on men's saddles—ride just like men."[71]

In 1890 a ten-week "pedestrian tour" of the High Sierra by Hubert Dyer, Fred Pheby, Neil Lakenan, and Joseph N. Le Conte included three burros loaded with food, blankets, ammunition, extra clothing, and rolls of film for their camera. In those days, packing parties could depend on the hospitality of sheep and cattle camps during their backcountry forays. Herders often shared food, shelter, and information with travelers. Cook's Cow Camp on Whitney Creek was a favorite stop. Hubert Dyer described his layover at Cook's Camp on

The well-dressed lady on the trail, circa early 1900s. —Ramsay Collection, Eastern California Museum

the 1890 trip. "Cook . . . told us to help ourselves to everything at his camp. . . . Once there we hunted out his freshly killed beef, cut off some deliciously tender steaks and sallied into his impromptu cupboard where two pails of fresh milk awaited us. . . . When bed-time came he gave us many extra blankets and comfortable quilts so that we slept like lords."[72]

Dyer's group met several other packing parties that summer, and at Cook's camp they were told of "a party from Visalia now within 9 miles of us and on their way to Whitney. They had considerable trouble with their pack animals and were in some-what of a demoralized condition all around. Since returning home I received a letter from [Cook] telling me of three or four parties that had set out for Whitney but two of them upon coming to the Rocky slide had given up and turned back."[73]

Several professional packers were operating that year. On the east side, guided parties from Independence and Lone Pine traveled the Hockett Trail on fishing and hunting trips

Bert Johnson's cow camp, Whitney Meadows. Early-day packers often stayed at cow and sheep camps. —Charles Morgan Collection

Tourist pack train, Lone Pine, California, 1890s. —Eastern California Museum

and on excursions to Mount Whitney. On the west side, Dyer and his friends met packer John Fox in the Visalia Big Tree Grove, later renamed the General Grant Grove, who led them across sheep trails to his camp at Cedar Grove on the Kings River.[74]

A year later, John Muir wrote of "Mr. J. Fox, bear killer and guide, who owns a pack train and keeps a small store of provisions in the valley for the convenience of visitors." Muir and his party engaged him to "manage our packs" and lead them down the rough trail into Paradise Valley.

With the formation of Yosemite, Sequoia, and Grant Grove National Parks in 1890 and the forest reserves in 1893, commercial tourist packing became even more popular, but the trails and access roads still were a mess. When Captain James Parker took over as superintendent of Sequoia National Park in 1893, he reported that "owing to the neglect of the Government the Giant Forest is not nearly as accessible as formerly. The Government has allowed the wagon road, which formerly led to a point 9 miles from the forest, to go to ruin, so that now it is impossible to get with a wagon to a point nearer than 19 miles distant, the 10 miles of this road intervening being so washed out as to be scarcely passable of pack mules."[75]

Most of the trails still followed the ancient Indian pathways, which were becoming rough and washed out from stock use. Heavy usage by sheep herders had nearly obliterated some of the higher routes. No bridges had been built over the larger streams. On the Tunemah Trail, one pack train of thirty mules lost nine of them in the five-thousand-foot descent into Simpson Meadow, and the trail into Kings Canyon was also a vertical drop.

"Unless you stick to the beaten path, where freighters have lost so many mules they have finally decided to fix things up a bit, you are due for lots of trouble," Steward Edward White told his readers. "Bad places will become a nightmare with you and a topic of conversation with whomever you meet."[76]

Visitors to the national parks depended on commercial pack outfits to lead them through the undeveloped terrain of the high country. From 1891 to 1907, several private concessionaires maintained the roads and trails and provided backcountry pack trips throughout the Yosemite area. They were loosely supervised by a California state agency in the valley and by cavalry units in the federal park.

During this period, the Yosemite Stage & Turnpike Company, run by the Washburn brothers of Clark's Station (now Wawona); the great Sierra Stage Company, operating on the Tioga road; the Yosemite & Transportation Company; William Coffman and George Kenney; and ranchers such as Tim Carlin of Tioga, Tom Jones of Beasore Meadows, and others out of Madera and Merced provided horses and mule transportation into the valley and backcountry. Young Thomas Reid guided tourists into Yosemite Valley from Hodgdon's Ranch at the end of the foothill road. The bigger companies erected stables, barns, and way stations along the park's improved roads.

People continued to come. In 1894, during a period of warm weather, it was reported that more people visited Sequoia National Park than at any time previously. In Yosemite, most of the valley's trails and bridges had been upgraded by the 1880s, and new trails were being built. Tourism in Yosemite's state forest reserve was burgeoning, drawing thousands of visitors each year.

SIX

Growth of the Packing Industry

1890s–1910s

Beginning in the 1890s the creation of three new national parks and the forest reserve system generated a consistent source of income for packers. To encourage tourism in the parks, the government launched major trail-building and maintenance efforts, hiring local commercial packers to haul supplies to the workers. Construction and improvement of a network of trails across Sequoia National Park began in 1903.

"It is desired that main trails be straightened and widened and made trails, instead of rambling cow paths as at present," Captain L. C. Andrews, acting superintendent of Sequoia and General Grant National Parks, advised. "It is assumed that my successor will be able to ride main trails next season without being brushed from the saddle or traveling 5 miles unnecessarily in order to go 2 miles."[77]

In 1914, after the cavalry moved out, the parks were left with little stock of their own, which created the need for still more commercial packers. As the years passed, government packers replaced many commercial pack outfits on trail crews, but both the parks and the national forests still hired outside packers throughout the twentieth century.

The three main types of government projects that packers supported in the early 1900s were fire suppression, trail construction and maintenance, and bridge construction, as well as miscellaneous work such as the construction and supplying of ranger stations and railroads. Trail-building crews usually consisted of fifteen to twenty-four men, with twenty-five to thirty mule-loads of camp gear and tools. They spent most of the summer season in one camp, working out in different directions. A construction-crew packer was required to haul large amounts of dynamite for blasting, gasoline for saws and jackhammers, full-size anvils for shoeing, large rocks for building, and dirt for major fills.

Crews responsible for maintenance, in contrast, were fairly small and moved often. A maintenance crew usually consisted of six to eight men, including a foreman, a cook, workers, and a packer. The packer would move camp for the crew every two to three weeks, depending on the number and condition of the trails to be repaired in an area. These moves entailed ten or more mule-loads and often required two days to accomplish. Sometimes the pack animals were used to help with the maintenance work by moving rocks, hauling dirt, and shuttling tools and equipment.

Maintenance work started early in the season. First, "log" or "saw" crews went to the receding snow line to cut away deadfall from the winter. A two- or three-man crew of packer and sawyers might need five mules or more, the lead "saw mule" carrying all the tools and equipment and the rest loaded with food and gear. After a big winter, log crews might require a packer all summer long, working uptrail as the snow melted, usually staying at each campsite only for a week or two, then moving on.

Bridge crews were deployed after the high waters of spring snowmelt subsided, during mid- to late summer. Pack loads for bridge crews could include cables, safety ropes, come-alongs, block-and-tackles, tree-climbing equipment, torches, iron or wooden beams, stringers and railings, decking, and tools, in addition to feed for the work animals and provisions for the crew. One or two packers would stay with the sawyers, helping with the hauling and any other work needing the strength of horses or mules.

All the trail crews required comfortable camps throughout the wilderness summer. Wood stoves, screened meat safes, copper boilers, large metal "river boxes" to be set in a stream for refrigeration, tents, and sometimes even showers were hauled in. Fresh meat, fruit, milk, eggs, and vegetables, plus a resupply of canned goods and mail delivery were guaranteed each week.

Packing decking for trail bridges, 1928. By the 1940s such decking was packed on the side rather than upright. —Yosemite Research Library

Other government projects of the period also brought business to the growing number of packers. The United States Geodetic Survey continued to send out surveying parties to create topographical maps of the High Sierra region. These expeditions spent whole summers in the backcountry and depended on mule packing for supplies. In 1890 a pack outfit carried nineteen thousand pounds of supplies to the barren base of Mount Conness for a geologic survey and mapping expedition.

Assisting the effort to create access to Mount Conness, packers also supplied the crews who came in to open the old Tioga road, build a bridge across Yosemite Creek, push through the snow to Tuolumne Meadows, dig out the trail to

Young Lakes, and build a new trail that included stone steps to the top of the peak. Packers then hauled building materials to the mountain, where the survey workers built eleven tent structures with milled-wood framing, an observatory, and three cement pillars to support instruments for triangulation. Muleteers brought firewood to the camp all summer long from the Conness Creek basin.

In addition to working directly on park development projects, packers reaped the benefits of the growth in tourism resulting from that development. One of the first operations to take advantage of the new opportunities was Broder & Hopping. In 1898 homesteader John Broder began a commercial packing operation out of Three Rivers when an attorney from San Francisco hired him to guide a party into the Giant Forest area. Realizing a profit from the venture, Broder decided to go into the business full-time. By the next year, he had gone into partnership with Ralph Hopping, opening Broder & Hopping in Giant Forest.

Meanwhile, in 1899, the Park Service received its first appropriation of money for development of the southern parks. Soon the area had so many visitors that Broder & Hopping ran a triweekly stage line from Visalia to the Kaweah Post Office at Three Rivers. The following year they expanded their operations to eighty-five head of pack and saddle animals, upgrading from three tents to ten and adding a cookhouse, along with new equipment and more employees. They called the new facility Camp Sierra.

Unfortunately, the partners shortly discovered that they had expanded too quickly, and before long they couldn't even pay wages. They took in Jim Griffin as a partner in payment for back wages, but the business never got out of debt. After Broder died, the entire outfit was sold at a sheriff's sale in 1908.

Other packing companies fared better. In the late 1890s, John Nelson and Carmel Wilson opened a commercial pack station at the Jim Aiken ranch, near Springville, to pack tourists and supplies into Camp Nelson. The station's facilities included corrals, a pasture for their own pack animals and those of visitors, and a place to park buggies and wagons. When the Tule River road was extended to Camp Nelson in 1922, Wilson and Charlie Smith, Nelson's son-in-law, moved to Nelson's resort.

In 1901 Charles Robinson expanded his Owens Valley mining pack train to include tourist packing, taking several parties over Kearsarge Pass into the backcountry. When Robinson's son Allie took over the operation, he directed even more resources into the growing tourist trade. The Robinsons handled all the Sierra Club High Trips from 1912 until World War II.

Throughout the 1910s, more packing businesses sprang up. Art Griswold, Frank Negus, "Little George" Dillon, and Otis Lawson operated outfits from their ranches in the Tule River area, and Owen Rutherford opened a station at Quaking Aspen. In 1914 Malvin Duncan and Jim McDonald started running trips from Camp Wishon. Wally Rutherford also headquartered there, with a Mr. Kirkpatrick taking over his business in 1918.

On the east side, the Olivas family packed supplies and guests into Lewis Camp on the Kern River for several years beginning in 1912. They hauled cables for a new bridge and wire for phone lines. They also continued packing for the Forest Service, carrying in all the equipment for the rangers who spent their summers in the backcountry.

The Inyo Sierra Guides & Packing Company's extensive brochure boasted, "With fifty head of stout, mountain-raised horses and mules, new equipment and comfortable saddles, we are prepared to take you to any part of the Sierras." Looking forward to increased tourist business with the completion of the railroad from Mojave into the Owens Valley, the outfit offered the services of ten experienced guides, packers, hunters, and trappers, including E. H. Ober, "the foremost authority on fish and game in the Sierras," and Joe Drouillard of Big Pine, "the most successful trapper of the Eastern Sierras."[78]

In Yosemite, the state gave a concession to Coffman & Kenney in 1886 to run a livery operation, which included stock rentals for tourists. By 1906 the cavalry had its own stables and barns in Yosemite Valley, but Coffman & Kenney continued to provide packing and riding services for tourists. Later they became part of the Yosemite National Park Company. The company's consolidation with Curry Camping Company in 1925 created the Yosemite Park & Curry Company. It was the main packing company for tourists in Yosemite Park. By 1932 National Park Service director Stephen Mather had consolidated several small Yosemite concessionaires into the Yosemite Park & Curry Company, and it became the sole packing concession authorized to work in Yosemite.[79]

The government also led its own parties. In 1915 Stephen T. Mather was appointed assistant to the secretary of the interior, who was in charge of the national park system. To create public awareness of the parks, he arranged a trip through Sequoia National Park to Mount Whitney that included government officials, politicians, and journalists.

The Mather Mountain Party was a pack train to outdo all others. Robert Marshall, chief geographer of the United States Geological Survey, made the arrangements for the trip. He wrote to Mather, "Groceries are bought, mules being shod, their tails roached and ginger injected into them, fishing poles tested and fishing permits secured; Dr. Simmons is packing his emergency kit; the beef are being fattened; the lamb stuffed; the trout starved; the buck located and the firewood piled."[80]

Seventeen guests plus cooks and packers made the trip from Giant Forest to Mount Whitney and Owens Valley. Frank Ewing, a park ranger acting as chief packer for the trip, led the party of thirty men and fifty horses and mules. The packs included such items as white linen tablecloths, napkins, silverware, china, newfangled air mattresses, and sleeping bags.

Not all packing parties were large ones in the early 1900s. Many were simply burro-assisted walking trips. Typical was the excursion of teachers Walter Smith and Archie Loomis of Exeter, California. "With two rented burros we outfitted ourselves for a month of mountaineering and struck out from Three Rivers early in August 1913," Smith wrote in an account of the trip. "We were tenderfoots but eager and we walked from Three Rivers . . . to the top of Mt. Whitney. Then back. . . . We were not so tenderfooted when we returned."[81]

Even on riding trips, poor trails and awkward loads often impelled guide and customers to walk for safety and to save the strength of the animals. The going was slow. Packing equipment and personal effects were bulky and heavy in the early 1900s. Blankets, hemp ropes, canvas tarpaulins, hunting knives, firearms, ammunition, wool sweaters, long fishing rods, portable horseshoeing outfits, medicine kits, dishes, and other items all took up a great deal of space and

Ranger-led Kings Canyon stock trip, 1926. Historically, rangers have been a part of many pack trips. —Sequoia National Park Archives

were deadweight on the animal. "Through the high country two miles an hour is a fair average rate of speed, so you can readily calculate that fifteen make a pretty long day," Steward Edward White cautioned in 1904. "You will be afoot a good share of the time."[82]

In addition to tourists and the Park Service, water and power companies needed the services of pack outfits, too. Several of them began to exploit the southern Sierra in the 1890s. As early as 1886 the Mount Whitney Power Company and the San Joaquin Electric Company employed pack trains to support their explorations of the backcountry in search of hydroelectric plant and reservoir sites. When the first power plants

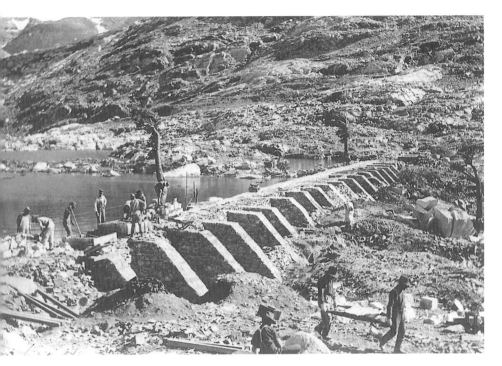

Mount Whitney Power Company dam under construction at Franklin Lake, Mineral King, California, 1904. Thousands of pounds of cement, sand, rock, wood forms, and construction supplies were hauled by mules to early-1900s power company dam projects. —Crowley Family Collection

were built on the Kaweah in 1886, the Kern in 1897, the Tule in 1909, and the Kings River in 1919, mule trains hauled supplies to the construction sites. On the Kaweah River, dams were built at Wolverton Creek and Monarch, Crystal, Franklin, and Eagle Lakes in the summers of 1904 and 1905.

"The thing that I remember about that dam building was the myriad of stock there was up there," the son of construction supervisor A. J. Robertson recalled. "There was horses and mules all over the place, because they had to carry all those aggregates by mules into those dams. The cement, the sand, the rock and everything was carried in there by the mules."[83]

In 1908 and 1909, on the east side of the Sierra, the massive Owens Valley aqueduct created significant packing jobs. The Los Angeles Department of Water and Power hired packers to haul supplies and equipment to crews working on the project. Later they provided similar services at the city's planned reservoir sites in Horseshoe Meadows and at Second Lake.

Preceding work on large dam, reservoir, tunnel, and power-station projects, expeditions went into the backcountry to survey the sites. Pack trains hauled surveyors' supplies up Big Creek, Stevenson Creek, the middle and south forks of the San Joaquin, and all their smaller tributaries. Surveys of the stream sheds were an ongoing process, especially in the water-rich drainages of the San Joaquin River. There, from 1894 through the 1930s, large pack trains supported survey crews and their backcountry camps in Blayney, Jackass, and Granite Meadows. On one well-traveled route, leading to a summer survey camp in Blayney Meadows, the workers made Mono Hot Springs a favorite stopover on the hot, dusty trail. By 1918 it had become so popular that the Forest Service installed a large concrete tub with a crude shelter by the main spring.

The packers' work supplying these crews could bring in money all summer long and sometimes almost into winter. In 1918 packer Dave Qualls took the last survey group of that year out of the backcountry in November, during a raging snowstorm. By the time the train reached Kaiser Pass, at 9,305 feet elevation, the snow was reported to be up to the animals' bellies and the riders had to raise their feet in the stirrups to clear it.

Aside from all these jobs, packers took other work where they found it. Carmen Olivas packed salt and wine for sheepherders and cattle grazers, as well as bags of compressed snow from Lone Pine Canyon for summer refrigeration in the towns of the Owens Valley. He also transported equipment for rangers in Sequoia and General Grant National Parks. Later, he hauled materials for the east side trail being built to Mount Whitney from the Owens Valley. In Yosemite, from 1905 to 1907, mule trains carried the materials and moved dirt for the building and grading of the roadbed of the Yosemite Valley Railroad.

One of the most unusual jobs was undertaken in 1909. Six years earlier, a military reservation for scientific and weather observations had been established on the summit of Mount Whitney. After the citizens of Lone Pine completed a pack trail to the summit in 1904, the Smithsonian Institution made plans for a stone shelter and three-room observatory, and in 1908 a packing contract was awarded to Charles W. Robinson of Independence.

The job entailed repairing the original trail, then hauling materials, personnel, and supplies to the top of what was then the highest mountain in the United States. Materials included steel, cement, glass, sheet metal, and wood; among the supplies were fuel, tools, camping items, and provisions. In all, the load was estimated at twenty thousand pounds.

Mount Whitney pack train on the summit, circa 1920. The original trails from both the west and east sides were built in 1881 and 1904 to facilitate stock travel. Stock is no longer allowed on Mount Whitney trails. —Harvey Collection, Eastern California Museum

Payment was five cents per pound on delivery, plus $1.50 per day for each saddle animal and three and a half cents per pound for firewood.

The twenty-two barrels of rapid-setting cement had to be specially packed for the mule trip, and the scientific instruments required extra wrappings and special packing, too. One instrument, a house-fly vane radiometer, capable of measuring a candle's heat at ten thousand miles, was taken up the trail "cradled in someone's arms like a newborn baby."[84]

All the materials had to be sorted and labeled, then packed to protect them from the weather. Each item was scheduled to be shipped only when ready for use. "It was reported that time after time just as a pack train arrived the workmen were ready to use the material they carried."[85]

On the last day of construction, fireworks and a huge bonfire were lit so that the people in Lone Pine could plainly see the celebration. Once the shelter was completed, other scientific studies followed: a study of the spectrum of Mars in 1909; continued studies of solar radiation; a Swedish study of atmospheric radiation in 1913; and weather observations by the U.S. Weather Bureau. These in turn led to other scientific expeditions in the surrounding area, all serviced by pack trains.

FISH STOCKING

As recreational fishing became more and more popular, the stocking of fish in the southern Sierra's barren streams and lakes became another job of packers in the late 1800s and early 1900s. Early efforts by individuals carrying a few fish fry in jugs and coffee cans gave way to commercial pack animals rented for the job. Officials at both Yosemite and Sequoia National Parks actively promoted fish planting to encourage recreationists.

In August 1873, on one of the first commercial fish-stocking ventures in the southern Sierra Nevada, A. B. Kitchen took a pack train to the South Fork Kings River, from where he carried two hundred fish fifty-eight miles over the Sierra summit to be planted in Big Pine Creek. Eighty of the fish survived the trip. Kitchen was paid one dollar for each fish.

In 1902 Anna Mills Johnston reported that her 1878 Mount Whitney climbing expedition met two fishermen at Kern Lakes who supplied Owens Valley with fresh fish. In 1881 J.W.A. Wright wrote of a fishing enterprise at Fish (Kern) Lake in which Dick Runkel, who had a summer ranch upstream, employed several men who caught hundreds of trout with hook and line. The fish were kept alive in fish pens in Kern Lake, and every two weeks up to three hundred pounds of them were packed the forty miles to Lone Pine, where they were sold at fifty cents per pound.[86]

Many of the early fish plantings, however, were initiated by settlers in sheep and cattle camps to provide variety in their own high-country diets. In the Yosemite area, cattlemen Lewis and Eugene Elwell stocked streams in the late 1880s and 1890s.

According to George W. Stewart of Visalia, the first planting in the mountains involved two men carrying rainbow trout in cans on pack animals from the Big Kern and Little Kern Rivers to the streams and lakes on the western slope of the mountains. The plantings were done at the Kaweah River headwaters around 1880, during a mining rush at Mineral King, when hundreds of miners were hungry for fresh delicacies. More plantings quickly followed.[87]

In 1897 Andrew D. Ferguson, rancher and oil man, was appointed Fresno County game warden, and he made the stocking of the Sierra streams his major project. On a salary of sixty dollars a month and twenty-five dollars traveling expenses, he supplied the Sierra high country with fish for four years. Using his own ranch horses, Ferguson spent an average of one thousand dollars a year beyond his pay to stock the mountain waters. Planting many of the streams of the San Joaquin River drainage, he worked south into the Kings River and Tehipite Valley. There, he carried adult rainbow trout by mule train into Crown Creek and small lakes in the area.

Not only were individuals hired to do the planting, but the Sierra Club also joined the endeavor. On the 1908 Kern River outing, members planted golden trout in several lakes and streams, and Kern River trout in Moraine Lake. The experiment was so successful that in 1912 the outing committee reported that "the trout planted by the club in 1908 have

Packing for a fish-planting trip, circa 1910. At center is Walter Fry, Sequoia National Park superintendent.
—Lindley Eddy, Sequoia National Park Archives

grown to very large size and the fishing will be superior to any we have enjoyed."[88]

Fish that Sierra Club members planted in Bench Lake in 1910 were reported in 1913 to have grown to two to three pounds. In 1912 the club stocked various streams with golden and rainbow trout while one member led a pack animal with cans full of fish to the head of the Kern-Kaweah. For several years most fish plantings were performed by private individuals and clubs, but with the creation of a fish commission, the state supplied thousands of small fish for planting.[89]

By 1909 the Fish Commission of California had organized its Fresno Division, and Andy Ferguson was hired to be the assistant in charge of the agency. With the help of former forest ranger Sam Ellis, who had his own "splendidly equipped" pack train, the men stocked thousands of fish from Tuolumne to Kern County using a thirty-mule pack train, the mules handpicked by Ellis. "It is the most pretentious work of pack-horse distribution of fishes ever undertaken anywhere," Ferguson wrote in 1914. "No canyons are too deep for us to penetrate in search of stock fish, and no mountains too high for us to cross when we must reach the headwaters of some important stream."[90]

Ellis discovered that "the golden trout were more tender and would not endure the hardships that the common rainbow could, nor would they carry the same number of hours on a pack animal."[91] The reason, the men learned, was that rainbow trout could hold themselves clear of the sides of the can for about eight hours, while golden trout could last only six hours. After that time, they tired and were injured or killed by bruising from the cans. Loch Leven trout lasted one or two hours longer than rainbows.

Around 1909 cattleman Alfred Hengst and his nephew, Bill, took two pack animals with two five-gallon cans each to Little Whitney Meadows and collected about one hundred one- to one-and-a-half-inch golden trout. Hauling them to Granite Creek, they depended on the motion of the mules to keep the water fresh. "Our theory was that the jolting movement of the animals would keep the water sloshing in the cans well enough to keep plenty of oxygen moving through the water," Hengst said. Whenever the pack train stopped, somebody led the mules around to keep the water aerated.[92]

Upon reaching a stream or lake, the planters simply dumped the five-gallon cans of fry into the water. The fish had an estimated fifty percent survival rate. This basic method was used by the Forest Service, the Fish Commission, and eventually the California Fish and Game Department, until trucks and airplanes replaced mules.

The relationships among packers, rangers, and game wardens were generally friendly. On fish planting trips, the planning, work, and care of the fish were shared by all. This spirit of cooperation would continue even through the hard times following World War I.

The stocking of fish dispersed several species throughout the Sierra and provided a major source of food on backcountry trips, which appealed to a growing population of recreational wilderness users. For the packers, the fishing business created a "double benefit," providing not only income but also opportunities to share a major interest of almost all back-country users. And, not least of all, it created hundreds of campfire fish stories.

SEVEN

Early Sierra Club Outings

1902-1920s

The founding of the Sierra Club in 1892 created a new form of recreation for hundreds of California city dwellers. Between 1902 and 1946, the club's annual High Trips brought commercial stock packing its biggest impetus to date. The Sierra Club's second expedition, in 1902, was the largest backcountry trip into the southern Sierra yet undertaken.

On the 1902 trip, over two hundred Sierra Club members were packed into a two-week base camp in the Kings River Canyon. After the main expedition, Sierra Club president John Muir took a group of twelve on to the Kern Canyon through the Giant Forest and Mineral King. The organizer of the outing was William E. Colby, who created the High Trips to entice Sierra Club members into the backcountry, hoping that the experience would help them better understand the need for wilderness preservation. Colby planned and led most of the early trips.

The packers for this outing were from Kanawyer's Resort at Millwood, and Broder & Hopping in Giant Forest. The participants rode by stagecoach part of the way, then traversed the intervening wilderness area over primitive trails either on foot or horseback. The logistics were nearly overwhelming. In 1902 Poly Kanawyer was almost bankrupted paying for the extra animals he'd bought to handle that year's twenty-five thousand pounds of food, camp equipment, and dunnage.

The Sierra Club handled members' requests for riding horses for its first two outings, but in 1903 the club relieved itself of the responsibility. "The experience of the [Outing] Committee in the past with regard to furnishing saddle ani-

John Muir in the Giant Forest, Sequoia National Park, 1902. Photo by George David Smith.
—Tulare County Library Archives

mals has been very unsatisfactory and the expense, trouble and annoyance connected there with have caused them to take this stand. The pack-train and the accommodation of walkers is the first and main consideration."[93]

For the 1903 Sierra Club trip to Mount Whitney, the Broder & Hopping outfit provided a pack train of eighty-five mules and saddle animals. Many of the participants rode, and thirty thousand pounds of personal baggage, provisions, and camp equipment were packed. The cost for each participant was five dollars for the five-week trip.

What was advertised as an easy trip of ten miles or fewer a day became a nightmare in logistics for the packers. In their month-long preparations, Broder & Hopping had not anticipated the number and difficulty of tasks: securing enough stock and packers, procuring and keeping track of supplies and equipment, grooming the trails, helping to construct the

Kanawyer's camp and store, Copper Canyon, South Fork Kings River, circa 1900s. The Kanawyers provided stock for pack trips. Years later, the Sierra Club used the camp. The site now is owned by Kings Canyon National Park. —Sequoia National Park Archives

base camp—Camp Olney on Lewis Creek—and even helping to build a temporary footbridge across the Kern for the hikers.

Once begun, the trip itself was fraught with problems. First, participants trickled into Mineral King all afternoon and into the evening, and the baggage wagons were delayed until almost nightfall. When the party started up the trail the next morning, June 27, snow still blocked the 10,587-foot pass at Farewell Gap. One member, Reverend J. C. McLean, reported:

> By 9 o'clock the snow had softened, making the footing very insecure. One of the animals, overcome by exhaustion and the effects of the altitude, fell dead in his tracks. Once or twice unwary riders were thrown headlong from their plunging horses and had to be extricated from the snow-banks . . . . Occasionally some floundering mule loosened from his pack

a dunnage-bag. . . . Then one or two packers would slide after it down the steep, snowy slope, berating the situation with a volubility that would have amazed a steamboat captain.[94]

It took from dawn to past midday to get all 110 people and sixty packed mules over the four-and-a-half-mile trail to Farewell Gap, after several Broder & Hopping wranglers "paved" the route on their way to build camp at the junction of Coyote Creek and the Little Kern. But the packers could not make it over the gap before dark. "We anchored a line in the snow, unpacked the mules and tied them up close," packer Ord Loverin recalled. "We didn't have down sleeping bags, just blankets and tarps and we like to froze sleepin' out that night."[95]

The next morning the half-frozen men slid the packs on ropes down the south side of the gap, then forced the reluctant mules after them. The steep climb up the new trail to Coyote Pass found many of the hikers struggling, and one woman's horse slid off the trail. The party also encountered rattlesnakes.

When the second contingent arrived at Camp Olney, the packing party's population swelled to over two hundred, and keeping track of everything became almost impossible. Bedrolls were lost. The cooks began to complain of food shortages, and Sierra Club members were obliged to supply hundreds of fish to satisfy the campers. One evening the catch was over six hundred golden trout.[96] Despite all the problems, the packers led two parties up Volcano (Golden Trout) Creek toward the base of Mount Whitney, and by July 12, 103 people stood atop the highest mountain in the continental United States.

The return trip down the new Wallace Creek Trail was somewhat easier, and the now-seasoned group experienced few unpleasant incidents on their way back to Mineral King. "The Club's third [outing] was so very far from perfect that perhaps Mr. Colby's determination not to 'quit on a failure' saved it from being the last," Marion Parsons reflected many years later.[97]

As the years passed, the Sierra Club expeditions continued to encounter difficulties. In years of high water, some animals were swept downriver at stream crossings. Snow often caused loaded pack animals to slide off the trail, step into air pockets surrounding hidden rocks, or fall through snow bridges covering under-the-snow rivulets. The first crossings of each year were especially hazardous. Rockfalls, washouts, destroyed bridges, tangled undergrowth, and downed timber often blocked the way. Sometimes the mules had to be unpacked before crossing steep snowfields, avalanche-furrowed slopes, or flooding rivers. In 1908 a young woman fell from a precipice in the Big Arroyo, and her body had to be packed out of the canyon.

Part of the packer's job was to make the trails passable. After the 1902 trip, when a group heading for Mount Brewer lost two horses on the hazardous Bubb's Creek Trail out of Kings Canyon, packers and rangers cooperated in brushing out the trails just ahead of the Sierra Club group. Some trails could not be made safe, however. In 1906 the High Trip un-

Breaking trail in the spring, circa 1920. Snowy early-season trips can entail numerous hazards, yet pack trains went into the backcountry as early as possible each year to accommodate the eagerness of customers and to enhance the packers' small profits. —Ramsay Collection, Eastern California Museum

sucessfully attempted to take mules over Glen Pass into Rae Lakes, and for several years afterward only knapsack excursions were allowed into the basin.

Starting with the Sierra Club's 1912 Kern River outing, the club, the Forest Service, and the boards of trade of Visalia, Lindsay, Exeter, and Tulare hired men to travel a day or two in advance of packing parties. The main trails were in the best condition they had been in for years.

After safety, the most important concern of commercial packers on the High Trips was to keep the participants comfortable and happy. The commissary for these large parties was immense. The Sierra Club hired its own cook and kitchen crew for each outing, and there was no skimping. Dried,

Loading a kitchen range for a Yosemite trail crew, 1939. These full-sized stoves had to be specially packed, usually upside down, and carefully padded. —Yosemite Research Library

bottled, and canned foods supplemented any fish the members caught, and the cooking staff served a "city menu" three times a day. "[Camp cook] Charlie Tuck was soon at home among three stoves and numberless cauldrons and stew pans," reported Josephine Colby of the 1903 trip. "He, with the aid of two sturdy assistants and one slip legged little elf of a Chinese boy baked and doled out his two hundred loaves of bread a day."[98]

On the 1902 trip Poly Kanawyer packed a cast-iron army stove, but it proved too heavy for the animals. After that the club used a lighter sheet-iron stove, specially designed by trip leader William Colby. The stoves folded into one piece, but each weighed more than two hundred pounds. Often three or four of these stoves were taken on a trip.[99]

Added to the commissary were canvas tents, tables, chairs, equipment, horse and mule shoes, and a myriad of other supplies. In addition, exhausted, sick, or injured campers sometimes had to be carried. Around one hundred pack animals carried 175 to 250 pounds each on these trips, which took a toll on the animals. Sore backs had to be treated, with very little "down time" to facilitate healing.

When the Broder & Hopping outfit was sold in 1908, the Sequoia region was left without a pack station large enough to handle the Sierra Club outings and other growing crowds of highcountry enthusiasts. The 1908 Sierra Club High Trip to Kern River utilized several small outfits around Grant Grove, Springville, and Camp Nelson. The following year, Earl McKee, Clarence Britten, and Clarence Fry started commercial packing out of Three Rivers, with only ten animals each. To accommodate large parties, they borrowed whatever additional horses and mules they needed from neighbors and friends.

In the meantime, motorized vehicles began to arrive. By 1913, throughout much of California, automobiles were using whatever trails and wagon roads were wide enough to accommodate them. They began chugging up the Colony Mill and Mineral King roads in Sequoia and worked their way into Yosemite Valley. By 1915 even Yosemite's steep Tioga road was improved to handle autos. As more and more roads were built into what had once been wilderness, mule packing was on the verge of becoming something of an anachronism. Tourists no longer needed pack trains to reach recreational spots in the mountains—they could drive to campsites, resorts, hiking trails, and viewpoints.

Mules were still needed for the backcountry, however, and it was the backcountry that began to draw increasing interest from nature lovers and recreationists, thanks in part to the Sierra Club, and several packers benefited from the interest. Between 1914 and 1918, Fred Maxon, Onis Brown, Tom Phipps, and Bill Canfield all started commercial outfits. In 1919 Chester Wright sold his sixty animals to the General Grant National Park Company, renamed the Kings River Parks Company, a subsidiary of the Yosemite National Park Company. By 1922 the concession had more than ninety horses, mules, and donkeys.

In the 1920s Sierra Club members began organizing their own outings in the Sierras. Some of these trips lasted up to

Sierra Club High Trip packers, with Allie Robinson (kneeling on left), Milestone Bench, July 1940. Large groups of packers are a phenomenon of the past. —Cedric Wright photo, Livermore Collection

eight weeks, at times with over two hundred guests. Although Allie Robinson was the chief packer for William Colby's official Sierra High Trips, the "ad hoc" outings also used other area packers. The trips brought in solid business for Ike Livermore, who handled several Sierra Club High Trips in the mid-1940s. In 1946, to supply the club's outing, Livermore not only purchased twenty bronco mules from a ranch in Fallon, Nevada, he also bought out the Chrysler & Cook and Barney Sears outfits, leased twenty mules from the Rock Creek pack station, and filled in with a few more from his Mineral King partner.

The Sierra Club High Trips continued into the 1950s. The packing facilities and practices improved until in 1931, on the twentieth outing, participant Marion Parsons reported, "the crowd, the packers, the commissary boys and girls, the cook, and the weather all conspired to make the month a perfect one in every way."[100]

EIGHT

Competition and Cooperation

1920s-1950s

The interest generated by Sierra Club trips in the 1920s gave birth to more packing outfits and higher profits. In 1928, "the most profitable season in the history of commercial packing, there were 480 head of animals in use and the gross receipts for the local packers [on the west side of the Sierra in the Three Rivers area] were over $100,000."[101]

Among the influx of tourists were wealthy would-be adventurists. Beginning in the early 1900s, several prominent American families, such as the Rockefellers of New York, gathered with friends to taste the delights of the western wilderness. The W. P. Fuller party took thirty-day trips each summer for thirty years, and the Crocker Bank party packed for twenty-eight years.

The growing tourist trade was not the only source of income for commercial packers. Providing services to cow camps and backcountry resorts brought in some income, too. But it was government contracts that provided the most reliable source of work. Commercial pack outfits supplied backcountry rangers in various survey, insect control, logging, firefighting, and other assignments. They also hauled materials for building and repairing ranger stations, fire lookouts, trails, bridges, dams, and camps. Government contracts alone were seldom enough to keep a pack outfit solvent, however, because the work for the Park and Forest Services was often performed at reduced rates.

There was a high level of cooperation between government agencies and commercial packers. Rangers became an integral part of many pack trips and often lifelong friendships developed. One example of the closeness between government workers and packers was the case of fish-and-game warden Walter "Shorty" Long. In between his backcountry patrols, during the lean Depression years he worked for packers Laurence Davis and Ray Buckman as camp cook, stock handler, and dishwasher, and he became a favorite of the wranglers.

The packers often cooperated among themselves, too, sharing wranglers, combining stock to accomodate large parties, and working together to brush out trails. Henry Olivas regularly hired surplus stock from Harold Gill and often rented "quite a group" from Allie Robinson.[102] Trust between the outfitters was strong enough that written agreements were seldom used. When Phil Buckman sold one-third of the Mineral King pack station to his nephew, Ray Buckman, in 1937, there were no formal papers but the agreement was fully honored.

In spite of the comraderie, with more and more packing operations open for business, there was tremendous competition among them. Highly individualistic, resourceful, and self-reliant outfitters jealously guarded their methods and knowledge. Each charged for his services according to his own criteria, even for government work.

The services provided by different outfits also varied. Some furnished equipment and others provided guides and cooks along with equipment, but some only delivered and retrieved customers' supplies to and from backcountry campsites. The methods and equipment each pack operator used also varied widely. Types of pack and saddle rigging, kinds of hitches and cinches used, methods of packing and guiding, veterinary practices, and other details depended on the particular outfitter's needs and preferences. Each was certain that his way was best.

In 1920 the going rate for pack trips in California's national parks was two to three dollars per day for each saddle and pack animal, six dollars per day for a guide or a packer with a horse, and six to ten dollars per day for an equipped cook. A longer trip with guide, packers, cook, saddle animals, pack animals, and supplies cost from fourteen to twenty-five dollars a day per person.

While the larger, better-stocked outfits began to realize profits, a small outfit with a string of fifty or fewer horses and mules could have a hard time. Some of the smaller operations were short-lived "bootleg" packers without licenses or proper equipment. They offered cut-rate prices, which forced legitimate packers to keep their rates low enough to compete.

The major pack outfits in the southern Sierra numbered thirty-six in 1920, fifteen of them operating on the east side, six on the Kern River, and eleven on the west side. These included two concessionaires, in Sequoia and Yosemite National Parks. By the end of the decade, the Forest Service reported that the vast majority of recreational backcountry users were hunting and fishing parties, and tourists going to and from Mount Whitney, of whom "probably 95 percent" hired commercial packers.[103]

In the years following the First World War, the packing industry felt the effects of a societal restlessness that the war may have created. Union power was growing, and mule wranglers were not exempt from the mood of the times. During the Sierra Club's annual trip one summer, leader William Colby recalled, Allie Robinson's packers "went on strike, cause not recorded; they saddled their horses and rode home, leaving the High Trippers to carry on doing their own packing."[104]

"The packers on the whole were a hard-working, underpaid group," according to Stewart Kimball, who acted as camp doctor on later trips.[105] They had always been underpaid, but now expectations of increased opportunities after the war were high. Instead, a postwar depression in 1921 saw thousands of businesses fail nationwide, affecting the packing business.

Another setback to the growing industry came in the summer of 1924. First, a drought created feed shortages, then a hoof-and-mouth epidemic broke out among livestock throughout most of California. The subsequent depression was felt not only in rural California, but also throughout the ranching areas of the Pacific Coast. As a result, in the Sierra's national parks and forests, roads were closed in order to prevent spread of the disease; disinfecting vats and fumigating stations were erected; and special permits were needed to move stock. The decline in park visitation continued into 1925.

Fortunately, the epidemic did not last long and the packers recovered quickly. By 1930 Forest Service officials listed seventy-three permitted packing operations. Another count in 1936 declared seventy: forty-eight on the west side and twenty-two on the east side, with 2,764 head of stock for hire.[106]

In spite of the downturn in business in the 1920s, there continued to be work for packers with the power companies. In 1921 a "sizable" pack party went into the backcountry to select sites for water-flow-gauging stations, and as late as 1923 there was a ten-day encampment of power company officials at Blayney Meadows.

The building of the O'Shaughnessy Dam in Hetch Hetchy Valley between 1919 and 1923 was too large a job for a packing operation, so a railroad was built to haul equipment and materials to the site. Nevertheless, horses and mules played a key role in the preliminary work, including the logging of the valley and the construction of the wagon road that preceded the railroad's entrance in 1918.

On the east side of the Sierra, in the spring of 1925, the work of extending the dam at Second Lake began. The small dam, built in 1895, was made higher to increase water

Packing a tandem load. Glacier Pack Trains. The saddle frames have swivels to facilitate easy movement of long pipes or lumber around corners. —Pat and Clay Stout Collection

Ord Loverin (top row center) with a few members of the Simpson party, 1925. This party was one of the largest stock-packing excursions ever to ply the backcountry trails. —Sophronia A. Britten Collection

storage for three hydroelectric plants on Big Pine Creek. Long lengths of pipe, lumber, and rails; an air compressor; and even two disassembled Fordson farm tractors were carried up the mountain trail on muleback. To transport some of the heavy equipment, two mules were packed in tandem.

After all the equipment had been hauled up to Second Lake, strong opposition developed to having an earth-filled dam in one of the Sierra's most beautiful basins, and the project was abandoned. A mile of railroad tracks along with sidecars, tractors, buildings, and debris remained at the lake until cleanups were organized in the 1960s and 1970s.[107]

Also in 1925, the largest saddle and pack train ever assembled on the San Joaquin River traveled from Jackass Meadows to Kings River. James Simpson, board chairman of Chicago's Marshall Field wholesale store, gathered with several members of prominent Chicago families and Sequoia National Park superintendent Colonel John R. White to visit the various reservoir and dam sites and to continue south through the High Sierra. Packer Ord Loverin led the thirty-day trip.

Meanwhile, the fish plantings begun in the 1870s expanded in the new century, creating continued employment for packers. By 1925 the Mount Whitney fish hatchery in Independence was in operation, raising rainbow, eastern brook, German brown, and golden trout fish fry to be packed out. The hatchery transported the fry to one of the pack stations, where the fish were loaded onto mules and taken to backcountry lakes. Fingerlings also were shipped to the west side of the Sierra by railroad, then packed up to Camp Nelson. From there, Carmel Wilson and his packers carried them on into the backcountry, two cans to a mule.

By 1935 packers, rangers, and fish and game personnel were spending "considerable time and trouble" planting fish, an estimated 30 to 150 mule-loads per year. Ultimately, however, the work was not completely successful, nor did it prove to be lucrative for the packers. The California Fish and Game Commission and some private parties paid the packers for their work, but the money usually covered only the rental of the stock. Moreover, the plantings did not always have good results. Eastern brook trout planted from the Mount Whitney Hatchery seriously depleted the original rainbows stocked in previous years. At least one packer objected so strongly to the infiltration of "brookies" that he took a contract to haul a load of them to a lake but dumped them into a canyon instead.

HARD TIMES

After the hit-and-miss prosperity of the 1920s, the Great Depression hit, taking its toll on Sierra packers. Fewer private parties had the time or money for long trips into the wilderness. Some commercial packing jobs were generated through the Works Project Administration (WPA), the Emergency Conservation Work (ECW), and the Civilian Conservation Corps (CCC) projects. However, most of the public-works camps were served via roads with motorized vehicles, and backcountry projects were often supplied by government pack trains.

The maintenance, repair, and improvements of park trails did use some commercial hauling. Among the trails worked on were the John Muir Trail; the High Sierra Trail between Giant Forest and the Kern River; the Junction Meadow Trail on the Kern River; the trail over Mammoth Pass; a trail into Devil's Postpile; and a trail to Sequoia's Pear Lake.

The Hamilton Gorge suspension bridge was constructed in September and October 1932 over an avalanche chute as part of the High Sierra Trail. More than two hundred pack trips delivered approximately forty-one thousand pounds of material, including tons of cable, steel, and concrete. Materials were hauled twenty-one miles from Mineral King via steep Black Rock Pass to the gorge. Five years later, this bridge collapsed and was carried down by an avalanche.

Pack train crossing Hamilton Gorge suspension bridge, 1935. —Sequoia National Park Archives

The so-called Ponderosa Highway, a six-hundred-mile-long, one-hundred-plus-foot-wide fire break that ran nearly the entire length of the Sierra, required transportation not only of the usual hand tools and camp items but explosives and thousands of pounds of arsenic (the latter was used in a futile attempt to prevent the regrowth of chaparral and forest vegetation in the fire-break corridor). In addition, CCC work on wilderness drift fences, fire lookouts, telephone lines, insect control, firefighting, and reforestation all required the hauling of supplies.

More typical of early projects for the Park and Forest Services were the ones Ike Livermore and Henry "Leakey" Olivas worked on in 1930. Livermore and Monroe Griggs of Atwell Mill packed all the materials for a fire lookout above Hockett Meadows. It took about twenty round-trips from the mill to the lookout. Olivas spent several years hauling wire-fence

Workers at Atwell Mill packing lumber for construction of Cahoon Lookout, 1929. Much of the lumber used for back-country buildings and trail work in the late 1800s and early 1900s came from Atwell Mill. —Sequoia National Park Archives

materials for drift fences in Templeton and Brown Meadows. In 1935 he packed two thousand posts from Jordan Hot Springs to the Monache, Casa Vieja, and Red Rock areas.

Unfortunately, such government work was not enough to keep the packing industry viable. Furthermore, private parties were no longer profitable either. "Living through drought years and depressions was hard sledding," Olancha packer Sam Lewis remembered. "By working at any sort of job that came up during off times between pack trips I did manage to hang on."[108]

Many packers picked up odd jobs such as hauling, providing day rides, and lending stock for parades and rodeos. For a lucky few, even Hollywood had work for packers. On the west side in 1925, Ord Loverin handled the stock logistics for a movie filmed in Three Rivers. On the east side and in the Kern River valley, brothers Pete and Henry "Leakey" Olivas, Ted Cook, Russ Spainhower, and Irvin Wofford found almost steady employment from the 1920s through the 1940s supplying stock and supplies for films made on location in the southern Sierra.[109] Their outfits provided horses, mules, cows, wranglers, extras, and even stagecoaches. Pete Olivas and Ted Cook became so involved in the movies that they joined the Actors' Guild.

Ethyl Olivas, wife of Henry, made lunches for the casts and crews of films shot in their area, and the family became very friendly with them. During one Hopalong Cassidy picture, Henry took his dog with him to the set. "One day this great big car drove up out here in front and [the driver] had Leakey's dog," Ethyl recalled. "He said, 'Leakey's dog got tired, so I had to bring him home.'"[110]

In spite of these occasional windfalls, most young wranglers, dependent on summer work, had a hard time finding jobs during the Depression. After his first backcountry trip in 1930, Ike Livermore found nothing available until August of 1933. "I was keen to go down to Mineral King, but there was no paying work for an extra packer," he lamented.[111]

The profits of each year made a difference in the wages that could be paid. By 1935 wranglers' wages ranged from thirty to ninety dollars a month. This included room and board between trips. For these wages and benefits, the hired men worked six or seven days a week for as many hours as needed, for periods up to three or four weeks in the back-country.

With costs, wages, and income so variable in the packing industry, pricing among outfitters became haphazard. In the early 1930s, packers started two associations, one on the west side and one on the east. These informal groups met to try to reach an agreement on pricing, but competition proved too fierce and no agreement was made. Then in 1934 an agent for change arrived. Ike Livermore, only twenty-three years old at the time, suggested that that all the packers on both the west and east sides get together and develop one true packer's association. In the midst of the Great Depression, the High Sierra Packers Association was born. First on the west side, then on the east, the association worked out guidelines for all packers with National Forest Service permits in the southern and central Sierra.

The packers agreed to cooperate on a very loose basis at first. Among the topics they discussed were methods of soliciting business, accounting procedures, rate structures, care of stock, equipment maintenance, fish-stocking methods, group liability insurance, joint advertising, and a campaign against the growing threat of wilderness roads. Gradually, the association became more formalized. To support better industry standards, the Forest Service encouraged membership. Livermore brokered a deal for insurance for association members from Lloyd's of London. Brochures listed all the association's Eastern Unit and Western Unit packers, with maps of the High Sierra showing where each station was located. By 1936, thirty-five outfits were members of the High Sierra Packers Association, approximately half of all the packers then in operation.

After suffering through depression, droughts, and increasing competition, packers faced new challenges with the Second World War. Just as the economy began to get better, wartime rationing limited travel and created food shortages. New restrictions due to the war also put a damper on backcountry trips: "No campfires will be permitted after dark," a memorandum to all packers warned in the summer of 1942. "In view of the fact that practically all back country areas are too remote to make provision for immediate transmission of blackout signals, it will be necessary that you do not allow campfires to burn during the hours of darkness."[112]

Of greater concern was gasoline rationing. Families on an "A" card coupon, which was what most residents of California had, were only allowed ninety miles per month for pleasure driving. At the annual meeting of the High Sierra Packers Association on April 20, 1943, officials from the Office of Defense Transportation (ODT) and the Office of Price Administration (OPA) outlined a plan to ease the situation. Since nearly all pack-station owners, as stock raisers, had virtually unlimited gasoline allowances for truck operations, it was agreed that the ODT would allow passengers to ride in supply trucks from rail stations to the pack bases.

The plan was not officially sanctioned, however. "At least ninety-eight percent of the travel to the California Parks since gasoline rationing went into effect has been a technical violation of gas rationing regulations," they admitted.[113] It was an unwritten agreement that the OPA would not enforce their regulations in the parks.

Even with these allowances, the war years were a near disaster for pack operators. In 1942 the Inyo National Forest listed only nine permitted packers, down from twenty-three the year before.[114] Worse than wartime regulations was a more serious problem: most of the young wranglers, as well as young male customers, were in the service. Even the owners sometimes served. Ike Livermore, for example, spent the entire war period in the service. Some packers requested that partners and employees be exempted to pack government supplies and fight fires in the backcountry.

With all the restrictions and with so many men and women away in the service, few tourists came to the Sierra during the war. Fees for tourists remained near depression levels, with horses going for two to three dollars per day and guides, cooks, and packers getting seven to ten dollars per day.[115] The outfits that survived depended in large part on government contracts. CCC projects and fighting a rash of summer fires helped.

Another significant source of work came from the ongoing geologic surveys. In 1947 Ed Sargent, owner of the Glacier

Pack Train outfit, employed four packers and guide Norman Clyde for a summer-long survey. Each packer was in charge of caring for three surveyors, their horses, and six pack mules.

Surveys took place during the winter as well. By the 1940s the California State Snow Survey had begun taking winter snowpack measurements. Packers cooperated in building and supplying the cabins and even helped take the surveys. Packer Earl Pascoe participated in some of the first surveys. "My father used to begin the trip every winter from the lodge at Road's End [on the Kern River] and make a one hundred and fifty mile walk through snow. It would take him two weeks," Earl's son Raymond recalled. "He would go around in the fall of the year with a pack mule and put food in all the Forest Service cabins. . . . Each winter, he would make the trip on snowshoes and measure the snow at each of these spots."[116]

Two snow-survey cabins were built in Yosemite National Park in 1947, in cooperation with the California Cooperative Snow Surveys. The construction materials were hauled by mule, and Joe Barnes out of Mather pack station was hired to supply and stock the cabins each year. The following year, Herb London of Rock Creek was given the contract to haul the materials for building a winter survey cabin at Summit Lake, at the headwaters of Rock Creek. Packer Clay Stout worked on the project. "I ended up with six weeks of steady packing of all the materials for that cabin," Clay recalled. "I took two aparejo loads every day, lumber, and one of them was tandem."[117]

Occasional government projects aside, times continued to be tough for the packing industry after the war. By the 1940s, overgrazing and other environmental concerns had prompted increasing government regulations that affected packer operations. Pasturing was curtailed and rules on building, maintenance of trails, camps, and stations, and animal care were established. Complying to many of these regulations increased packers' costs. Changing times were making mule transportation less and less profitable.

Park contracts were becoming more scarce as not only the automobile but also other forms of transportation increasingly replaced mule power. In the 1920s small motorized vehicles augmented mule trains to haul materials and supplies up trails near roads. Later, airplanes delivered supplies, fish plantings, and eventually tourists into the backcountry. By the 1950s helicopters had come into limited use.

The packers' hunting and fishing business also diminished. With the establishment of Kings Canyon National Park in 1940, a large portion of deer-hunting country was eliminated, seriously cutting into business. In 1949 motorized boats were prohibited on backcountry lakes, and outfitters were made responsible for the safety of any hand-propelled boats their guests brought in.

Nevertheless, it was not all bad news. After the Second World War, the economy improved, interest in and access to the wilderness grew, and people had time for longer vacations. The introduction of new lightweight materials ushered in the age of backpacking and modernized the traditional equipment of stock packing. Even so, many packing businesses were earning "just enough to get by," according to Pete Olivas.[118]

After a small boom in the early 1950s, some packers left the business, while others adapted the best they could. Ike Livermore used his interests in the different pack stations as tax write-offs because they always were losing money. Bob Cooper in Monache Meadows depended on his neighbors after each packing season to supply him with work to earn his board. When the Buckmans of Mineral King sold their resort to the Disney Corporation in the 1960s, Gem Buckman told a friend what a relief it was to be able to go into a store and buy something without having to ask the price.[119]

While established outfitters struggled, a new style of packer flourished. By 1950 backcountry commercial stock packing was no longer a simple matter of guiding expeditions into the wilderness. In tourist areas it was show business. Johnny-come-lately packers wore black Stetsons pulled low over the eyes, heavy chaps, clean shirts, and handlebar mustaches groomed to perfection. With a practiced western drawl and tight-lipped smiles, they sat around the campfire telling tales borrowed from Hollywood movies and singing songs heard in western bars. Full-service pack trips evolved into specialized cultural experiences, built out of myth and fable. The costumes and performances were simply a way of enticing more customers and soliciting larger tips.

Mules with boats maneuvering on the trail. Restrictions on boating in backcountry lakes have eliminated scenes such as this.
—Ramsay Collection, Eastern California Museum

This brand of entertainment was actually not so new. Steward Edward White wrote a description of such "imitation bad men" in Yosemite in 1904: "Each morning one of these men took a pleasantly awe-stricken band of tourists out, led them around in the brush awhile, and brought them back in time for lunch. They wore broad hats and leather bands and exotic raiment and fierce expressions, and looked dark and mysterious and extra-competent over the most trivial of difficulties."[120]

"Today things are different," Johnny Jones groused in his memoirs. "There are too few pack stations and too many operators I call 'candlestick makers.' . . . They'll buy a pair of fancy boots and a great big sombrero and without knowing which end a mule feeds, they are supposed to be packers."[121]

Right or wrong, comfortable packing trips led by pseudo-cowpokes were where the money was. By the early 1970s old-timers Ord Loverin, both the elder and younger Earl McKee, Dick Wilson, the elder Davis family, Sam Lewis, Allie Robinson, Bruce Morgan, and Ike Livermore were all gone from the business.

PART II

LAND USE
AND PROTECTION

NINE

The Conservation Movement in the Sierra Nevada

1875-1906

Ever since European settlers first touched the shores of the Americas, land had been considered an expendable resource. In the minds of those who dared to step into the "unhallowed" wilderness, it existed to be conquered, subdued, and used to man's purpose.[122] As long as the frontiers were open, unrestrained use of public lands was an accepted practice. In fact, the United States government encouraged it. Throughout the nineteenth century, in an attempt to secure American rights to the entire continent, the government backed exploration and settlement across the expanding western frontier. The Homestead Act of 1862 and other legislation opened tens of millions of acres to settlement, allowing nearly unrestricted use of the land.

In the Sierra Nevada, activities were essentially unregulated, including the cutting of timber, the diversion of streams and rivers into canals, the free grazing of livestock, the construction of trails, and the running of supply pack trains across the southern mountains. Even as late as the mid-1900s, as some old-timers remembered, the Sierra was considered open to all. Cattlemen, sheepherders, miners, foresters, surveyors, adventurers, tourists, and packers all shared the trails. The only rule, unwritten, was that if you used it, you took care of it.

In the vast open spaces of the West, it was difficult to imagine a time when population demands could despoil the wilderness. But it already had happened in the East, in what had once been thought a wilderness too huge to be totally occupied. Now, as accounts of gold and other treasures in the West spread eastward, opportunists arrived in the Rocky Mountains and on the Pacific Coast to reap a share of the natural wealth.

As unregulated exploitation of the land increased in the Sierra, the awe-inspiring beauty of the landscape was all too quickly being lost to commercialism. Public desire to conserve not only water and timber resources but also the natural magnificence of the Sierra Nevada prompted concerns over the unchecked private ownership and commercial use of the mountains.

In Yosemite Valley, after quasimilitary expeditions expelled the Indians in 1851 and 1852, private enterprises settled into the area to take advantage of ranching opportunities and the growing tourist trade. Although only 653 people visited the Yosemite Valley between 1855 and 1864, many of them, including some who had political clout in the East, realized what a loss the private appropriation of such scenic lands was bringing to the public.

A concerted movement to save Yosemite from exploitation persuaded Congress to grant control of the valley and the Mariposa Big Tree Grove to the state of California in 1864, specifying that it be held for "public use, resort and recreation." In 1866 California accepted the grant, essentially making the area the first wilderness park in the United States and setting a precedent for the future National Park system.[123]

Nevertheless, pressure on land in the Sierra Nevada continued during the 1860s. Demand for wool, meat, minerals, lumber, and water escalated with California's growing population. Trails were cleared to accommodate large pack trains carrying supplies to mining camps and small mountain communities. Wagon roads were built to lumber mills and growing towns. Following the drought years of 1862 through 1864, sheep and cattle by the thousands were led from the dry plains and foothills to high mountain meadows, and the unregulated grazing continued through the rest of the nineteenth century.

By the 1870s the environmental damage caused by lumbering, grazing, and other pressures made the need for conservation increasingly apparent. As unregulated use began to threaten the watershed for California's expanding irrigation systems, as giant Sequoia groves began to be cut, and as more and more prime mountain meadows were homesteaded, citizens, journalists, politicians, and businesses issued a call for preservation.

Then Scottish-born John Muir appeared on the scene. With a background as a wilderness explorer, amateur geologist, and conservationist, he began a series of writings and public lectures in 1875 promoting his theories of Sierra Nevada glaciation and the need for government control of its forests. Muir's descriptive essays garnered a devoted audience.[124]

As public consciousness of the consequences of wilderness destruction rose to a new level, President Rutherford Hayes appointed staunch environmentalist Carl Schurz as Secretary of the Interior in 1877. Four years later, the federal Division of Forestry was created. Its function was mostly to gather and provide information, and although it lacked power to enforce regulations, it was the precursor to the U.S. Forest Service. In 1890 the area surrounding the state-managed Yosemite Valley became Yosemite National Park, and in the same year Sequoia and General Grant National Parks were also created. The following year saw the Reservation Act passed, stipulating that the immense Sierra Reserve become part of the public land system. But outside the parks, unregulated exploitation continued to be the norm, depleting the Sierra's resources.

It was not until the turn of the twentieth century that the concept of forest management as political policy was considered. President Teddy Roosevelt made conservation a central part of his administration. He created the U.S. Forest Service in 1905 and appointed Gifford Pinchot as its chief. The nation's approach to wilderness use was in transition.

TEN

Federal Land Management

1906–1950s

When the national parks and forest reserves were created to protect the wilderness, rules and regulations inevitably came with them. Of particular concern was overgrazing. In 1906, for the packing industry using forest reserve lands, it all became official. According to U.S.D.A. Forest Service regulations:

> The Secretary of Agriculture will prescribe each year the number of stock to be allowed in each reserve. The period during which grazing will be allowed will be determined by the Forester. The Supervisor will issue grazing permits in accordance with the instructions of the Forester.[125]

All grazing, including that of commercial pack stock, was included in the new regulation. Now the government, not the packers, would decide where their stock would graze. The practice of dotting the public landscape with campsites, shanties, and fences wherever one wished was no longer acceptable. All such construction had to be approved, and enclosures were limited to one acre.

Furthermore, commercial interests no longer had unrestricted use of the mountains. Permits were required for any use of public land. By 1920 a concessionaire's permit was required for commercial operations within the national parks, and independent stock packers using park trails had to be approved and authorized. The Forest Service soon followed suit with their own packing permits.

Livestock owners were charged for winter grazing in the national forest lowlands—in 1906 the fee was thirty-five cents per head for cattle and horses, and by 1926 it had reached forty-seven cents per head. Restrictions on the maximum number of stock that could be grazed were extended to include corporations as well as individuals. Temporary grazing permits, called "on-and-off" permits, designated that no more than fifty percent of a company's or individual's stock could be grazed within a national forest at any one time.

In Yosemite Valley, concessionaires were given permits for grazing in allotted meadows; remaining meadows could be used by the public. Often fences were erected and idle horses pastured wherever the feed was good. But by 1929, after automobile roads allowed easy transport of goods and materials, a program of eliminating all fences in Yosemite Valley was initiated, thus closing most of the pasturage in the valley.

Not only were the lower ranges used for winter pasture being restricted, but base-camp pastures were too. In 1920 at the Giant Forest pack station, it was still customary to allow camping parties to range stock for four hours on the adjacent meadows. But the next year, the Park Service met with the commercial packers to discuss the damage being done by their stock. "All your horses are still roaming the Giant Forest campsite, where they break down water connections, obliterate trails and make new ones, and trample down the meadows," superintendent John White chided.[126]

Commercial packers knew how vulnerable the high mountain meadows were to overgrazing. Most pack outfits moved their camps when an area showed signs of overuse, not only to preserve the health of the meadows for future use, but also to serve the more immediate concern of animals straying at night if there wasn't enough feed to keep them close to camp. Unfortunately, there were those who did not follow these practices.

Overgrazing affected upland meadows on both national park and Forest Service lands. In 1926 backcountry reports concerning a lack of horse feed in Hockett Meadow and the Kaweah's South Fork forced several Sierra meadows to be restricted or closed. For the first time, the Giant Forest was closed to grazing. In the Sierra National Forest in 1931, officials limited use to "wrangling purposes only" at Jackass Meadows near Florence Lake, Clover Meadow, Dinkey Creek, Cliff Camp, and several other central Sierra areas. If a large

Lower Paradise Meadow, Kings Canyon National Park, 1940. By the mid-1930s many meadows were overgrazed and restrictions became necessary. —Sequoia National Park Archives

party was camped at one place for several days, the stock had to be contained somewhere away from accessible feed.

Not everyone cared to adhere to the new rules. Inyo National Forest ranger H. H. Simpson reported in 1931, "At present, commercial packers are prohibited from turning their stock out on the open range, except when under actual hire status. This restriction has not been satisfactorily observed and much dissatisfaction among the cow men has developed."[127]

The regulations attempted to limit not only grazing areas but also grazing seasons. Packing companies were charged a fee for using winter ranges in the foothills but not for grazing on park lands during the summer packing season. Therefore, "The longer that these stock remain in the mountain meadows, the less the cost of over-wintering . . . This fact has contributed to the overuse of Park grazing lands," a memorandum from Yosemite assistant forester Emil F. Ernst noted to the superintendent in 1935.[128]

In response to what had come to be called the "company grazing problem" in Yosemite in the 1930s, recommendations were made to place restrictions on the Yosemite Park & Curry Company's "promiscuous" grazing, especially during the spring and fall months, with rotational grazing in specially defined areas.[129]

The concessionaire resisted the proposal. "[Our] policy of spring grazing, as well as use of the Wawona area is not thoroughly understood," Yosemite Park & Curry Company president Don Tressider informed the park managers in January 1936.

> This practice has come about in recent years, not primarily through a desire to reduce our expenses, but through a fundamental change in operating conditions. . . . Now we find that animals used at Tuolumne Meadows, Mather, and on our High Sierra Circuit represent a substantial part of our business and it can readily be seen that since those areas do not even become accessible until June 15 or later we are faced with a problem.[130]

Adding to the company's grazing crisis was the fact that the early 1930s had been drought years, so their winter range was now running out of both feed and water by March. The only place to feed the animals was in higher elevations. The park made some concessions, but the grazing meadows continued to show rapid deterioration, especially with the drought. In the spring of 1935 another report recommended further measures.

The report brought several closures and restrictions to Yosemite's park areas. All high country north of the Tuolumne River was closed, and the area between the Tuolumne River and the Tioga road was restricted. The Wawona Meadows were relegated to a shortened grazing season. The mid-elevation wet meadows were put on a spring and fall rotation system and some were closed completely to spring grazing. Furthermore, limits were put on the number of stock allowed in the parks at any one time.

The changes were not easy on the Yosemite Park & Curry Company. The logistics of feeding became more difficult, as stock had to be moved to and from the mountain-based pack stations seasonally, and feed had to be hauled up to the corrals to supplement grazing. The expense of moving approximately two hundred horses and mules in and out of the park and the need to buy more feed depleted the already small profits made by the Yosemite Park & Curry Company's backcountry operations.

In spite of the efforts in Yosemite and elsewhere to control it, grazing pressure in the Sierras continued to increase as recreational packing gained popularity. "Recreational grazing problems develop chiefly at strategic meadows used as overnight stopping places on main routes of travel," Sequoia and Yosemite regional wildlife technician E. Lowell Sumner Jr. reported in 1936. "Famous scenic routes which support the most travel thus tend to suffer the most severely. . . ."[131] He concluded, "Hardly a meadow in the Sierra remains in its primitive state. Unless active protective measures are taken now, the chance that these meadows will recover completely is slight."[132]

The problem extended beyond overgrazing. From its inception, the commercial packing industry depended on wealthy individuals, corporations, and clubs as the core of their recreational business. The larger the party, the more money they made. And the heavier the damage. Not only were meadows being overgrazed, but major campsites were being destroyed. Ever larger and more elaborate campsites—including toilet areas, fire and garbage pits, and stock compounds, as well as the trampled tracks between them—were creating almost irreparable damage.

"There is a positive saturation point beyond which further concentration of people will destroy the very thing which they seek," Sumner noted, "and in some areas this saturation point has already been exceeded."[133]

With this increasing pressure, conservationists began to worry that the Park Service would be unable to withstand the growing demands for development. While the Forest Service had reserved two million acres of Primitive Areas against any future development, the Park Service continued to struggle with the need to provide facilities for its growing number of visitors.

Barney Sears's Lone Pine pack train at Golden Trout camp, circa 1930s. By this time, some backcountry camps had permanent structures and amenities. —Frasher Collection, Eastern California Museum

In Sumner's view, further development should not be the Park Service's first priority. "To the local parks properly belongs the function of handling huge crowds," he wrote in the 1936 report. "To the national parks, on the other hand, properly belongs the function of preserving superlative natural regions, including wilderness areas, as little changed as possible for the benefit of posterity. . . . Already those who want more roads, more public campgrounds, more gas stations and more trails to scenic points have obtained these improvements for themselves throughout approximately 99 percent of all recreational areas in California, including most of the choicest portions of the national parks."[134]

Yet Sumner believed the problem was naturally self-limiting. "Of those few who do enter the wilderness, a still smaller number are willing to leave the beaten path; the remainder will seldom be so numerous as to destroy the wilderness atmosphere." This would have been the case, that is, if not for commercial packers. It was they who enticed otherwise reluctant visitors into the backcountry. Destruction in those areas "is largely accomplished by efforts to coax large numbers of less venturesome individuals into the wilderness by the construction, even in remote places, of ready built camp sites and extensive systems of easy trails, which require the exercise of a minimum amount of energy and ingenuity on the part of the visitor."[135]

The Sierra Club made its own contributions to the problem. The club was created in 1892 to promote awareness of conservation issues, yet it also encouraged wilderness use, paradoxically causing more damage. One of the club's original goals was to entice more people into the Sierra, with the idea that they would grow to care about the mountains

A 1920s mule train at Franklin Pass, Mineral King, California. Until the 1940s, large mule trains of sometimes more than two hundred animals were the norm. Concerns about backcountry degradation caused officials to set increasing limits on the size of trains. Today no more than fifteen animals per party are allowed in the parks, twenty-five on Forest Service lands, and there are efforts to lower those counts. —Fresno Bee Files

and therefore make certain they were protected. But the idea backfired. The thirty-nine commercially packed Sierra Club High Trips between 1902 and 1946, each with some two hundred people and at least seventy-five pack animals out for periods of a month or more, further degraded the backcountry.

Even in the beginning, the Sierra Club noted their large outings' effects on the environment. Its High Trip of 1902 had over two hundred participants, with "some 25,000 pounds of personal baggage and camp equipage," residing for five weeks at Kings River Canyon. The next year's High Trip to Kern Canyon was even larger.[136] In 1913 the Outing Committee reported that lack of feed for animals in the Tehipite Valley prevented any stay of longer than one night. Still, as late as 1922, when the club camped in Cahoon Meadow for several days, the pack stock was allowed to graze freely, and there was practically no feed remaining when they left.

"Muir could hardly have anticipated the day when men—practical men at that—got together and agreed that we should stop building roads into California's high mountains, much less the day when they should begin to worry about traffic on the trails," Sierra Club director David Brower wrote in 1948. "Yet that day has come. And the Sierra Club's High Trip, being the largest single contribution to wilderness travel today, is the one which many men worry most about."[137]

By the late 1930s, it had become apparent to nearly everyone that the Sierra Nevada could no longer sustain increasing numbers of people, roads, and commercial enterprises. Regulations increased throughout the 1930s, '40s, and '50s. Ranger districts were set up in the forests to monitor use, to note packer practices, and to enforce regulations. The number of campers, stock, and days of usage were carefully recorded in reports. Packers were required to repair camps and trails and to limit their camps to designated areas.

Conservation concerns of all types were addressed in the new rules. Fire safety, camp sanitation, and fishing and hunting laws were created and updated. A strict prohibition of firearms, explosives, and fireworks in the parks was enacted. Corral and facilities maintenance, soil-erosion prevention, and care of stock were all defined in packers' regulations.[138] In 1947 the Sierra National Forest informed the Yosemite

Park & Curry Company that it would no longer allow park concessionaires to pack hunting parties into the forest.

During these decades, sanitation issues were particularly targeted for regulation, and complying to some of the new laws was challenging for pack operators. Building toilets to government specifications and fly-proofing them was expensive, and they were almost impossible to maintain. At the Broken Bar Pack outfit headquarters, Art Frost was instructed to construct a new toilet in a concealed place "built of surfaced material, the cracks battened, the roof should be shingled, the seat covered, a good door provided, and the pitt [sic] made fly proof, and the structure painted or stained. . . . The vault should be four feet deep."[139]

The rules were stringent about all sanitation issues. Frost also was told that before his packer's permit could be renewed he had to clean up the headquarters, burn all debris, and haul cans to the government garbage dump or bury them with at least a foot of dirt. In the 1940s the Park Service required that manure be removed from corrals at least twice a week and scattered, not piled, along the road slopes under supervision of a park road foreman. Also, fly traps or flypaper had to be placed around buildings or corrals. In the 1930s and 1940s several requests for construction of corrals, outbuildings, and improvements to existing facilities were denied.

Property rights to facilities and infrastructures also changed as emphasis on public ownership of park lands developed. In 1944 Hugh Traweek and Don Cecil at Grant Grove were informed that the water system they had put in at their pack station was considered property of the government. "Traweek asked about 'selling his concession at Cedar Grove.' I told him that he had nothing to sell, except possibly his own physical installations," superintendent John White wrote in a memorandum.[140]

Furthermore, to address the continuing problem of overgrazing, the government instituted new stock-feeding practices. It had become necessary to assign special areas to users. Grazing of surplus commercial pack and saddle stock was relegated to specified ranges. In 1940 the Cecil Pack Train was assigned to Jerkey Meadow, Hugh Traweek to Long Meadow, and Dick Wilson to Cub and Hotel Meadows. Grazing areas were allowed a maximum of twenty-five animals at a time.

The difficulty of enforcing permit regulations was an ongoing concern for the Park Service. For years, especially during World War II when there was a shortage of rangers, the pack-station operators could agree to the conditions of their permits while their wranglers ignored many of the stipulations. Or they could operate clandestinely without any permit at all.

In May 1944 park rangers J. H. Wegner and Walter Fry made a lengthy tour visiting park-area packing operations. "There seems to be much laxity or misunderstanding or both existing regarding the necessity of first securing permits to operate within the Park," Wegner reported after the trip. "Everyone contacted wanted the privilege to operate inside the Park but many were reluctant to commit themselves to the obligation of securing liability insurance as required. . . . It is strongly suspected a number of those in this situation plan to try to get by as they evidently have in the past—without a permit."[141]

In fact, almost no one Wegner and Fry contacted had a permit. Archie Dean of Independence had never procured one and had not seen a ranger in his region for ten years. Sam Lewis was bitterly against the idea of insurance and reluctantly accepted permit forms. Bob Welch, who required all his guests to sign a "responsibility release" in advance, wasn't interested in a park permit. On the west side, Frank Negus, out of Springville, had nothing but complaints, and Jack Ducey of Prather, John J. Dale of Dinkey Creek, Fred Cypert of Springville, Roy and Laurence Davis of Mineral King, and Craig Thorn of Silver City all failed to return signed permits. In Yosemite, Tom Jones of Beasore Meadow did not always get a permit or pay his per-head fee, and Billy Welch of Mather blatantly used William Meyer's permit.

Packers who did try to work with the government didn't always get what they wanted. In 1944 Earl McKee was allowed to graze his stock in the Cow Creek area, but the following year his application for grazing rights in three park pastures was denied. He was advised, "in view of current conditions and the likelihood of the Government having to increase the number of pack and saddle animals in the near future, it will be necessary to conserve all present available feed for future use, and there will be little if any likelihood that Government feed for this stock will be available."[142]

Still, Earl McKee and many other packers were coming to accept that they had to live within limits, not only to promote conservation, but also to maintain their good working relationships with Park Service and Forest Service rangers and administrators. "We have got along pretty good for nearly a quarter century," McKee noted. "The next one-quarter ought to be easier."[143]

Cooperation did not always come easily, however, and the permit issue persisted. The 1948 superintendent of Sequoia National Park, E. T. Scoyen, was not pleased with the continuing laxity. "This entire matter of packing permits in Sequoia seems to have been handled outside the regulations for a good many years, and apparently without objection on the part of the Director or anyone else," Scoyen complained. "Stricter regulation of these packing operations is something we must have."[144]

It was almost impossible to keep up with the permit problems. In May 1949, nine pack outfits took trips into the parks without signed permits and nine others had not submitted rate schedules and liability information. While the need for supervision and patrolling grew, funding was always lacking. By 1949 the five-dollar fee for a packer's permit did not even cover the cost of issuing it, let alone monitoring who did or didn't have permits. "I would say that $25 each would more nearly cover the cost," Sequoia Kings chief clerk B. F. Gibson estimated.[145]

The problem spread beyond permit issuance and compliance. Late filing of financial reports, schedule rates, and itineraries was epidemic. Tourist complaints of poor care of stock were frequent, and adequate cleaning of corrals was rare. Grazing violations continued. The building of unauthorized trails, which damaged the environment and created maintenance problems for trail crews, was a practice that packers were loathe to relinquish, for exclusive access to special lakes and hunting areas could bring in extra business.

In the meantime, packers were finding it harder and harder to keep pace with the times, even as business flourished. Interest in mountain recreation was still growing, horseback rides and hiking becoming popular. The packing business enjoyed the modest boom, but with it came higher costs and stricter regulations. Better management became crucial. The industry could not remain the unstructured enterprise it once had been.

Paperwork began to require hours of attention. There were seemingly endless records involving liability insurance and performance bonds; schedules of proposed rates for stock, equipment, and services; annual financial reports; and logs showing number of stock and days they grazed, number of patrons, days of service, destinations, and other details.

Added to the paperwork was an increasing need for facilities maintenance. As years passed, base operations required ever more attention and upgrades. For many operators it was both financially and physically difficult to keep up with it all, so stations gradually degraded. In the meantime, costs of feed, salaries, stock, equipment, supplies, and insurance kept escalating.

Grazing and trail regulations also continued to increase. By 1950 loose-herding of pack and saddle stock was prohibited on the trails except in areas designated hazardous. More and more grazing areas and trail camps were closed. Even temporary corrals now required permits and the use of government corrals was restricted.

"We are restricted more and more and are only able to take [pack trains] through narrower and narrower corridors, and there are fewer and fewer grazing lands," Charles Morgan complained. "With so few areas, eventually there aren't going to be any packers."[146]

ELEVEN

Self-regulation and Compliance
in the Packing Industry

1920s-1950s

For the fragile mountain ecosystems as well as for the packers and the government agencies overseeing them, survival
depended on cooperation. All the rules and regulations in the
world would make no difference if the wilderness users were
not willing to follow them. By the 1930s, making certain the
most popular backcountry routes were protected from overuse had become one of the top priorities for all concerned.

At the same time, the government agencies also realized
the need to keep good pack outfits in business. It was only
with their cooperation that both the public and the natural
resources could be served. As the director of the National
Park Service wrote to Sequoia superintendent John R. White
in 1922:

> You ask[ed] to be advised relative to the Service's attitude
> toward private individuals who conduct packing operations
> from the Three Rivers district through the present Sequoia
> National Park and into the region of the proposed Roosevelt
> National Park. As most of these packers have for a consider-
> able time been conducting parties into the area which will be
> included in the enlarged national park, and are well and favor-
> ably known . . . I feel that we should not put any unnecessary
> restrictions on their operations, but rather should encourage
> them in every way we can.[147]

As late as the 1930s, foothill ranches such as the Maxon ranch, shown here, served as staging grounds for backcountry pack-train excursions. —Three Rivers Historical Society

Efforts to accommodate pack operations extended to the smaller operators as well as to the large concessionaires. In the 1930s the Yosemite Park & Curry Company agreed to allow three small pack outfits to handle their packing business in outlying areas of the park. The company signed an agreement with the San Francisco Recreation Commission to handle a saddle and pack service for the city's municipal camp in Hetch Hetchy Valley, then subcontracted the job to Joe Barnes at Mather for one percent of the gross revenue. The Yosemite Company agreed to furnish one-half of the stock needed, "for which Joe Barnes will pay the Company seventy-five cents per horse per day including saddle, bridle and blanket."[148] The association between the Yosemite Park & Curry Company and Joe Barnes was a long-lived affair, lasting from 1932 into the mid-1960s.

Viola Chubb, one of a handful of women outfitters, was another subcontractor to the Yosemite Park & Curry Company.

In 1938 she paid the concessionaire twenty-five cents a head for all stock used in the park out of her headquarters at Jackass Meadows on the Beasore road, while the company paid her twenty-five dollars a year to be its agent. In return, she was required to limit the area of her operations to approved boundaries; to have her stock, saddles, equipment, and personnel subject to their approval; and to provide them with the names and addresses of all her customers.

Most agreements were mutually beneficial and the outcomes successful. But not always. The contract between Bob Bright, owner of the Aspen Valley Lodge on the old Tioga road, and Yosemite Park & Curry Company in the 1930s caused friction between the latter and the National Park Service. As an early pioneer of the area and owner of private land within park boundaries, Bright saw no reason to accommodate either the park or the concessionaire. In 1938 he had asked the park for a permit to use park trails but had been offered a subsidiary agreement with the Yosemite Park & Curry Company instead.

"We have considered your plan, but as we can not see any gain to our business by using your stock, and only a lot of trouble, we have made up our minds to try out free horse service with hotel accommodations," Bright responded to Yosemite Park & Curry Company president Dr. Don Tressider.[149] Bright's plan was to get his own franchise with the Park Service.

The government had reasons of its own to oppose Bright, and it prevailed upon Tressider to resist him. "If the Brights obtained a direct packing privilege from the United States they would start to promote Aspen Valley, thereby increasing possibly the patronage to Aspen Valley Lodge and building up the value of the property which eventually the Government expected to buy," Tressider wrote in a 1939 memorandum.[150]

Although he held rights to all stock usage in Yosemite, Tressider felt the Park Service's insistence upon the subcontract created bad publicity for his company. However, realizing the need for cooperation, he followed their wishes. The whole argument was soon moot: in 1940 the building of the new Tioga road isolated the Aspen Valley Lodge and made the packing operation obsolete.

Subcontracts with the Yosemite concessionaire were not the only means of working within park boundaries. In the

1940s, although the authorization for their use of park trails was designated experimental, two to six packers based on adjacent Forest Service lands were approved for travel in the Yosemite backcountry.

Working with specific pack operations was a start in conservation efforts. But with major trails and popular campsites continuing to degrade, the government needed the cooperation of private groups as well. In 1941, acknowledging its own need to address the problem, the Sierra Club formed a committee on pack-stock grazing in the California national parks to help define the problems and goals of grazing management. In cooperation with the Park Service and assisted by E. Lowell Sumner Jr., at that time regional biologist for the Park Service, the committee drafted a report in December 1941.

> Mr. Sumner's report and the committee's observation show that many meadows subject to pack stock grazing are seriously deteriorating, and that some are almost past recovery. . . . In such meadows, as the result of over-grazing, breaking up of sod by grazing too early in the season, replacement of forage grasses and sedges by weeds and the inroads of brush and trees, aggressive constructive steps designed to restore the forage should be taken at once. If this is not done the forage value of the meadows will be completely destroyed and there will result a condition in the National Parks as serious as that of which we have complained in some parts of the National Forests.[151]

The club's recommendations included the relocation of drift fences, published instructions and signs posted for packers and private parties, the publication of maps showing the locations of available meadows, limitations on the use of critical meadows to one overnight stay for each party, better administrative control of the pack stock of trail crews and other park employees, and the employment of additional rangers to control grazing.

Many of these measures were put into place, but abiding by the restrictions wasn't always easy or even possible. Two parties arriving at the same time to use an area, inadequate feed at approved sites, and animals with minds of their own all made compliance difficult. Finally, the Park Service realized "the absolute necessity" for careful scheduling and park approval of any large parties traveling into the high country.

In cooperation with the Sierra Club, the Park Service formulated restrictions on the number of animals that could be used on a trip before an approved itinerary was required. In 1946 a suggested limit was proposed at fifty, but in consideration of packers' input, the number settled upon was seventy-five.[152]

"The larger trips such as the American Forestry Association Trail Riders and Sierra Club High Trip require a minimum of 75 head to furnish adequate packing capacity for a mobile type trip," packer Ike Livermore wrote to the Sequoia National Park superintendent in 1947. "It is obvious there are many meadows that should never be visited by a big party. On the other hand, there are many grazing areas left in the mountains where 75 or even larger numbers of stock do not create damage."[153]

Packer Charles Morgan pointed out that the alpine grass was tough enough to handle heavy use. "It has a very dense root system and it's very impervious to hooves. You can hardly take a knife and cut it."[154] Yet the grass was not the main concern. Damage to stream channels and to the soil, the introduction of alien plants, and the disruption of wildlife also needed to be considered.

The Sierra Club's first High Trip after World War II added its own restrictions. "As a conservation measure," read the outing announcement for 1946, "the High Trip will this year be strictly limited to a maximum of 125 members. This is essential in order to reduce the number of pack stock so as to minimize the very serious grazing load up on the high mountain meadows."[155]

But even 125 people was too many, Sumner reported in 1947. "Degree of damage to meadows in the High Sierra and rate of disappearance are closely related to their strategic importance as stopping places. Therefore, the most vital meadows are now most endangered."[156]

In response, the Sierra Club continued adding more conservation practices. There now was careful planning of High Trip itineraries to avoid small but critical meadows. Feed was carried to places where the packers had formerly grazed their stock. Night riders sometimes pushed the grazing stock two or three miles from frequently used meadows. The larger groups avoided convenient fenced pastures that could quickly become overgrazed.

All the club's plans were coordinated with the Forest and Park Services and with other pack train outfits to avoid over-concentration of travel in particular areas. Itineraries allowed two layover days for every moving day so that packers could relay supplies to each new camp. Less environmentally destructive options for backcountry trips, such as burro, knapsack, and base-camp spot trips, were introduced.

In spite of the increased cooperative conservation efforts, large pack parties continued to enter the backcountry outside the parks without following the same strict guidelines. They camped in the most scenic places whether their numbers might harm the area or not. They fished out planted streams. They left behind dusty, blackened, trampled campsites filled with makeshift human comforts. And they still overgrazed popular meadows. It was hard for some of the old-time packers who had plied the mountains for years to accept the idea that they might be damaging the land on which they depended.

"I would like to think that all the early packers had some knowledge and interest in conservation," Charles Morgan said. "Where we had stock we would camp in areas that could handle them. It was responsible use. We would never camp that many people in an area where there was a lot of pressure. We would camp where it was ecological, off the beaten path where there was little use. We didn't leave any impact."[157]

"I do recall when I was a kid I saw some old time guides lead parties with 40 or 50 head of stock," Yosemite area's Johnny Jones remembered. "They would loose herd the pack stock which were all trained to stay in line. Riding through where they were camping you might see some of their people, but you would never see either their camp or their stock. Camps were out of sight, away from streams and meadows. The stock was back up a little canyon. Little gate barriers held the stock well away from the trails and camps. Most stockmen and back packers I know love the mountains and talk about protecting the wilderness."[158]

But nostalgia for simpler times had to give way to the reality of change. As more and more people went into the backcountry, these same packers came to realize that some restrictions were necessary.

It wasn't just commercial pack operators who contributed to the problem. Equestrian clubs and individual horse riders were traditional vacationers in the wilderness. Local ranchers and their families were among the first recreationists in the Sierra. As soon as trails were opened in the 1850s and 1860s, nearby ranch families explored them. The Dennison, Jordan, Hockett, Broder, Smith, and Porter families in the Tule and Kaweah areas; the Dusy, Fox, and Kanawyer families on the Kings; and the Carlin, Elwell, Reid, Errera, Rusk, and Smith families on the Merced and San Joaquin were among the ranchers known to have used the backcountry beyond their grazing grounds to fish, hunt, and relax. On the east side of the Sierra, ranchers Carmen Olivas and Charlie Robinson took family and friends on recreational pack trips long before they started charging fees for the service.

Often such trips were community events, with several families from local towns gathering to travel into the backcountry. That tradition continued for years with private horse and mule parties using Sierra trails without restrictions. By the early 1900s, several riding clubs from all over California began to gather for summer trips into the backcountry. As their numbers grew, so did reports of abuses including overgrazing, spoilation of campsites, and contamination of streams and lakes.

However, by the 1940s riding clubs had become an integral part of conservation efforts. They too began to emphasize careful treatment of the environment. They also helped with the maintenance and management of wilderness areas, conducting light trail maintenance, cooperating to define and regulate wilderness grazing and camping practices, and performing backcountry clean-up duties.

In 1948 commercial packers also responded to the concern. The High Sierra Packers Association formulated its own self-regulation. The Eastern Unit created a packer's code, and many of the recommendations contained in it were incorporated into Forest Service regulations. The code promised ecologically sound practices and operations that would please both customers and government agencies.

The code stipulated that only physically fit, well-shod animals would be rented, that all equipment would be kept in serviceable condition, and that pack stations would be kept neat, orderly, and in good repair. Members of the association would not use more stock than were needed on trips nor graze stock on National Forest lands when they were not in service. They would solicit business only from established headquarters, cooperate in preventing and suppressing fires, maintain clean camps, and unload and keep stock out of camping areas.

E. Lowell Sumner at a campsite trash dump near Charlotte Creek and Bubbs Creek Trail, Kings Canyon National Park, 1940. —Sequoia National Park Archives

Furthermore, association packers agreed to assume responsibility for the safety of their patrons, to preserve trails by not permitting shortcuts, not to drive loose stock on narrow trails, and to close all gates after passing through drift fences. They would observe all agency rules on the use of feed and public pastures, graze stock of large parties away from popular areas, and obey all state fish and game laws. In addition, to combat the degradation of campsites in the high country, the Packers' Association in cooperation with the Sierra Club inaugurated a program for camp cleanup in heavily used areas.

Such measures had become a necessity for the pack station operators of the High Sierra. Long gone were the industry's beginnings as haul companies for mining camps and small communities. Modern stock packing was for recreation. Pack trips were for the hunters and fishers, climbers and nature lovers who wanted guides. Their customers expected service and good food, and they wanted a few civilized amenities without seeing signs of the civilization that provided them. Degraded campsites, rutted trails, overfished streams, and overgrazed meadows were simply bad for business.

Tobe Way fishing camp, Hutchinson Meadows, 1930s. From the 1920s to the 1940s, camps were comfortable, even elaborate. Some were considered permanent, their constructed amenities used year after year by commercial packers. —Frasher Collection, Eastern California Museum

PART III

THE PACKING LIFE

TWELVE

Making a Go of It

"Looking back on it, it has been as flat as a pond," packer Sam Lewis wrote of his life. "Mostly hard work and privation as I was living it, with a few highlights, a good share of obstacles, and a lot of competition from other men attempting to make a go of it in a hard land."[159] Lewis was one of the more successful packers in the southern Sierra Nevada. But it wasn't easy in a profession filled with economic hardships, changing priorities, and the vagaries of nature.

Originally, Sam had no intention of becoming a pack outfitter. His ambition was to run cattle and raise horses. In 1914, at age nineteen, he rode out of Los Angeles looking for open country "where I could shout, sing or cuss and take a deep breath."[160]

Sam found his country at Little Lake, in the foothills just south of Owens Valley. There, road-station owner Riley Hart paid him forty-five dollars a month with board for breaking horses. After two months, Sam left Little Lake for other jobs, but he returned the next year to run a pack outfit for the new owners of the Little Lake station, race driver Bill Bramlette and his wife. At the same time, Sam started a homestead ranch in the Rose Springs Valley. But he soon found he couldn't make a living raising cattle on the meager grasses of the eastern desert foothills.

"I was too ignorant to realize all it would take to raise cattle," Sam wrote later. "I lost both the time and the money I invested in cows. But during those years I found that horses could survive here on this range and that people would pay to be packed into the Sierra to fish and hunt in an area where there were no roads."[161]

Sam Lewis, 1968. —Meng Collection, Eastern California Museum

When the Bramlettes decided to sell the pack station in 1919, Sam found a backer and bought it. For the next forty-five years, he was a packer.

Ike Livermore was another example of this special breed of men. Born of well-to-do parents, educated in private schools, he was a young man with many opportunities. Like Sam, Ike did not intend to become a packer.

Ten years after Sam acquired his pack station, Ike was pursuing his youthful desire to work on a trail crew. In 1929 he had been promised a summer job on a Mendocino National Forest crew, but the Forest Service ran out of money. "You might try going to different rangers around the Sierra," one Forest Service employee advised him.

In May, eighteen-year-old Ike rode his motorcycle up and down the length of the Sierra on both the east and west sides.

But everywhere he inquired he was given the same story. Times were hard, budgets were depleted, there were no jobs available. Finally he found himself at the entrance station to Sequoia National Park with ten dollars left in his pocket. He told his tale of woe to the ranger on duty there. "Why don't you try some of the packers?" the ranger suggested.

"What's a packer?" the young man asked.[162]

Fortunately Ike knew how to shoe a mule, and he landed a job at a pack station in the road-end mountain community of Mineral King. There he worked as bull cook (assistant to the head cook), shod horses and mules, and did odd jobs at the corrals. Occasionally he took customers on short day rides, but he didn't go out into the backcountry all summer.

It wasn't until the next summer, 1930, that Ike finally got the chance to work in the Sierra wilderness. Again at the Mineral King pack station, he spent the entire season packing into the backcountry. Then the effects of the Depression hit, and there were no pack trips for the next two years. In 1933 he packed out just two Sierra trips.

After graduating from Stanford University, Ike entered Harvard Business School. There he learned an important fact: he missed the West and the mountains. In the summer of 1934 he returned to California and his packing job. At the end of the season he mounted his motorcycle and rode the Sierra foothills again. But this time he wasn't looking for work. With a questionnaire in his hand, Ike headed out to study the packing business.

Between the Tioga and Walker Pass roads, Ike contacted thirty-three pack outfits, interviewing most of them at length. He compiled a list of seventy-one pack outfits operating on both sides of the central and southern Sierra, noting their locations, number of stock, rates, revenues, and expenses. He learned their equipment, methods, and routes, and discussed their hopes and worries. Then he returned to Stanford and used the report to write his master's thesis, subsequently earning an MBA.

By that time, Sam Lewis had been in the business over twenty years. He was married with six children, all of whom were involved in the family operation. Living far away from any school, their education had been intermittent. Still, all of them graduated from high school, and one went on to college.

*Sam Lewis with wife Olive and their daughter Barbara,
1954.* —Meng Collection, Eastern California Museum

Sam had built his business slowly and with his own sweat. Little Lake station was on the railroad line from southern California and had a hotel for Sam's clients, but Sam wanted his own headquarters. After 1920, when the automobile became more common, he moved the station to his homestead in Rose Spring Valley. With his own equipment, he constructed a road between the base operations and a main trail leading into the mountains. He kept the business small, catering to private parties rather than larger groups.

"I worked all the angles I could to entice customers," Sam wrote. "It took years to build up a regular clientele . . . who were able and willing to pay their way and who encouraged others of their kind to come."[163]

After a road was built in Kennedy Meadows in 1933, Sam lost his hunting and fishing grounds there and had to change his pack route. He bought the packing rights of Jim Cowan and began to pack up Haiwee Canyon, some twelve miles from his home. With the property rights came campsites at Dutch Flats and Deer Mountain, adding to one he already had at Troy Meadow. Later he built another one at Casa Vieja.

To support his new location, he built a primitive road from the highway and erected a pack station at the Portuguese Benches, where springs provided sufficient water. At his four mountain camps, he built six log cabins. He also set up several tent camps, all four to eight hours' ride into the backcountry. His wife, Olive, helped run the pack station, cooked for guests, raised the family, took care of the homestead ranch, "and never did that woman ever complain," Sam remarked fondly.[164]

The Sam Lewis homestead. Portuguese Flat, Olancha, California. —Drew Collection, Eastern California Museum

Building a business without much capital wasn't easy. Until after World War II the Lewis homestead didn't have a toilet, electricity, or running water. When Sam wasn't busy with his packing business he kept money coming in by working for others. He did road work for the state and county and for private interests, worked on mining and farming projects, broke and shoed horses, and did odd jobs for anyone who needed something done. "I wasn't afraid to work," Sam wrote.

"For fifty years my life was . . . developing a primitive area—working at many jobs from breaking horses, cow punching, working roads, doing team work with my wagon scraper and plow, a lot of work with just pick and shovel, which at the time was the only way I could do it. . . . Out away from town the only jobs were labor. Not having much education or much brain power I took pride in my strength and willingness to use it."[165]

Ike Livermore, in spite of his privileged background, did not have an easy time either. In the beginning, he took seasonal accounting jobs in order to leave his summers free to pursue the packing business. Getting his start during the Depression, he had to work hard to get business. Then, just after he was married in 1943, the navy sent him overseas.

After the war, with a family starting, Ike worked in the lumber industry. But he still kept his summers open, building his packing business. In 1937 he bought an interest in the Mineral King Pack Station and in 1946 bought two outfits on the east side from which he formed Mt. Whitney Pack Trains. He founded the High Sierra Packers Association and served as its executive secretary. He also brokered all the stock for five Sierra Club High Trips and personally packed several others. For a time in the 1940s, Ike was the largest outfitter in the Sierra.

Still, the financial rewards were slim. "Dina and I were starting to have our second child, and I could see that packing is not the greatest business in the world to support a family, so I tapered off," Ike recalled.[166] Instead he worked for large corporations and for the state to raise his five children in comfort. All of them attended private schools and college. Three of his sons helped out at the pack stations for several years, but none of the Livermore children went into the business.

Mineral King Pack Station, circa 1940s. —Barbara Hansen Collection

Dina and Ike Livermore and their family. Back row: Samuel, Edith, Pauli, Norman III; Front row: David, Dina, Ike. —Livermore Collection

In 1947 Ike reluctantly agreed to sell his share in Mineral King to his partner Ray Buckman. Four years later, he turned over full management of his Mt. Whitney operations to Bruce Morgan. Still, Ike refused to relinquish his interests in the business entirely. He remained involved with Mt. Whitney Pack Trains until the early 1970s when, after years of financial and permit problems, he and the Morgan family transferred their operations to Rock Creek's Herb London and Bob Tanner.

By 1950 Sam Lewis was beginning to feel the effects of his working life. After developing arthritis, he, too, began to taper off. Not only was his health weakening, but with all the postwar advances in machinery and materials, manual labor was no longer in much demand. Ten years later, at age sixty-five, Sam turned his outfit over to his son, Sam Junior. Sadly, the younger Sam Lewis lost the whole operation some years later.

THIRTEEN

"Characters"

"What I've done is no great monument of much consequence to future generations," Sam wrote in 1968. "We all do the best we can with what we have to work with. However, it is heart breaking for me to see that all my life of hard labor has no lasting value."[167]

Packers are a breed of their own. Strong-willed nonconformists, the term "character" would describe many of them. Cecil "Buck" Cooper and Ted Cook loved to recite Robert Service poetry, scaring children with their renditions of "Dangerous Dan McGrew" and "The Face on the Barroom Floor." Others were the quiet sort. Ed Thistlewaite was a tall, lean man who talked to his mules. "Pretty mule, pretty mule," he would soothe them.

Tom Phipps, partner of Roland Ross in one of the Mineral King operations, was known as an old horse trader. "He'd sell you a blind horse," Earl McKee Jr. recalled. "He'd trade anything. He'd trade his car he was driving. It didn't matter to him."[168] Then there was Mineral King's Phil Davis, who was rumored throughout the late 1920s to have fallen in love with the wife of his head packer, Tommy Carrol, and traded two strings of mules for the right to marry her. Later he lost his Forest Service packing permit, reportedly for polluting the Mineral King stream.

Red Altum packed out of the Red's Meadow station, on the east side of the Sierra. "He started his day with a jaw full of Beechnut Chewing Tobacco flavored with a good sized hunk of Day's Work [tobacco]," Dan Farris recalled. "When he got that going just right he would pull out a Roi Tan Banker cigar, bite off the end and of course add that into the chew. Then

147

he would light the cigar, take about two draws from it then let it go out. He wouldn't relight the cigar but as the day grew longer the cigar grew shorter as he added it into the chew 'for body' as he put it. You could track Red anywhere in the Sierra just by following the tobacco stains on any flat rock he passed."[169]

Many packers began their careers at a young age. Earl McKee had a string of five mules at age thirteen. Bill Welch became a guide for the Yosemite Park & Curry Company at the tender age of ten. In the 1930s wrangler John Alltucker helped drive stock up the Mineral King road when he was only eight years old. He became an assistant packer and guide at age ten and took his own pack train out when he was thirteen.

Pete and Henry "Leakey" Olivas started packing when they were five or six. The brothers inherited a pack station from their father, Carmen, and often packed for the Forest Service as their father had. In the 1970s Henry ran afoul of regulations, refusing to leave his Monache Meadows compound after he retired.

Many packers in the early days defied the rules. In the 1930s T. J. Gilliam packed "aeroplane" customers out of Monache Meadows without permission or permit. After the Forest Service finally gave him one, he didn't always bother to renew it. Fred Cypert and Harold Gill operated almost totally outside the regulations and were posted on the Park Service "wanted" list. "Confidential memorandum for all outpost rangers to keep watch of packers Cypert and Harold Gill," a memorandum from the superintendent cautioned. "Reports of these two men are not too good."[170]

William Stanford "Billy" Ball was quite a colorful talker. He claimed to have been a Hollywood electrician and the first man to wire Catalina Island. At one time, so he said, he owned an ocean liner. On coming into dock one day, he fell off and was crushed between the boat and the dock, causing him to suffer severe "heart attacks" thereafter, notably after nights of prolonged drinking. Married six times, the last time to a woman forty years younger than he, he outlived four of his wives and was nearly eighty years old when his youngest son was born.

Billy owned the Snow Pack pack station north of Little Lake until he supposedly lost it in a poker game. Records show that in 1932 his outfit was sold in a sheriff's auction after a mortgage foreclosure, for the sum of $531.82. Nevertheless, the next spring he applied for a grazing permit.

Some packers were unusually skilled. Ed Sargent was a master with the lasso. He could pick one horse out of a corral of forty galloping heads and lay the rope gently over the one he wanted. Marcellus Brown was so strong, it was said, that he could hold a mule without tying it down, shoe it while it kicked him, and just laugh.

Barney Sears, "a mountain of a man with a beard, pot belly, and an 'S' curved pipe," had much the same reputation. When stock wouldn't behave he hit them, sometimes knocking them to their knees.[171] "There was no mule alive that he couldn't walk up to, pick up a hind foot without the rope on, put a shoe on, and that mule could not get its foot away from him or kick loose, because he was so strong. He'd just pick it up and hang on until the mule would give up."[172]

Born in 1867, Barney lived like an old desert prospector at the Cottonwood pack station. He captured and broke wild horses for his large string of pack stock and raised brood mares in the Lava Rock Desert near Death Valley. The mule colts he bred were so tough that nails couldn't be driven into their hooves—they worked shoeless on rough granite trails throughout the Sierra.

Barney may have been tough, but he was fair. He paid top wages, keeping his workers for years. At age seventy-seven, he admitted that he was getting too fat to ride like he used to, saying he was starting to get tired before his horses did.

Not all in the packing trade were men. Helen "Toady" Parish ran the Parish pack station in Monache Meadows, depending on neighbor boys to help her while her husband drove trucks. Viola Chubb ran an efficient outfit out of Jackass Meadows on the west side. She gained a reputation for toughness in her dealings with the concessionaires of Yosemite National Park.

One notoriously forgetful packer, Archie Dean, known for abandoning pack parties in the backcountry, depended heavily on his wife, Mary, to run the outfit. A scrappy businesswoman, Mary intimidated the formidable Three-Corner-Round outfit when they didn't pay their rent. Her daughters became packers long before it was common for girls to do so.

Drinking problems were not uncommon among packers. Lee Maloy loved his "potato juice," as did Fred Burkardt. Earl McKee fired one packer three times because of drinking but kept taking him back because he was such a good worker. After a night of drinking in camp, Walter Pratt would awaken everybody in the morning by jumping in the creek and yelling. It was "to get the blood going," he always told the campers. "All old packers are either dead drunk or dead, period," became a popular campsite joke.[173]

Actually, most packers were sober, hardworking men who had garnered their education in the wilderness.[174] They were men like Jim Kindred, who had been a master sergeant in World War II, sang funny songs off-key, loved bronc mules, and could outdance any ten men. "He was a mountain goat and just tougher than heck," Earl McKee recalled.[175]

"Absolutely fearless" around mules, Jim could tame any animal. The only thing he couldn't make work was his old Chevy, which always lost its brakes going down the Mineral King road. Whenever it gained too much speed, Jim would run it into the embankment, tearing pieces off the fenders and leaving a line of scraps along the side of the road.

Earl Pascoe, who started packing at age twelve with his father, had his own string of six burros by age sixteen. He worked in the business for forty years, running a lodge and pack station called Road's End. His was considered one of the best outfits on the trail.

Frank Coleman was a Yosemite Miwok Indian who worked for Coffman & Kenney in the early days. Weighing close to three hundred pounds, he had to ride an extra-large horse, and he could carry a ninety-four-pound sack of cement under each arm. Yet he confessed to a deep fear of bears.

Another Native American from Yosemite was Alvis Brown. Born in El Portal, he packed for the Park Service for thirty-two years and was known as the best packer in the country. Out in the backcountry, he and the other packers lived off canned food and whatever fish they caught, supplementing their diets with native plants and an occasional quail. Fellow packer Bob Barrett believed Alvis was the most accomplished Indian dancer he had ever seen. Alvis believed in spirits, and there were certain places he did not like to stay.

Onis Brown, no relation to Alvis, ran wild horses on the Carizzo Plains at the southern end of the San Joaquin Valley. He was a packer for forty years, beginning in 1914. Earl McKee Sr. said Onis knew more about the backcountry than any man he ever knew, and it seemed he had a shortcut to every place in the Sierra.[176] Onis trained his own horses and dogs, teaching the dogs tricks as well as how to lead the horses.

Ben Harris—packer, guide, hunter, teamster, and noted teller of tall tales—was a man to be trusted in spite of his stories. After a trip guiding a greenhorn into the woods, Ben turned up with the man's body strapped to a mule. "Feller died about six days ago, so I brung him down," he explained. When asked why it had taken five days to get him down, Ben answered, "He paid for a seven day trip and old Ben don't go back on his word. So I kept him up there 'til his time was up."[177]

Ben Harris, a packer, teamster, handyman, and teller of tall tales.
—printed in *Fortnight Magazine,* November 1955, from the Crowley Family Collection

FOURTEEN

Mules and Their Tales

The packers weren't the only "characters" in the mule-packing business. The animals themselves had unique personalities and were as full of flaws, virtues, and quirks as their masters.

Billy was a bucker. Shorty loved to have his nose rubbed. Coso defied all mule logic by his distaste for barley, and he once ran back home to his original desert country, not to be found for a year. Then there was Doris, "black and shiny, hard to catch, pretty enough to win a ribbon in the mule beauty contest. She was the sauciest number in the corral."[178]

The mules, burros, and horses in an outfit could contribute significantly to a trip's success or failure, and sometimes the animals starred in adventure stories of their own. Many packers developed special bonds with their animals and thought of them as much more than mere livestock.

Exceptionally smart or strong mules were invaluable to their owners. John Crowley's lead mule, Bess, had the ability to gauge distances to avoid rubbing her pack on obstacles, and her human colleagues relied on her uncanny instincts to help decide what fork to take on unknown trails. Bess could lead the other pack animals around barricades, and she would stop and "blow" to alert the packer of snakes on the trail. She used her talents for her own benefit as well, stealing sacks of barley from under her sleeping wrangler's head.

Earl McKee Jr. had a mule named Fritz that could carry five hundred pounds, including bridge decking of four-by-twelves eight feet long. Fritz learned to stop, look around, back up a little, and turn whenever he hit something. Eventually he seldom ran into anything.

*A member of the party, Bruce Morgan, Charley Gilman, mule "Doug,"
and a wrangler on the trail to Mount Whitney. Some mules were so
personable that they were allowed to join in on various activities, including campfire story-telling sessions.* —Livermore Collection

John Crowley with his lead mule, Bess. —Crowley Family Collection

Another McKee mule was Gus, a huge creature over sixteen hands high that packed the heavy commissary boxes. One day when the pack train was loose-herded through a boulder field, Gus came upon two overhanging rocks that the smaller mules passed under easily but that were too low for him. Gus stopped, looking all around for a better way. He started one way and another, but he couldn't get around the overhang. Finally he got down on his knees and crawled through without hitting his pack.

Gus was so careful and good at judging distances that when the elder Earl McKee died in the Sixty Lakes Basin in 1960, Gus was chosen to carry the body out.

Tommy Jefferson's mule Jed, named for explorer Jedediah Smith, was "always pioneering off by himself, usually in some tasty bit of bunch grass that keeps him too busy munching to check on the where-abouts of his fellow mules."[179] Jed was probably the most intelligent mule the Mount Whitney Pack Trains ever had. He had been jerk-line leader on a twenty-mule team and knew all the tricks of the trade. One autumn, when a herd of stock was trapped in Horseshoe Basin by an early storm, Jed was the only one to survive. He was found far down the mountain below the snow line, totally unharmed.

Not all pack animals were such assets to their owners. Training, shoeing, loading, and leading them could all present difficulties for packers. There were always one or two mules in an outfit that refused to be packed or shod. Ord Loverin had one in his Giant Forest stock that had to have his front feet roped and tied to a tree before he could be packed. Cognac appeared to be the gentlest of mules, but he didn't care for bareback riders, "unloading" them as quickly as he could. He didn't always like the pack loads he was given, either. On a trip in 1937, Cognac broke away and "busted" his kyack, strewing its goods all over.

On a 1903 Broder & Hopping trip, a mule named Corbett tried to kill anyone who attempted to shoe him. "He had already crippled two men and bit another when we tried to put shoes on him," Ord said. "We had to throw him, muzzle him and stretch him out and then hammer the shoes on. When he walked down the trail his tracks looked like he was going sideways, the shoes were so crooked."[180]

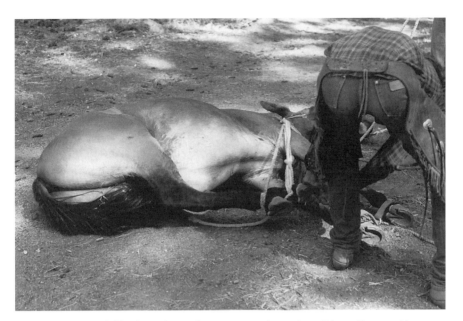

Shoeing a difficult mule, Cedar Grove pack station, Kings Canyon National Park. When mules are brought in from winter range they can be obstinate and dangerous to shoe. Here, Ord Loverin has a "wild" mule grounded and its legs trussed to do the job. —Tim Loverin Collection

Fifteen years later, when Ord was shopping for stock, he heard about a mule for sale that turned out to be Corbett, twenty years old by then and as mean as ever. Feeling an affinity for the old codger, Ord bought him for ten dollars and used him for three more years in spite of his continuing terrorization of the wranglers.

Working with broncs was another challenge for packers. Charlie Robinson and his son Allie used bronc mules to fill out their stock for large Sierra Club High Trips. On one of the 1930s trips, fifty Robinson wranglers decided they wanted to take a ride to the top of Mount Whitney, and Charlie agreed to let them go if each one rode one of the bronc mules. The trip up was easy, but on the way down the mules decided to run down the precarious switchbacks, scattering rocks and the wranglers' curses all along the way.

Most packers loved their mules and treated them well. But there were times when patience wore thin, and some handlers could be mean and even cruel. In 1929 Frank Eggers of Mineral King became so angry with a bronc burro he was trying to break that he pulled out his knife and cut off both her ears.

On the trail, there were always mules that balked at any hint of danger and ran at any sudden noise. There were those that would lie down under a load they decided was too heavy or unbalanced. One day, on approaching a rickety old swinging bridge, Charles Morgan learned what could happen when a mule was displeased.

The bridge had no guards and the split-log planking was patched with rocks. The three smaller mules at the head of the string moved onto the bridge, but the three larger ones

Pack train crossing a small suspension bridge. Mules kicked and wore holes in the boards, which could make the crossings treacherous. Some mules would balk at crossing such a bridge. —Ramsay Collection, Eastern California Museum

at the back balked. When the big ones pulled back, the lead mules instantly lay down on the bridge to avoid being pulled off. In the process, one mule in the middle was jerked off the decking and left dangling by her lead ropes over the rushing waters.

The only way out of the predicament was for Charles to cut the halter rope and let the mule drop into the river. As the animal tumbled down end over end, her pack came loose. After she hit the water, she worked her way about a hundred yards downstream into a chest-deep eddy, where a surprised wrangler eating lunch caught her and led her back to shore.

The army horses and mules sold after World War II were advertised as gentle and easy to ride and pack, but this proved to be untrue for most of them. Ben Loverin and Earl McKee had an army mule they once packed with blasting powder on one side, food on the other, and a gas stove on top. When the stove started clanking, she stampeded, and by the time they caught up with her two miles later, the eggs and dynamite were all mixed together.[181]

Before backpacking became widespread, burros were the favored pack animal for most self-sustained walking trips. Burros are small and easy to pack but slower-moving than horses or mules. Burros are also curious, intelligent, and often just as exasperating as any mule. On a trip through the Yosemite high country in 1911, J. Smeaton Chase and his party used horses, mules, and burros. One burro, a recalcitrant male, delighted in devising means to rid himself of his load. "By practice he had developed an abominable sagacity, and could judge to a nicety the space between trees or below branches that would ensure the maximum damage to his load. Into those places he would charge and stand shoving and straining with sullen fury, hoping to dislodge his pack; and the only way to force him out was by hammering him steadfastly on the muzzle."[182]

On the other hand, the party's jenny, or female burro, was a confiding creature, as willing and placable as the jack was difficult. But even she had her quirks. "During breakfast she would stroll about the camp, receiving our remainders and enjoying the conversation; but when the time came that the detested 'chores' engaged all our attention she would edge off and melt imperceptibly into the brush."[183]

Enticing the burros to work called for flexible tactics. One burro named Adam could be induced to action by a single word or the toss of a small pebble. But with one named Teddy, it took three sharp words, each progressively louder, accompanied by a strong prodding. "I note that the centre of intelligence in the burro appears to lie about the middle tract of the back," Chase noted. "At least the first movement of response arises there. A slight, almost imperceptible elevation of that region is followed by a downward jerk of the head; the ears wag responsively; last of all the legs receive the percussion, and the tough cylinder of the trunk lurches forward."[184]

Teddy had a fear of being left behind and getting lost. On occasion, usually when he was in a field of good feed on a rest stop, he would forget his careful watch. Upon realizing that the other animals had moved on, he would run at a canter, ears rigid and with "an expression of ludicrous anxiety" as he hurried to catch up.[185]

Some of the most remarkable stories about mules and other pack animals occurred on the hazardous trails of the Sierra. While mules are known for sure-footedness, these trails, especially in the early days, were so rough that even the most agile mule could fall off. Yet the ability of a mule to recover in such falls could be amazing. When William Brewer and his companions on the 1864 Whitney Survey team tried to negotiate the infamous Kings Canyon Trail, their pack mule, old Nell, fell and rolled down an estimated 150 feet. She lost her pack but emerged unfazed. The men put the pack back on her, including what was left of a burst bag of flour, and continued on their way.

Horses, too, could recover surprisingly. On the same survey trip, a pack horse named Buckskin fell off the trail, "turned a complete somersault over a bowlder [sic] and landed below squarely on his feet, when he kept on his way as if nothing had happened."[186]

Elizabeth Pass, on the High Sierra Trail out of Giant Forest, was notoriously perilous. Allie Robinson told of watching an entire string of mules roll in single file down four hundred feet of the pass, come up on their feet one after another, and follow the packer on down the trail. Other mules did not fare so well on the pass, however. In 1905 Steward Edward White, his wife "Billy," for whom Elizabeth Pass is named, and their

Near the crest of the Mount Whitney Trail, at its junction with the High Sierra Trail, 1930. Sierra pack animals must be sure-footed and stay calm on narrow trails on sheer cliffs. —John Diehl, Sequoia National Park Archives

friend Wes created a primitive stock trail over the pass. At one point they forced their horses and six pack animals up a ridge above the headwaters of Cloudy Canyon. Struggling across soft snow and ice crust, one horse fell onto the rugged rocks, followed by the mule Jenny. "She started confidently enough, following Bullet's lead, but soon had the bad luck to thrust one hind leg through a thin spot and down into a deep hole."[187]

After they finally got her to her feet, her eyes "fairly glazed with terror," she went down again, then again. "The last ten feet she floundered forward on her fore knees, never attempting to get more fully to her feet."[188] Poor Jenny survived the ordeal only to have to cross more snowfields, narrow ledges, a ten-inch log hung across a "slide rock" (a steep slab without footing), and a vertical grass slope to make it over Elizabeth Pass.

Of course, not all animals survived such dangers. In the late 1890s, fish and game warden Andy Ferguson and his crew were trying to maneuver a pack train carrying fish from the Middle Fork of the Kings River up the incredibly steep and difficult Tehipite Trail. Near the foot of the trail one mule fell and landed on his back between two trees. Mac, the mule wrangler, stopped to extricate the mule while the rest of the crew walked on. Then, on nearing the top of the canyon wall, one of the saddle horses slipped and fell to its knees.

In trying to pull itself up, the horse fell over backwards off the trail. It fell fifty feet, struck the ground, fell another fifty feet, then disappeared over a bluff. Ferguson shouted to Mac, on the trail below, to look out. Jumping behind a tall pine tree and looking up, the wrangler saw the horse sailing overhead, hooves up. Then he heard the crash of its body half a mile below. Although all his mules made it up the trail, Mac left Ferguson's crew at the first opportunity.

On another of Andy Ferguson's fish-planting trips in the late 1890s, while trying to forge a trail into the headwaters of the North Fork Kings River, Ferguson came upon a series of connected benches on the side of a granite wall. He and his helper, Ken, worked their pack train down the benches only to find the last one impassable. "There it lay at our very feet," he reported. "The stream for our tired fish, grass for the horses, rest and supper for ourselves, but, alas, a hundred feet of smooth granite, steeper than the roof of a house was between us and our goal. To go back was impossible. We had brought our stock down over ground which no laden animal could climb back over. Dark was fast approaching and the prospect was anything but pleasing."[189]

Ferguson forced his riding horse, Conejo, over the edge of the cliff onto a snowfield and slid down to the meadow below. Leaving Conejo, Ferguson then climbed back up for the mules. "Taking them one by one, we led the mules to the brink as I had done Conejo. To line them down the slide, as I pulled a mule's forequarters toward me, Ken, using the mule's tail for a fulcrum, swung his hindquarters in the opposite direction. Thereafter, there was nothing the mule could do but slide—and I slide with him. Thus we took the entire string into camp without spilling so much as one drop of water."[190]

Several packers told stories of whole pack strings sliding on their haunches down the early-season snows of high passes. "It is truly astonishing to see with what ease and care these

The bravest of mules. Glacier Point, Yosemite, circa 1930s.
—Pat and Clay Stout Collection

useful animals pack their heavy loads over deep snow," James Hutchings noted in 1856, "and to notice how very cautiously they cross holes where the melting snow reveals some ditch or tree beneath; and where some less careful animal has 'put his foot in it,' and as a consequence has sunk with his load into trouble. We have often watched them descending a snow bank when heavily packed, and have seen that they could not step safely, they have fixed their feet and braced their limbs and unhesitatingly slid down with perfect security, over the worst places."[191]

In addition to working on routine pack trips, some mules did special "high-profile" jobs. For years, in the early 1900s, mules hauled wood and red-fir bark to the 3,254-foot Glacier Point above Yosemite Valley for evening firefall spectaculars, one of Camp Curry's major tourist attractions. It was also popular for tourists to have their photographs taken perched on Glacier Rock, which jutted from Glacier Point's sheer cliff facing. One day, Herbert Earl Wilson, the firefall tender for the Yosemite Park & Curry Company, lured a brave mule onto Glacier Rock to have its picture taken.

FIFTEEN

The Good, the Bad, and the Park Service

For the Park Service, finding an outfit with a cooperative owner or manager, sufficient monetary backing, good equipment, good stock, and competent wranglers was rare. It seemed that even the most trusted outfits could end up having problems. Ord Loverin's was a good example.

The problem started in 1922, when Theophil Leonard Fritzen, manager of the Kings River Parks Company, voiced a complaint to the Sequoia National Park superintendent regarding the Sierra Club's Francis Farquhar. Farquhar had organized a party that planned to leave from the Kings River Parks Company's Giant Forest area, but he had chosen independent outfitter Ord Loverin as its pack supplier and guide rather than hiring Kings River Parks' own services. "I am quite willing to assume all of the responsibility for engaging Ord Loverin instead of the Kings River Parks Company or anyone else," Farquhar informed White. "I sought the best arrangements that I could make both as to reliability, service and rates."[192]

The Park Service ordered the concessionaire to allow Loverin's outfit to use their facilities for the trip, and it grudgingly complied. The Kings River Parks Company had already suffered difficulties. The onset of a severe drought had created feed problems in the area, then an epidemic of hoof-and-mouth disease had broken out. Most discouraging, they had registered deficits of over five thousand dollars for their Grant Park packing operations in 1920 and 1921.

Ord Loverin.
—Sophronia A.
Britten Collection

In 1924 the Park Service suggested that Loverin take over the concession. Kings River Parks Company's parent, Yosemite National Park Company, was more than willing, knowing they were lucky to get Loverin. "It was only with great difficulty that we persuaded anybody to take over the Kings River Parks Company's pack and saddle stock, which had been a losing proposition for years," superintendent John R. White admitted years later.[193]

Born in the foothill community of Eshom Valley, California, Orlin Loverin, nicknamed Ord, had been raised with horses. When he was still a teenager he had teamed for the Hume-Bennett Lumber Company and had shown his business acumen by starting his own freighting company there. He soon moved his operations to the Kaweah area, and in 1903, when he was seventeen years old, he was hired as one of Broder &

Hopping's packers for the Sierra Club High Trip from Mineral King to Mount Whitney. He also hauled construction materials for the Mt. Whitney Power Company's flumes and dams.

After working on a muleteering job in Death Valley with his friend Bert Belknap, he returned to Three Rivers and joined forces with Earl McKee to pack guests on extended tours into the High Sierra. Successfully packing large parties of wealthy people for periods of up to two months, Ord earned a loyal clientele.

It seemed no young man was more impressive than Ord in his mule-handling experience and knowledge of the mountains. In 1923 Carl Akeley, well-known African explorer and naturalist, dedicated a book to him as the best outdoor man he had ever known. So when Ord agreed to take over the Kings River Parks Company operations, the Park Service was pleased.

The honeymoon lasted two years. In addition to Ord's own good stock, the Yosemite National Park Company offered him ninety-two more head at four dollars a head for horses and mules and five dollars for burros. The company also let him use its barns, corrals, and tack without charge for the first year, with an option to buy after that. The Park Service allowed him to haul equipment from the closed Kings River Kanawyer's Camp to Giant Forest so he could set up a small camp there.

Ord's new operation was an immediate success. "Mr. Loverin is maintaining first-class riding horses in the Park," an attorney for the General Grant National Parks Company wrote in 1926. "On the Alta trip we all remarked on how superior the horses were to those usually found at mountain resorts."[194]

By 1924 Ord had netted nearly $3,500. In 1926 he rented a good summer horse pasture in Alta Meadows, which pleased the Park Service, for it kept the meadow from being used for cattle grazing. Ord Loverin seemed to be doing everything right.

But the bubble was about to burst. In the spring of 1926, the Park Service granted a twenty-year contract to a new concessionaire, the Sequoia & General Grant National Parks Company, for the operation of all trail transportation in Sequoia National Park. From the first, the company's officers,

Hazen H. Hunkins and Howard H. Hays, were dubious about Ord Loverin continuing his pack and saddle operations, but the park was insistent. "Unless the company treats Loverin in a liberal manner there is a possibility of trouble in this matter as Loverin is highly thought of by many influential people," John White informed the national park director.[195]

Right away, disagreement arose over the commission Ord was to pay the new company. While letting him retain all profits from the pack-train business, the company requested ten percent of the gross receipts on the lucrative saddle-horse operation. That would be nearly fifty percent of the net, Loverin argued to the Park Service. Finally Ord agreed to pay five percent of the gross profit collected on his saddle-horse, burro, and pony operations.

The new company remained dissatisfied with Ord, accumulating a list of complaints during the 1926 season. Loverin was absent from the Giant Forest headquarters too often, they claimed. The saddle-horse business had been handled in "a rather loose and unbusinesslike manner," and Loverin had failed to send the company a financial statement. The trips often got started late, and one pack party complained of an "improper attitude" toward the patrons. A guide on duty was seen to be drinking.[196]

Of even greater concern was the discovery that, after an accident over which the concessionaires were threatened with a lawsuit in July 1932, Loverin did not have the required liability insurance. He had never paid the premium, nor had he paid for the 1933 season.

Furthermore, he had broken his contract in arranging for a friend to haul hay and drive customers to his pack station rather than having Sequoia & General Grant National Parks Company do it. When the company attempted to confront Ord, Hunkins and Hays claimed that Mrs. Loverin displayed a hostile attitude toward them. To finish the 1926 season on a particularly sour note, the Loverins removed their saddle horses from the park before the advertised closing date of operation without notifying the company.

In response to Sequoia & General Grant National Parks Company's complaints, superintendent John White defended Ord. He pressured the company into signing a three-year lease with the packer, rather than the usual one year. In addition, the contract stipulated that the Park Service would have the final say in any disagreement that arose.

By the time the first three years had passed, however, the Park Service had complaints of their own about Ord's operation. In March 1930 White informed Ord that his base camp at Giant Forest was spreading over too much ground and was beginning to look like a resort. Then in September, the Johnson Brothers, cattle permittees on national forest land, found fifty-five head of Ord's horses grazing in one of their fenced hay meadows. While Ord's employees were blamed for the incident, forest supervisor M. S. Benedict ordered the outfitter to make good on the damages, and in order to control hired packers, he mandated that identification cards be issued.[197]

In spite of the problems, when George Mauger, new general manager of Sequoia & General Grant National Parks Company, alleged that Ord owed the company five hundred dollars and said he wanted to terminate the contract, the Park Service again came to Ord's defense. John White remonstrated with, "My own observations are that he has been satisfactory. . . . This packing business in the High Sierra is a very complicated problem."[198]

By 1933 the conditions between the Loverin packing operation and Sequoia & General Grant National Parks Company had deteriorated so much that the concessionaire refused to extend Ord's contract. "It is impossible for us to work with you under the conditions of the last year," George Mauger wrote Ord in April. "Last season our complaints from tourists about your service were frequent. . . . We cannot afford to be tied up in any arrangement where our liability on account of the saddle horses might put us out of business."[199]

For Ord, the effects of the Depression were making compliance almost impossible. Business was bad, money was scarce, and wages, stock feed, and other expenses were eating up most of his small profits. Meanwhile, his horses, once the best in the Sierra, were getting old, and his equipment was wearing out. He could not hire enough hands to take care of basic operations, let alone to meet all the regulations.

He finally worked out a one-year contract with Sequoia & General Grant National Parks Company, but the conditions in it were overwhelming. The insurance policies had to be paid and the amount owed on the subcontract brought up to date.

The existing corral was to be abandoned and rebuilt in another place. A horse rack (hitching rail with feed bins) had to be fixed near the Giant Forest Lodge with a man always in attendance during business hours. No loitering would be allowed around the corrals or horse rack. A sufficient variety of stock had to be provided for customers, and a thorough overhaul of all the equipment was required. All new personnel had to be approved by both Mauger and the superintendent.

Ord tried to limp through the season with as few packers and expenditures as possible. On July 18, 1933, it was reported that Ord's men had not kept the Huckleberry Corral clean. Ord was ordered to clean it up, but his men did not comply. In 1934 Earl McKee was given Ord's packing contract, and the man who had run one of the best pack outfits in the Sierra had lost his business. By the end of 1933, Ord had already sold his park interests, but he couldn't bring himself to sell everything. He kept thirty-five head and returned to Three Rivers, where he continued to handle a few large parties.

As late as 1947, there were still complaints about the Loverin operations, including grazing infractions and packing without a permit. But by then, Ord was no longer in the business; his brother Ben ran the outfit.

Not all packers had such a hard time. One example was the Three-Corner-Round Pack Outfit, which had its share of problems, yet managed to stay in business. If its long-term success was unusual, its story was too.

The Three-Corner-Round was founded in New Hampshire in 1918 as a summer camp for teenage boys. Its main activity was packing and hiking trips—sometimes in the mountains of South America and India, but most often in California. Yosemite and the High Sierra were the operation's favorite playgrounds for almost forty years.

The outfit used burros exclusively. Each boy was in charge of five burros carrying supplies and equipment for six to eight weeks, with a total of seventy burros on each trip. Members were expected to master nine skills by the end of a trip. Chief among them were mountain climbing, the use of block and tackle, bread making, scouting and patrolling, trail building, and bronco breaking. The groups scrambled up peaks and built burro trails over high passes into secluded basins that were considered difficult even for foot travel. A trail built in

1940 over Forbidden Pass out of Sixty Lakes Basin into the Gardner Basin was one of their major accomplishments. In earlier years, three Sierra Club members and an entire geological survey party had been killed in attempting this pass.[200]

In 1940 the Cleveland Museum of Natural History took over ownership and operation of the Three-Corner-Round outfit. It appeared that the museum planned to augment its natural history collection by having the boys collect high-mountain wildlife and botanical specimens in the area that had just become Kings Canyon National Park. B. P. Bole Jr., the museum's board chairman, petitioned the new park administrators for a permit to collect the specimens. "We have utilized the Three-Corner-Round Pack Outfit, which we own and operate, for the purpose of making these collections," Bole wrote to the Sequoia and Kings Canyon officials.[201]

Guy Hopping, assistant superintendent, issued Bole a scientific collector's permit in 1941 with the statement that, while the park encouraged the group to make further biological studies, "we are interested in keeping much of the new park unmodified, even with trails." He also stipulated that the collecting be done by adults rather than boys.[202]

The next year, superintendent John White withdrew the permit. "We are very much opposed to collections of specimens within the Park, when they may be procured equally well outside the Park," White informed Bole. He suggested the group obtain permission to gather specimens from Sequoia National Forest.

At that point, World War II intervened and the operation was inactive for four years. In 1947 Bole returned to the Park Service with a request for a new permit, which was once again denied.[203] In response to the denial, Bole wrote, "We note your refusal to grant us a permit to collect small mammals within the high country of Kings Canyon National Park, which this institution, the Three-Corner-Round Society, helped to create. . . . In view of the fact that all we wanted to do was catch a few mice in order to teach our boys museum collecting methods, and incidentally preserve the three or four birds which would probably get caught in such mouse traps as we might set out, we do not entirely understand your failure to grant our request."[204]

In spite of the Park Service's denial of the permits, Three-Corner-Round continued to allow its boys to collect specimens in the park, as well as to build unauthorized trails, hunt, and plant fish without permission. Letters directing the group to cease and desist were ignored, as were orders from rangers sent out to the outfit's often nearly inaccessible camps. Bole answered each charge with justifications and continued to do as he pleased.

By 1950 the Cleveland Museum had disavowed any connection with Three-Corner-Round. In 1951 superintendent E. T. Scoyen wrote to questioning members of the Sierra Club, "The first impression was that they were sponsored by the Cleveland Museum of Natural History. However, it finally worked out that this was so only to the extent that the sponsor of the group was a member of the staff of that institution. I am inclined to think this is purely a commercial venture."[205]

It was a well-organized operation. Even the beleaguered Park Service had to admit that, and the Forest Service registered no complaints. The boys were broken into small groups that impacted the wilderness minimally, and they always camped high, off the main trails where the animals wouldn't have to compete for feed. Superintendent White acknowledged that they were one of the best-managed outfits around for "going light" in the wilderness. If there were problems, the benefits the boys gained from their experience seemed to counterbalance them.

Unfortunately, the operation insisted on returning to the same areas in the park almost every year. As more backpackers visited the high country, more complaints were registered against the outfit, and commercial packers complained of decreased forage around the group's camps.

Eventually the Park Service declared Three-Corner-Round a concession, requiring it to pay the costs and comply with the resulting restrictions. Even so, the outfit ignored the requirement for a packing permit every year after 1947, and as late as 1959 the park was still issuing violation notices for the group's illegal grazing practices. But by then the operation was dissolving. Only seven boys and twenty burros were scheduled to be taken out in the summer of 1959, and the venture went out of business soon afterward.

SIXTEEN

Trail Stories

A good sense of humor was one of the most important attributes a packer could have. Practical jokes, funny incidents, and lively yarns helped keep the daily workload bearable. Stories of adventures and tragedies—both true and exaggerated—also kept listeners riveted around the campfire.

Telling tall tales to customers was a favorite occupation and one on which successful pack operations thrived. George Dyer liked to tell the story of a mountain lion stalking a skittish woman's tent all night. The lion wore its path into such a deep ditch that in the morning only its switching tail could be seen, still going round and round.

Ben Harris told of the time he and his riding mule were chased by Indians. Trapped on a bluff and circled by warriors, Ben and his mule decided to jump. About halfway down their fall to certain death, Ben remembered that the mule he was riding was the best trained of the lot and in desperation he hollered, "Whoa, mule, whoa!" Obeying his command, the mule stopped and gently floated to the ground.[206]

Much trail humor took the form of practical jokes. Changing "ducks," or rock trail markers, to lead a group to a vertical cliff was a favorite prank. A packing crew once teased a cook from San Francisco who was afraid of rattlesnakes by rigging a hair rope under his bedding and, just as he was falling asleep, shaking it to move like a snake. Another packer hung a dead snake on a stick at a sharp turn to spook the next packer's horse. As it turned out, the second packer took a different route, and on the jokester's return trip his own horse saw the snake and bucked the wrangler off.

Playing pranks on rookie wranglers was a common amusement, such as the time twenty-six-year-old Charles Morgan devised a test for the new hires in the Mount Whitney outfit. After Bruce Morgan, Charles's father and owner of the outfit, left the station for a few hours, Charles put his plan into operation. "Charles decided . . . we would have an agility test for the new hands to see if the first year men could keep their job," fellow wrangler Ed Turner recalled years later. "You had to walk down the hitch rail, a fifty foot long two-inch pipe, without falling. You had to tree climb. . . . You had to run up the road to the creek, run through it, and run back, and must show that you got wet. . . . We had advised the guys that if they didn't pass they would be put on a Greyhound bus and sent home."

All was going well until a blue pickup truck drove into the yard. Bruce Morgan had returned from town sooner than expected. "Bruce walks up to Charlie—I am standing there with my watch trying to act like nothing is happening—when here

Bruce and Grace Morgan, Mt. Whitney Pack Trains.
—Charles Morgan Collection

comes a kid all covered with water all over his Levis saying, 'How did I do?' Here comes a kid walking down the hitching rail, and another kid sliding down a tree. Bruce says, 'What in the hell is going on here!'"[207] Bruce sold his son a thirty percent interest in the business a few months later.

Packers played jokes on the customers, too. The packers of a "fancy" party, on being told that they couldn't eat or camp with the customers, promptly "lost" all the stock. Claiming to be going to look for the animals, the wranglers went off to play poker for a week.

Tenderfoot customers were the source of many a laugh for packers. There were the ones who burned their clothing trying to dry them by the campfire, and the one who tried to tape a horse's foot after it had lost a shoe. A woman once asked for her picture to be taken atop a mule without realizing that its "fifth leg" was down. Another time, two women were warming themselves by the campfire when a rattlesnake slithered out of some rocks. The wrangler swore he detected two wet spots on the ground where the women had been standing.

Customers asked endless questions about the backcountry, the pack animals, and the wrangler's lives. John Crowley was frequently asked about a mule's sex life. "Being a teenage packer, my response was always made with a red face," Crowley admitted. With some experience he learned to tell the questioner that yes, there are both male and female mules, and yes, they do attempt to breed, but their efforts are always fruitless.[208]

Unexpected transformations in a customer's perspective could occur on a packing trip. During the 1915 Mather Party outing, Congressman Frederick Gillett, a confirmed bachelor at age sixty-five, became so enamored of his mule, Jenny, that he decided "there was really much more in womankind than I had thought in the past years." He got married the same year.[209]

Stories of wild animal encounters were a favorite campfire entertainment. One night, Bert Nice was sleeping in the "kitchen" to guard the mess. An old doe kept coming in, trying to get to the soap that deer like so much, and Bert kept having to run her off. In the middle of the night the whole camp was awakened with a commotion that was louder than usual. "Bert, what the hell happened?" one packer asked. "I just bit a bear," Bert grumbled. A bear had come in to get to the food, and when Bert reared up to yell, he actually got bear fur in his mouth.[210]

Not all trail stories were humorous. When he was a young wrangler, Ike Livermore saved his brother from drowning in Dead Man Canyon north of Elizabeth Pass. Frank Chrysler told of breaking his leg and having to straighten it out in the crotch of a tree before riding alone out of the high country.

Nearly all packers had lightning stories, including tales of trees bursting, hair standing on end, and rocks buzzing. Once, a lightning bolt killed a whole line of mules, but the woman leading them survived. Troy Hall told of the time he was packing in Dusy Basin when lightning knocked off his hat. Marian Moreland was hit in Little Cottonwood Meadows; the lightning burned off her rain poncho and killed two mules and a horse while leaving her unconscious on the trail.

Poisonous plants, such as western water hemlock, larkspur, monkshood, and nightshade, were also threats that

Lillie Neal on top of Mount Whitney, 1926.
—Charles Morgan Collection

could throw a packing party into sudden peril. In the fall of 1926, young Lillie Neal and her fifty-year-old friend, Mrs. Lathrop, undertook what was publicized as the first trip to Mount Whitney taken by women without male escort. They packed their own mules for the trip.

"For four days we never saw a single person and during that time our horses all were poisoned and we thought they would surely die," Lillie wrote of their adventure.[211] The women didn't have "a ghost of an idea" where they were at the time, but they had camped by two meadows that seemed to have enough feed for their three horses. Just before going to sleep they heard their pack horse, Maud, yawling and groaning, and they found her frothing at the mouth. Soon the other two horses were afflicted, too. The women stayed up most of the night with the animals, leading them around and force-feeding them handfuls of soda and salt. By daylight, Maud was barely well enough to put the pack on. They walked the other two horses until noon, when the animals were finally able to eat and drink.

Sometimes packers were given warnings about poisonous plants and other hazards along the trail. In certain cases the wording was almost literary. One report in 1903 cautioned, "Along Soda Creek [out of the Big Arroyo] are a series of meadows enticing to both beast and man. These are the 'Poison Meadows,' but they do not look so attractive when one observes the whitening skeletons of riding and pack animals that have died in this paradise up under the sky."[212]

"WARNING—DANGER—Danger to pack stock from poisonous plants. Six horses have died in this meadow," a sign for Lower Goddard Canyon warned in 1942. "Beware of Larkspur and especially water hemlock. Note: Water hemlock is harmless to people unless eaten. The ancients got rid of their criminals and surplus philosophers by making them drink a deadly potion of it."[213]

In addition to its hazards, the trail had its annoyances. Occasionally a pack train ran into unfriendly backpackers who refused to give way, forcing the whole train to stop and move to one side, tearing down embankments and trampling vegetation. In 1938 packing customer Charles W. Kellogg told of a conflict his group had with some hikers. "A twist in the trail brought us unexpectedly face to face with a group of hikers, holding the center of the trail and refusing to budge. They gaped in awe at the bipeds on muleback. The mules all took exception to this inspection and retaliated by side-stepping daintily but dangerously in a lovely Polka. Fred [the guide] muttered to himself an unflattering opinion of hikers in general and this group in particular. 'Get off the trail,' he bellowed. 'Expect these animals to walk off the edge?'"[214]

However, on the same trip, another small group of hikers joined Kellogg's party at one night's dinner. They all sat around the campfire and played games into the night. Most of the time, a smile and a friendly greeting were all it took to make friends in the wilderness.

The end of a long day. Left, Allie Robinson; second from right, Ike Livermore. —Livermore Collection

SEVENTEEN

Rewards

In spite of all the hard work, long hours, and eternal problems, the packing business could be fun. Backcountry trips were unforgettable experiences not only for the customers, but also for the packers. A perfect blend of wilderness experience and social interaction, a pack trip could inspire individual triumph and group cooperation, swearing and laughter, isolated fear and shared beauty.

Mental pictures snapped in an instant would be imprinted for life. Two little children riding in kyacks, one on each side of the pack, the patient mule carefully adjusting its steps to the bouncing load, plodding without a misstep up the rocky trail. A delighted face at the presentation of a Dutch-oven birthday cake. The impossible antics of a lovesick mule trying to attract the attention of a pretty mare. Evening shadows creeping up an eastern canyon as the west-facing peaks glowed gold.

"Spring reawakens a dream," Yosemite's Joe Barnes reflected toward the end of his packing career. "Trails that rim and wind about snow clad peaks, deep lush meadows knee deep in flowers, sweat, dust and mosquitoes. Hard tail pack mules laboring up a rugged pass. At this point a stranger begins to think there's no beyond, then like a mystery it suddenly unfolds. Its secret exposed leaves him stunned and breathless. Man! Wake up, this is God's country."[215]

It wasn't just the beauty of nature that made life in the backcountry so memorable. It was the people, too. "I best remember Dr. Ray on long hard miles in the saddle," Barnes recalled about one of his favorite customers. "A tense sun, its heat quivering in the dust, chewing brown mule tobacco, a

*A day on the trail. The approach to
Mather Pass.* —Sequoia National Park Archives

grin that always overshadowed weariness, casting a fly that
outsmarted the trickiest rainbow, gay evening camp fires with
stories that are unforgettable."[216]

The magic of the campfire never changed. "No matter how
hard a day's walk or how unpleasant a day, we invariably
had jolly camps," Hubert Dyer wrote of his 1890 trip. "The
cracking fire, the bubbling coffee and sizzling trout or bacon,
always cheered us up."[217]

Around the campfire, the packers and customers shared
songs, stories, jokes, and routines that sometimes had been
planned for days. Discussions of politics, philosophy, and the
effects of grazing in the wilderness were interspersed with
bear stories, tall tales, and memories of the day. Ukuleles, gui-
tars, and voices blended in changing renditions of perennial
campfire songs. A beautiful mouth-organ concert might be

accompanied by the clang of mule bells from a dark meadow somewhere in the distance.

As the fatigue of the day made the eyelids heavy and the fire's embers began to glow orange, stars filled the sky with such clarity that it seemed one could touch the very edges of infinity. Campers warmed their backsides one last time at the fire before climbing into cold bedrolls, then, lying still, listened to the whisper of soft breezes in the forest and the peaceful murmur of a stream. Later they might hear the rustle of a deer or an errant mule looking for a midnight snack. At dawn, packers and customers climbed out of their tents into the silver-frosted morning, awakened by the aromas of simmering coffee and frying fish mingled with pine.

For many of the tourists, these were first-time experiences. The "flatlanders" learned to take soapless baths in icy snow-melt creeks and to wash their clothes by pounding them with rocks in a river. They endured puffed eyes, blistered noses, and cracked lips and experienced sleeping under a poncho in the rain. As the strange magic of the trail overtook them, they learned to savor small satisfactions—a piece of hard candy, a breeze on a hot trail, the cheery "ya-hoo" of packers coming into camp.

On unhurried layover days, the customers learned the thrill of catching "the big one" or took a day hike up a mountain, afterward regaling the others with embellished details of their adventure. They could cheer on the wranglers as they roped anything they could find—pack boxes, buckets, even children. Waiting for dinner, they might surreptitiously lift the lid off the Dutch oven to find a roast, bread, or cobbler.

When there were families on the trip the children added their own dimension of wonderment and delight. After hiking and riding all day they would climb rocks, fish, gather wood, play games, instigate snowball fights and river dunkings, and try to emulate the packers.

For the packers, trips were not novel events, they were a way of life. It was an odd mix of hardship and pleasure, loneliness and comradery. Untying frozen rope knots in the icy morning, playing poker late into the night. Sweating under the high-altitude sun, then sharing a tin cup at a refreshing stream. Sitting in the glow of the fire after everyone else has gone to bed, keeping an eye on a coyote skirting the perimeter of the

Sierra Club High Trip, Hutchinson Meadow, 1937. Ike Liver-more practices his lariat twirling talents. The High Trips had a tradition of staging a "bandana show" of all the brightly colored kerchiefs carried by trip participants (background).
—Livermore Collection

mule herd and hearing the punctuated yelping of its pack in the distance.

Out in the backcountry, keeping in touch with family, friends, and sweethearts was hard. It meant taking letters to a remote ranger station where, if you were lucky, a letter might be waiting for you. It might mean trying to contact a girlfriend you haven't seen in weeks on a ranger's old crank phone, its party-line sputterings making the words almost unintelligible, only to discover the next day that everyone in the High Sierra had heard every word.[218] Occasionally, a short romance would bloom between a young packer and a customer's daughter, so parting at the end of the trip became a heart-wrenching experience.

In spite of the sacrifices, the simple pleasures of the packing life were what counted. Rubbing down the tired mules and horses after a long day on the trail, inhaling the pungent odor of the animals' sweat-soaked blankets and hides and feeling them slowly relax their quivering muscles. The peaceful sound of creaking leather and the soulful braying and snorting protests of the animals. The stinging pleasure of skinny-dipping in the bitter waters of a crystal clear lake. The taste of fresh campfire coffee. The brilliant glitter of sun on snow. It was beauty. It was fulfillment. It was happiness. It was the best that life could be.

Whatever the frustrations of being a mule man, he could never have any true regrets. Sam Lewis knew that for a packer, there really was no choice. "You had dreams and visions to work for, and every effort was expended to bring about the realization of those dreams. Even yet, my thinking is geared to the horse, and the freedom that goes with primitiveness."[219]

Afterword

Ecologically, the High Sierra is a fragile area, threatened by the loss of a growing number of species. Also threatened are the packers who helped build its history. A changing culture, rising costs, and evolving backcountry policies are all taking their toll on the packing industry. Problems of the last two centuries have become portents of extinction in the new millennium. Little incentive remains to keep the industry alive.

There has been a marked change in the American public's attitude toward vacationing in the last fifty years. Easy access to recreation has become the norm. Rather than a long retreat, hurried travelers take short and varied excursions throughout the year, and potential destinations are nearly limitless. The ancient rituals of animal transportation are too time-consuming for those with a modern mind-set. Mule packing belongs to a quieter world.

Still, if backcountry travel is to be fully enjoyed and appreciated, and if our wilderness areas are to be kept open, packing has an essential function. The 1986 Stock Use and Meadow Management Plan of Sequoia and Kings Canyon National Parks states, "The use of pack and saddle stock is still recognized as a traditional, historically and culturally significant and legitimate activity that will continue in the backcountry of Sequoia and Kings Canyon National Parks."[220]

In practice, continuing the tradition is difficult. Conservation concerns limit the number of backcountry trails and camp areas open to stock use more each year, and some hikers' and environmental groups want to keep all stock off the trails. The perennial lack of funding for trail maintenance in the national parks and forests also restricts opportunities for packing. Even more limiting are the spiraling costs of running an outfit. The prices packers must charge to balance the expenses of employees, stock, feed, maintenance, equipment, insurance, and fees are rising beyond what the market will bear. Today's mule men often lose money to carry on the life they love.

Packers are no longer mountain men, characters out of the old West. They have been forced to become ordinary businessmen. Still they follow their dreams, struggling to keep a unique and historic way of life from dying. How long they can succeed is the question.

Pack train at Farewell Gap out of Mineral King.
—Three Rivers Historical Society Archives

APPENDIX A

Historical Pack Outfits of the Southern Sierra Nevada

The following information on packers was gleaned from many bibliographical sources, all listed in the Notes. Because so few records are available, this list does not include all organizations and individuals who have packed out of the Southern Sierra, particularly in the early years. Some names are omitted and dates may be approximate or incomplete, as they are based on whatever information was available. The most helpful resources for the 1920s to the 1950s were the records of the National Park and Forest Services, including actual permittees of each year. Dates given for packers who did not operate during World War II do not show that break. All packers are listed alphabetically, followed by area of base headquarters with known dates or approximate decades of known operation in parentheses.

EAST SIDE

Baker, William F.: Big Pine (1924).
Ball, William S.(Billy): Olancha (1930–1932).
Bell, A. R.: Independence (1923–1924).
Barrett, R. L.: Independence (1936–1937).
Barrett, R. L., and Allie Robinson: Independence (1941).
Bauer, Ralph: The Oaks, Olancha (1946). The Oaks Pack Station.
Bernardin, Lionel R.: Independence (1940).
Bole, B. P., Jr.: Independence, Aberdeen (1920–1950 and beyond). Three-Corner-Round Pack Outfit. The pack outfit first got a packer's permit in 1942 but no longer maintained one after 1947.
Boothe, Dudley, and Alice Houghton: South Lake (1950). Rainbow Pack Outfit.

Bramlette, Bill: Little Lake (1915–1919). Little Lake Pack Station. Sold to Sam Lewis in 1919.

Brown, Edward W., and D. E. McGuffen: Bishop (1931–1932). Mc-Guffen set up a separate operation in 1933.

Brown, George: Pine Creek, Big Pine (1934–1944). Pine Creek Saddle and Pack Train from 1935 to 1943, with O. Y. Mankins.

Brown, Vance: Hilton Lakes, Bishop (1930–1946). Hilton Lakes Resort Co.

Burkhardt, Fred: Olancha (1938–1940).

Burkhardt, Fred, and Richard Burns: The Oaks, Olancha (1923–1934). The Oaks Pack Train.

Burkhardt, Fred, and Wendell Gill: Olancha, Rock Creek (1938–1950 and beyond). Broken Bar Pack Outfit. Bought from Dan McComber in 1938.

Burkhardt, Fred, and Henry Olivas: Olancha (1934–1937).

Burns, Richard, and Frances Gragg: The Oaks, Olancha (1935–1946). The Oaks Pack Train. Frances Gragg operated alone from 1945 to 1946.

Bush, Perry: Bridgeport (1940–1947). Leavitt Meadows Pack Station.

Carter, Dud: Manzanar, Independence, Onion Valley (1930s). High Sierra Pack Trains. In partnership with Archie Dean in the early 1940s.

Chrysler, J. Frank, and Daniel N. Cook: Lone Pine Creek, Carrol Creek (1926–1934).

Chrysler, J. Frank, and Edward H. (Ted) Cook: Lone Pine, Tunnel Meadows (1934–1945). Tunnel Air Camp and Mt. Whitney Pack Trains. Bought Carrol Creek outfit from O. F. Dearborn in 1935. Sold to Ike Livermore in 1946.

Chrysler, J. Frank, and A. L. Hoegee: Lone Pine (1923–1925).

Clark, Frank W. (Bill): Bishop (1923–1924).

Cline, Asa and Everett: Shawhawk (Minaret) Summit, Mammoth (1925–1927). Sold to W. H. Patten in 1928.

Cline, Wilfred: Deadman Creek, Mammoth (1931–1935). Center Pack Train.

Collins, Jack, and Ed Mankins: Pine Creek, Bishop (1949–1950). Pine Creek Pack Station. Jack Collins alone in 1950.

Cook, Dan W.: Olancha (1923–1937).

Cook, Ted: Tunnel Meadows (1934–1936). Tunnel Air Camp. Sold to Bruce Morgan in 1936.

Cowan, James: Dunmovin, Little Lake (1923–1937).

Cruse (Cruz), W. D.(Bill): (1923–1924).

Cunningham, J. F. and T. H.: Mono Hot Springs (1949–1950s). High Sierra Pack Station.

Dean, Archie C.: Independence, Onion Valley (1912–1950 and beyond). Became High Sierra Pack Trains.

Dearborn, Ollie F.: Carroll Creek, Lone Pine (1912–1929).

Dow, G. W.: Jordan Hot Springs, Lone Pine (1933–1935). Jordan Hot Springs Pack Station.

Foote, W. H.: Independence (1930).

Fowler, C. E.: Lone Pine (1930–1936).

Freeland, Frank: Rock Creek (1945–1946). Rock Creek Pack Station.

French, Fred: Kennedy Meadows (1930).

Frost, Arthur (Art) C.: Rock Creek Lodge, Bishop (1922–1934). Broken Bar Pack Outfit. Sold to Russ McComber in 1935.

Garner, Cliff: Crestview, Bishop (1939–1941).

Garner, William J. and Dolly: Convict Lake Resort, Bishop (1935–1949). Sold to Paul Martin and Ivan White in 1949.

Gill, Harold: Onion Valley, Independence (1939–1947).

Gill, Wendell: Camp Nelson (1937), Rock Creek, Bishop (1939–1944). Rock Creek Pack Train. Also received packing permits from 1947 to 1950 and beyond. Frank Freeland operated the outfit from 1945 to 1946, after Wendell joined Allie Robinson (1944–1948).

Gilliam, T. J.: Monache Air Strip, Monache Meadows (1931).

Goss and Foote: Independence (1929–1930).

Gragg, Frances E.: Olancha (1945–1946).

Halliday, Harry: Parcher's Camp, South Lake, Bishop Creek (1924–1936). Became Rainbow Pack Outfits in 1937.

Halliday, Warren J.: Parcher's Camp, South Lake, Bishop Creek, Green Lakes (1937–1944). Halliday's Rainbow Pack Outfit.

Hamer, Fred H.: Big Pine (1924).

Hyers, Stoddard, and Pitts: Independence (1935–1937). Circle Dot Pack Train. Hyers and Pitts from 1937 to 1938, then Pitts alone from 1939 to 1941.

Jean, Walter, and H. L. Womack: Jordan Hot Springs (1930). Walter Jean alone in 1931.

Jensen, Elmer: Silver Lake, June Lake (1946). Frontier Pack Outfit.

Kinney, Ernest, and Spray: Big Pine Creek (1943–1947). Pine Creek Pack Outfit.

Kreider, C. M.: Manzanar, Independence. (1940s). Kreider's High Sierra Pack Trains.

Labachotte, P. E.: Big Pine (1924–1927).

Lewis, Sam N.: Portuguese Bench, Little Lake, Haiwee Canyon (1919–1958). Lewis & Son.

Livermore, Norman B., Jr., and Bruce Morgan family: Sage Flat, Carroll Creek, Whitney Portal Road, Lone Pine (1946–1972). Mt. Whitney Pack Trains and Monache Pack Train.

Lof, Hans: Bishop (1923–1926).

Logan, Robert H.: Big Pine Creek (1925–1931).

London, Herbert, and Donel Tanner: Rock Creek Basin, Bishop (1950 and beyond). Rock Creek Pack Station. Bought from Burkhardt and Gill. In 1972, London and Tanner with Tommy Jefferson also acquired the Mt. Whitney Pack Trains outfit.

Lumpkin, Charles and Helen: McGee Creek, Bishop (1947–1950 and beyond). McGee Creek Pack Station.

Lynn, Jack: Virginia Lakes, Bridgeport (1940–1947). Virginia Lakes Pack Outfit.

Mahan, Archie G.: Devil's Post Pile, Mammoth Lakes (1944–1950 and beyond). Red's Meadow Pack Train.

Mankin, Dee, and Jack Collins: Pine Creek, Bishop (1948–1950 and beyond). Pine Creek Pack Outfit.

Mankins, Oma Y., and George Brown: Big Pine Creek (1934–1943). Pine Creek Saddle & Pack Train. Mankins alone from 1943 to 1948.

Martin, Paul, and Ivan White: Convict Lake Camp, Bishop (1949–1950 and beyond).

McComber, Russ and Dan G.: Rock Creek Lakes, Bishop (1935–1938). Broken Bar Pack Outfit. Sold to Burkhardt and Gill in 1938.

McGuffin, D. E., and Ed Brown: Lake Mary, Mammoth (1931). Lake Mary Pack Outfit.

McGuffin, D. E., and R. Smith: Lake Mary, Mammoth (1932). Lake Mary Pack Outfit. McGuffin alone from 1933 to 1938.

McNinch, Glenn: Mammoth (1948–1949).

Mintzer and Frost: Rock Creek Lodge, Bishop (1926–1934). Broken Bar Pack Outfit. Mintzer joined Frost in 1926 after a year on his own.

Moore, Bob: Cottonwood Creek (1930s). Bought Cottonwood Lakes Pack Station sometime after Barney Sears sold it to Sonny Vintage in 1948 and operated it from 1950s to 1960s.

Morgan, Bruce: Tunnel Meadows (1936–1946). Tunnel Air Camp.

Morgan, Bruce, and family, with Norman B. Livermore Jr.: Sage Flat, Carroll Creek (1946–1965). Mt. Whitney Pack Trains. Morgan's son Charles and his wife, Mary, and Morgan's daughter Barbara and her husband, Tommy Jefferson, ran the outfit from 1950 to 1965. In 1964 Charles's participation ended with Jefferson taking over the operation and running it until 1972. In 1972 the outfit was turned over to Tanner and London, with continued management by Jefferson for several years.

Olivas, Carmen: Olancha (1890s). Commercially serviced both mines and Sierra vacationers. Lone Pine Canyon, Independence (1901–1934). Olivas Pack Train.

Olivas, Henry and Carmen: Olancha (1923–1924). One-Bar-One Pack Train.

Olivas, Henry and Ethyl: Sage Flat, Olancha, Monache Meadows (1938–1985).

Olivas, Henry, and Fred Burkhardt: Lone Pine (1934–1937). Burkhardt bought out Olivas in 1937.

Overhaulser, Edward C.: Lone Pine (1923–1933).

Overton and Offutt: Shawhawk (Minaret) Summit, Mammoth (1929–1930).

Parcher, W. C.: Parcher's Camp, Bishop (1923–1924).

Parker, George V.: Onion Valley, South Fork Oak Creek, Independence (1930–1950). Parker's Camp & Pack Train.

Parker, George V., and Albert M. Blunt: Onion Valley, South Fork Oak Creek, Independence (1925–1929).

Parker, Lee: South Fork Oak Creek, Independence (1930). Parker's Pack Train.

Parnell, W. P.: Mammoth (1946).

Partridge, Wallace: Bishop (1935–1944). Sold to Jesse Johnson and Ed L. Sargent in 1944.

Patten, W. H.: Shawhawk (Minaret) Summit, Mammoth. (1928–1929). Sold to Overton and Offutt in 1929.

Pattison, Jim: Bridgeport (1949–1950 and beyond). High Sierra Packers.

Pearce, Jay: Green Lakes and Devil's Gate, Bridgeport (1946–1947). Green Lakes Resort Station and Devil's Gate Pack Station.

Pearson, Clyde: Hilton Lakes Camp, Bishop (1947–1950 and beyond).

Pierce, Lee: Independence (1924–1932).

Pitts, L. H.: Independence (1935–1941).

Porter, George C., and son: Little Lake (1929).

Powell, W. P.: McGee Creek Canyon (1945–1946).

Purnell, Clarence: Jordan Hot Springs (1941–1948). Purnell Brothers Pack Outfit.

Purnell, Clarence, and Tom J. Mader: Jordan Hot Springs (1949–1950 and beyond).

Raymer, Fred and Edith: Convict Lake, Bishop (1927–1935). Edith alone after 1928.

Roberts, Charles A.: Bishop (1923–1930).

Robinson, Allie: Onion Valley, Symmes Creek, Oak Creek, Taboose Creek, June Lake, Independence (1928–1941). After World War II, also Leavitt Meadows, West Walker. Robinson Pack Trains and Leavitt Meadows Pack Train.

Robinson, Allie, and Fred Burkhardt: Independence (1941–1943).

Robinson, Allie, and Wendell Gill: Independence.(1944–1948).

Robinson, Charles W., Independence (1872–1928). Robinson Pack Train & Auto Camp. Base operations on lower Onion Valley Road from 1901 to 1928. Sold to son Allie Robinson in 1928.

Sanford, Stephen H.: Parcher's Camp, South Lake, Bishop (1922–1924). Sanford Brothers Pack Station.

Sargent, Ed L.: Glacier Lodge, Big Pine (1945–1950 and beyond). Glacier Pack Train.

Schober, R. J and Art C.: North Lake, Bishop Creek (1931–1950 and beyond). Schober Brothers Pack Train. Bought from Tobe Way in 1931.

Sears, Barney H.: Cottonwood Lakes, Olancha (1923–1948). Cottonwood Lakes Pack Station.

77 Corrals: Pumice Flat near Devil's Postpile (1920–1930s).

Shelly, Alfred: Parcher's Camp, South Lake, Bishop Creek (1945–1949). Rainbow Pack Outfit. Bought from Harry Halliday in 1945.

Siebenthal, Orrind: Big Pine (1930s–1940s).

Spainhower, Russell: Taboose Creek, Independence (1909). Drove pack stock for the Los Angeles aqueduct construction.

Spainhower, R. B.: Manzanar, Lone Pine (1941–1942).

Spear, Raymond W.: Lone Pine (1923–1928).

Steward, J. C.: Big Pine (1945–1950 and beyond).

Streckewald, Hovey, and Herbert London: Rock Creek, Mammoth (1947–1950 and beyond). Rock Creek Pack Station.

Summers, Charles: Agnew Meadows, Mammoth Lakes, Bishop (1940–1949). Agnew Meadows Pack Station.

Summers, Jack: Mammoth, Bishop (1950 and beyond).

Summers, Lee: Agnew Meadows, Lake Mary, Mammoth (1946–1950 and beyond). Mammoth Camp Pack Outfit.

Summers, Lloyd: Agnew Meadows, Lake Mary, Mammoth (1925–1946). Mammoth Camp Pack Outfit. Taken over by Lee Summers in 1946.

Tatum, Slim: June Lake, Mammoth (1930s–1940s).

Thelan, Horace P.: Mabel R.R. siding above Little Lake, Kennedy Meadows (1922–1933). Kennedy Meadows only (1933–1950 and beyond). Kennedy Meadows Pack Station.

Thorington, Cecil: McGee Creek, Bishop (1934–1944). Sold to W. P. Powell in 1945.

Wampler, Joseph C.: Whitney Portal, Lone Pine (1950).

Way, Roy (Tobe): North Lake, Bishop Creek (1923–1931). Sold to R. J. Schober in 1931.

Way, Roy: Mammoth, Bishop (1923–1948).

Wilson, Wally: Lone Pine (1928–1936 and 1938–1941).

Wilson and Chevis: Lone Pine (1936–1937).

Womack, H. L.: Jordan Hot Springs (1930).

WEST SIDE

Aiken, Jim: Tule River (1880s–1890s).

Ainsworth, Chet: Dillonwood, Springville (1948).

Anderson, Ted: Dinkey Creek (1930s–1940s).

Averill, D. R.: Pine Crest (1940).

Avila, J.: Dinkey Creek (1949). Sleepy 2 F Pack Train.

Barnes, Joe: Mather, White Wolf, Yosemite (1930–1969).

Bash, William (Bill): Coolidge Meadows, Trimmer (1930–1941).

Beaty, Pemberton: Weldon (1930s).

Benadom, Viola: Dunlap (1930s).

Berry, H. M.: Posey (1930s).

Berryhill, Claude: Blayney Meadows (1930s).

Bittner, Louis J.: Sonora, Dardanelles, Kennedy Meadows (1947).

Branscom, Floyd: Mariposa (1930s).

Bright, Robert (Bob) L.: Aspen Valley, Yosemite (1937–1940). Aspen Valley Lodge.

Britten, Clarence: Three Rivers (1924–1926).

Broder, John: Three Rivers (1898).

Broder, John, Ralph Hopping, and Jim Griffin: Giant Forest (1899–1908).

Brown, Billy: Jackass Meadows (1930s).

Brown, Onis J.: Three Rivers, Lemon Cove (1915–1949). Silver City (1949).

Brunnette and Stribling: Blanchard (1947). Cherry Valley Packers.

Buckman, Phil, and Frank Eggers: Mineral King (1929). Mineral King Packing Company. Bought from Phil Davis in 1929. Sold to Ray Buckman and Ike Livermore in 1937.

Buckman, Ray: Mineral King, Three Rivers (1948–1953). Mineral King Packing Company.

Buckman, Ray, and Norman B. Livermore Jr.: Mineral King, Three Rivers (1937–1947). Mineral King Packing Company. Buckman alone from 1948 to 1953. Sold to Lee Maloy in 1953.

Bunn, Walter T.: Dinkey Creek (1940s). Diamond X Pack Trains.

Burns, Glenn T.: Huntington Lake, Clovis (1930s–1954). Huntington Lake Stables.

Burton, J. Frank: Mountain View Resort, Posey (1930s).

Canfield, G. W. (Bill): Three Rivers, Exeter (1917–1930s).

Carlin, Tim: Hardin Lake, Yosemite (1915–1938).

Carrol, Tom: Three Rivers (1930s).

Cecil, Ernest: Cedar Grove, Badger (1930s–1940s). Cecil Pack Train.

Cecil, J. A.: Big Meadows, Badger (1930s). Cecil Pack Train.

Chubb, Viola: Jack Ass Meadows, Bass Lake (1935–1939).

Clodfelter, Dan: Three Rivers (1870s–1880s).

Coffman, William F., and George W. Kenney: Yosemite Stables (1906–1915). The Coffman & Kenney stables were absorbed in 1915 by the D. J. Desmond Co., which became the Yosemite National Park Co. in 1919. That, in turn, merged with the Curry Camping Co. to become the Yosemite Park & Curry Co. in 1925. The stables still in use today were built in 1927. In 1993 the company name was changed to Yosemite Concession Services.

Coker, R. T.: Big Meadows, Badger (1930s).

Combs, Nate R.: Blayney Meadows, Prather.(1940s). Diamond D Guest Ranch.

Crabtree, Rae M.: Coolidge Meadows, Balch Camp, Academy (1940s). Arrow-Heart Pack Train and High Sierra Guide Service.

Cunningham, John E. "Shorty," and son John: Florence Lake, North Fork (1948–1950 and beyond). High Sierra Pack Station. Son bought into the operation in 1968 and bought out his father in 1980.

Cunningham, Tom H.: Mono Hot Springs (1940s).

Cunningham, Vaud: Huntington Lake (1922–1941). Sold to Floyd Fike in 1941.

Cypert, Fred H.: Springville (1940s).

Dale, John: Dinkey Creek (1930s–1940s).

Davis, Eugene: Mineral King (1920–1924). Sold to Phil Davis 1924.

Davis, Eugene, and Jim "Bumble Bee" Kame: Mineral King (1901).

Davis, Laurence S. and Roy: Mineral King, Woodlake (1924–1950 and beyond). Davis Corrals. Bought from Bert Smith in 1924. Laurence and Roy Davis were partners, with Clarence Britten also acting as guide and minor partner.

Davis, Phil: Mineral King (1924–1929). Sold to Buckman and Eggers in 1929. Three Rivers (1930s).

Davis, Roy: Mineral King, Three Rivers (1923–1924).

Davis, Samuel B.: Cedar Grove, Woodlake (1949–1950 and beyond). Bar Seven Pack Station.

Dean and Wacaser: Kings Canyon (1940s).

Dillon, George, and Art O. Griswold: Dillonwood, Tule River, Balch Park, Springville (1910s–1940s). Balch Park Pack Trains.

Dillon, W. F.: Bass Lake (1930s).

Ducey, Jack E: Prather, Academy (1940s).

Duncan, Malvin, and Jim McDonald: Camp Wishon (1914).

Dupzyk, Fred: Bass Lake (1930s).

Eggers, Frank: Three Rivers (1930s and 1940s).

Ellis and Scott: Kings Canyon (1916). Cascada Pack Outfits.

Fenton, F. J.: Dinkey Creek (1940s).

Fike, Floyd E.: Huntington Lake (1945–1980). D & F Pack Camp. Bought out Vaud Cunningham in 1941 and Glenn Burns in 1954.

Fox, John: Cedar Grove (1890s).

Fraga, Dave: Dinkey Creek (1950 and beyond).

Fry, Clarence: Three Rivers (1909–1918).

Gill, Fred W.: Three Rivers (1941).

Gill, Wendell: Camp Nelson (1937).

Green, Duty: Springville (1895–1916).

Greigg, Walter: Quaking Aspen, Lloyd Meadow, Balch Park, Springville (1930s). Aspen Meadow Pack Station.

Griswold, Art: Springville, Balch Park (1920s–1930s).

Guinn, Charles B.: California Hot Springs (1930s).

Hamby, George: Fish Camp (1930s).

Harris, Ben F.: Mineral King, Farmersville (1920s–1930s).

Hobbs: Balance Rock, Posey (1930s).

Johnson, Clyde: Crown Valley (1930s).

Jones, Thomas: Bass Lake (1910s); Beasore Meadow, Coarsegold (1920s–1953).

Kame, Jim "Bumble Bee": Mineral King, Three Rivers (1890s). In 1901 Kame took Eugene Davis as a partner.

Kanawyer, Poley: Millwood (1901–1921). Barton's on Kings Canyon Highway (1921–1940s). Hume Lake (1930s).

Kurzi, Frank: Kennedy Meadows, Dardanelles, Sonora (1940–1946).

Lawson, Otis: Tule River (1910s).

Lemm, Milo: North Fork (1930s).

Loverin, Ord: Three Rivers, Giant Forest (1916–1946). Operated out of Giant Forest from 1924 to 1933.

Maloy, Lee, and Mrs. Earl McKee: Giant Forest, Three Rivers (1946–1953). McKee-Maloy Pack Trains. Maloy bought the Mineral King Pack Station from Ray Buckman in 1953.

Mankins, Oma Y.: Hume Lake, Dunlap (1940s). Bar Seven Pack Train.

Maxon, Fred: Three Rivers (1914).

McComber, D. G.: Camp Nelson, Springville (1940s).

McKee, Earl: Three Rivers, Hospital Rock, Giant Forest (1901–1948). At Giant Forest from 1934 to 1946.

Meyer, Horace: Yosemite (1938–mid-1960s).

Meyer, Wilson: White Wolf, Yosemite (1948).

Moyle, Chester: Mariposa, Merced (1920s–1940s).

Negus, Frank: Tule River (1910s); Balch Park, Springville (1920s–1940s). Balch Park Pack Station.

Nelson, John, and Carmel Wilson. Jim Aikin Ranch, Springville, Camp Nelson (1890s–1922).

Nelson, Smith: Camp Nelson (1922–1930s).

Parker, Milton: Bass Lake (1949). Sierra Pack Camp.

Parker, J. C. Jr.: Merchant of Visalia (1860). Supplied animals and supplies for trips to the Cosos Mines.

Phillips, Newt J. and Lloyd: Jerseydale, Fish Camp (1910s–1930s).

Phipps, H. A., and son: Mineral King, Lindsay (1927–1930s).

Phipps, Tom, and Roland S. Ross: Mineral King (1918–1929). In 1927 Phipps sold half interest to Ross.

Qualls, Dave: Huntington Lake (1910s–1920s).

Robinson, J.: Coolidge Meadows, Shaver Lake Heights (1930s).

Ross, Fred: Blayney Meadows (1941).

Ross, Roland S.: Mineral King, Three Rivers (1927–1950 and beyond). In 1927 Ross bought out Tom Phipps.

Rutherford, Kenneth and Owen: Camp Wishon, Springville (1930s).

Rutherford, Owen: Camp Wishon (1910s). Sold to Kirkpatrick in 1918. Quaking Aspen, Springville (1920s).

Rutherford, Owen, and Chester Wright: Three Rivers, Grant Grove (1908–1919). Sold outfit to Kings River Parks Company in 1919.

Rutherford, Owen A.: Springville (1940s). Rutherford Pack Station.

Ryder, Worth, and Fred Askins: Giant Forest (1920–1924). General Grant National Park Company. Sold to Kings River Parks Company in 1924.

Smith, Bert: Mineral King (1874–1924). Sold to Laurence Davis in 1924.

Smith, C. B.: Quaking Aspen, Springville (1936). Camp Nelson Pack Train.

Smith, Charles, and Carmel Nelson: Camp Nelson, Springville (1922–1936). Camp Nelson Pack Train.

Snider, Ed: California Hot Springs, Pine Flat (1920s).

Sovulewski, Gabriel: Yosemite (1899).

Spangler, Charles A: Springville (1940s).

Studor, Wilbur: Posey (1930s).

Thorn, Craig S.: Silver City, Three Rivers (1929–1948). Silver City Pack Station.

Tibbits, Roswell: California Hot Springs (1930s).

Traweek, Hugh: Hume Lake, Cedar Grove (1930s–1940s). Bar-Seven Pack Train.

Wacaser, H.: Hume Lake (1940s). Dean & Wacaser Pack Station.

Wass, Fred: Fish Camp, Cathay (1935–1936 and 1941–1947).

Welch, William (Billy): Mather, White Wolf, Yosemite area (1951–1954).

Wilson, Dick R., and Dick R. Wilson Jr.: Wilsonia, Cedar Grove, General Grant Grove (1925–1945). Wilson Pack Trains.

Wissbaum and Mathison: Dardanelles (1947). Douglas Resort.

Womack, H. L.: Springville (1930s).

Wright, Chester: Giant Forest (1910s–1920s).

Yosemite National Park Company: Yosemite, Wawona, Tuolumne Meadows, Mather (1923–1925). Became Yosemite Park & Curry Company (1925–1950 and beyond). Several managers through the years included Jim Helm, Jim Barnett, Jess Rust, and Bob Barrett.

KERN VALLEY

Brady, Pat and Peter: Kernville (1930s).

Calkins, Harold M.: Durrwood on the Kern (below Road's End), Kernville (1920s–1930s). Durrwood Pack Outfit.

Greig, Mrs. Walter: Quaking Aspen Meadows (1920s–1930s).

Howe, J. C.: Fairview (1920s).

McNally, John: Fairview, Kern Plateau (1934–1966). Fairview Pack Outfit.

Pascoe, Cecil J., and sons: Camp Pascoe, Road's End, Kernville (1920S–1930s). Bar 53 Pack Outfit.

Pascoe, Earl V.: Belleview, below Road's End, Kernville (1920s–1950 and beyond). Pascoe's Pack Train and Pascoe's Lodge & Pack Station.

Welch, Robert E. (Bob): Belleview, below Road's End, Kernville (1920's–1940s). Kern River Pack Train.

Wofford, I. L.: Kernville (1930s).

Wortley, Ken and Chester: Fairview, below Road's End (1928–1934). Sold to John McNally in 1934. Fairview Pack Outfit.

APPENDIX B

Historical Backcountry Campsites of the High Sierra

The following list of campsites in the High Sierra, although incomplete, is included as a beginning reference. The names and locations of campsites listed here were gathered from numerous sources, including articles, trip journals, oral histories, letters, memorandums, Park Service and Forest Service records and reports, maps, and place-name accounts. Because camps could be made almost anywhere and many were unnamed, hundreds of campsites are not listed.

In the early years of packing, especially from the 1870s through the 1890s, camps were made wherever there was feed, firewood, water, and a fairly level spot on the few trails of the time. Sheep, hog, cattle, mining, and lumber camps were popular campsites, but any area that had the necessary amenities and lay within a day's travel from the last campsite could be used.

As the years passed, camping parties tended to concentrate in the spots that had beauty and comfort as well as the essential needs. Itineraries were planned around special campsites. As feed diminished through overuse, government regulations required planned itineraries for large parties, with restrictions on and even closures of some of the overused campsites.

Although Sierra stock packers did business over a large backcountry area, often taking hunting and fishing parties into more northerly areas, the camps included here range across the High Sierra region of the greatest packing activity, from Yosemite south to Kernville. Some base camps used before the advent of automobile roads are included.

The campsites are grouped according to river drainage areas and listed alphabetically. Place names that were found in available accounts of the times are included. Some are areas that contained more than one campsite and/or changing campsites throughout the years. Approximate decades or beginning dates of use as stock trails are shown. Various forks of the main rivers are noted with each individual camp listing.

Baker and Big Pine Creeks
Big Pine Lakes: Big Pine Creek, early 1900s.
Palisade Basin and Lakes: Big Pine Creek, early 1900s.
Palisade Creek: Big Pine Creek, 1910s.
Sanger Meadows: Baker Creek, 1910s–1930s.
Sugarloaf: Onion and Baker Creek, 1910s.

Birch Creek
Birch Lake (above Big Pine): Birch Creek, 1920s.
McMurry Meadows (sheep and cattle camp): Birch Creek, 1870s.

Bishop Creek
Andrew's Camp (Resort): South Fork, early 1900s.
Donkey Lake: Middle Fork, 1930s.
East Lake: Middle Fork, 1890s.
Green Lake: South Fork, 1870s.
Lake Sabrina (Sebrina): Middle Fork, early 1900s.

Cottonwood Creek
Cottonwood Creek and Meadows (later Big Cottonwood Creek): 1860s.
Cottonwood Lakes: Cottonwood Creek, 1880s.
Horseshoe Meadow: Cottonwood Creek, 1940s.
Little Cottonwood Creek: 1910s–1930s.

Diaz Creek
Diaz Meadow: Diaz Creek, 1880s.

Kaweah River
Alta Meadows: Headwaters Middle Fork, 1870s.
Aster Lake: Marble Fork of Middle Fork, 1920s.
Bacon Meadow: Middle Fork, early 1900s.
Bear Trap Meadow: Marble Fork of Middle Fork, 1880s.
Bearpaw Meadow: Middle Fork, 1930s.
Big Meadows: Giant Forest area, Middle Fork, 1870s.
Blossom Lakes: South Fork, 1900–1930s.
Cabin Meadow (originally Sheep Camp): Marble Fork of Middle Fork, 1880s.

Cahoon Meadows: Marble Fork of Middle Fork, 1880s–1920s.

Cliff Creek: Middle Fork, 1870s.

Cliff Creek Crossing: Middle Fork, 1930s.

Coffee Pot Canyon: East Fork, 1910s–1920s.

Deer Creek (Hamilton Lakes): Middle Fork, early 1900s.

Giant Forest (originally Log Meadow, Tharp's Camp): Marble Fork of Middle Fork, 1870s.

Halstead Meadow (Pasture): Marble Fork of Middle Fork, 1870s.

Hamilton Lakes (Deer Creek before 1929; became a commercial backcountry camp): Middle Fork, early 1900s.

Hart Meadow: North Fork, 1880s–early 1900s.

Hockett Lakes: South Fork, 1860s.

Hockett Meadow: South Fork, 1860s.

Horse Creek: South Fork, 1930s.

Hyde's Mill: North Fork, 1870s.

Ladybug Camp: South Fork, 1860s.

Lion Rock (Meadow): Middle Fork, 1860s–1890s.

Little Wet Meadow: Middle Fork, 1930s.

Log Meadow (Tharp's Camp, later Giant Forest): Marble Fork of Middle Fork, 1860s.

Lone Pine Meadow, Creek (formerly Heather Meadow): Middle Fork, 1890s.

Long Meadow: Wolverton Creek, Middle Fork, 1880s.

Mehrten Meadows: Middle Fork, 1920s.

Mitchell Meadow: South Fork, 1910s–1920s.

Moose Lake: Headwaters Marble Fork of Middle Fork, 1860s.

Pear Lake: Marble Fork of Middle Fork, 1920s.

Redwood Meadow: Middle Fork, 1860s.

River Valley: Middle Fork, 1930s.

Round Meadow: Middle Fork, 1880s–1890s.

Rowell Meadow (originally a sheep camp): Marble Fork of Middle Fork, 1870s.

Sand Meadows: Hockett Meadows area, South Fork, early 1900s.

Sheep Camp (later Cabin Meadow): Marble Fork of Middle Fork, 1880s–early 1900s.

Tamarack Lake: Lone Pine Creek, Middle Fork, 1930s.

Tharp's Camp (Log Meadow, Giant Forest) Marble Fork of Middle Fork, 1860s–1870s.

Tuohy Meadow Sheep Camp: South Fork, 1870s–1880s.

Visalia Big Tree Grove (became General Grant Grove): North Fork, 1890s–1950s.

Weston Meadow Cow Camp: Middle Fork, 1880s–1890s.

Wet Meadows: Middle Fork, 1900–1930s.

Wolverton's Cabin: Marble Fork of Middle Fork, 1880s.

Kern River

Bake Oven Meadows (early sheep camp): South Fork, 1890s–1930s.

Beach Meadows: Main Fork, early 1900s.

Big Arroyo (originally Jenny Lind Canyon): Main Fork, early 1900s.

Big Five Lakes (originally The Five Lakes): Big Arroyo area, Main Fork, 1890s.

Big Pine Meadow: South Fork, 1860s.

Big Whitney Meadows (formerly Whitney Creek Meadows): Main Fork, 1870s.

Bog Meadows and Creek (originally Long Meadow, renamed Ferguson Creek in 1920s): Main Fork, 1900–1930s.

Broder Cabin: Little Kern, 1930s.

Broder Ledge: South Fork, 1930s.

Broder Meadows (cow camp): Monache area, South Fork, 1860s–1870s.

Bullion Flat: Little Kern, early 1900s.

Burnt Corral Meadows: Little Kern, 1870s.

Burton's Camp (later Corral Meadow): Main Fork, 1890s.

Casa Vieja Meadows: West side Monache area, Main Fork, early 1900s.

Chagoopa Creek (Plateau): Main Fork, 1940s.

Chagoopa Falls (junction Chagoopa Creek and Kern River): Main Fork, 1880s.

Click's Creek: Little Kern, early 1900s.

Click's Sheep Camp (Martin Click Camp): Little Kern, 1870s–1880s.

Corral Meadow (formerly Burton's Camp): Main Fork, 1920s.

Cow Camp: Rattlesnake Creek, Main Fork, 1920s.

Coyote Lakes (Creek, Basin): Main Fork, 1930s.

Crabtree Lakes (Creek): Main Fork, 1940s–1960s.

Crabtree Meadows (originally a cow camp): Main Fork, 1890s.

Dark Canyon Camp: Lower Main Fork, 1890s.

Deer Mountain: Little Kern, 1930s.

Dutch Flats: Little Kern, 1920s.

Edwards Camp (Bullion Flat): Little Kern, 1870s–1880s.

Edwards' Meadow (Soda Springs near Little Kern Lake): Main Fork, 1910s.

Ferguson Creek and Meadows (originally Long Meadow, then Bog Meadows): Main Fork, 1900–1930s.

Fern Camp: Kern Canyon, Main Fork, 1880s.

Forester Lake: Upper Kern, Main Fork, 1930s.

Funston's Meadow (became Lower Funston Meadow): Main Fork, 1860s.

Funston's Kaweah Meadow (became Upper Funston Meadow, then Sky Parlor Meadow): Chagoopa Plateau, Main Fork, 1860s.

Golden Trout Creek (Golden Trout Camp, formerly Whitney Creek, then Volcano Creek): Main Fork, 1870s.

Guitar Lake: Mt. Whitney area, Main Fork, 1870s.

Guyot Flat (Sand Flat, Guyot Creek): Mt. Whitney area, Main Fork, 1910s.

Hell's Hole Camp: Main Fork, 1930s.

Jenny Lind Canyon (Big Arroyo): Main Fork, 1870s.

Jerky Meadows: Main Fork, 1920s.

Jordan Hot Springs (originally Jordan Junction; became a commercial backcountry camp): West side Monache area, Main Fork, 1860s–1980s.

Junction Meadows (Junction Camp): Main Fork, 1880s.

Kennedy Meadows (before road built in 1933): South Fork, 1880s–1930s.

Kern Canyon Ranger Station: Main Fork, 1940s.

Kern Lakes (originally Fish Lakes): Main Fork, 1870s.

Kern Flat and Potholes: Main Fork, 1900–1930s.

Kern Hot Springs: Main Fork, 1890s.

Kern-Kaweah Canyon: Main Fork, 1890s.

Lake South America: Main Fork, early 1900s.

Langley's Camp (Langley Meadow below Guitar Lake): Main Fork, 1880s–1890s.

Lewis Camp (Runkle's Place before 1898, later also called Old Dick's Place; became a commercial backcountry camp): Main Fork, 1880s–1980s.

Little Claire Lake: Soda Creek, Big Arroyo area, Main Fork, 1890s.

Little Five Lakes: Big Arroyo area, Main Fork, 1920s.

Little Whitney Meadows (originally Long Meadow): Main Fork, 1930s.

Lloyd Meadows (originally a sheep camp): Main Fork, 1870s.

Lost Canyon: Main Fork, 1890s.

Milestone Bench, Creek: Headwaters Main Fork, 1930s.

Monache (Monatchy) Meadows: South Fork, 1870s.

Mulkey Meadows: South Fork, 1890s.

Parole Camp: Little Kern, 1870s.

Poison Meadow: Main Fork, early 1900s.

Quinn's Horse Camp (originally Quinn's Sheep Camp): Little Kern, 1860s–1930s.

Ramshaw Meadows (originally a cow camp): South Fork, 1860s.

Rattlesnake Creek (Upper and Lower): Main Fork, early 1900s.

Red Rock Meadows: Toowa area, Main Fork, 1900–1910s.

Rifle Creek: Little Kern, 1930s.

Rock Creek (Upper and Lower): Whitney area, Main Fork, 1880s.

Rock House Meadow: South Fork, 1880s–1910s.

Runkle's Ranch (above Kern Lakes): Main Fork, 1870s.

Runkle's Place or Camp (later Lewis Camp): Main Fork, 1880s–1890s.

Sacatar Meadow: South Fork, 1900–1930s.

Sand (Sandy) Meadows: Whitney area, Main fork, 1870s.

Shotgun Creek: Little Kern, 1930s.

Silver Lake (originally Shotgun Lake): Little Kern, 1930s.

Siberian Outpost: Main Fork, early 1900s.

Sky Parlor Meadow (originally Funston's Kaweah or Upper Funston Meadow): Main Fork, 1860s.

Soda Springs (Flats): Near Runkle's Place or Lewis Camp, Main Fork, 1870s.

South Fork Meadow (became Tunnel Meadow): South Fork, 1880s.

Strawberry Meadows: South Fork, 1930s.

Templeton Meadows (originally a sheep camp): South Fork, 1870s.

Timberline Lake: Mt. Whitney area, Main Fork, 1930s.

Trout Meadows: Main Fork, 1860s.

Troy Meadows: South Fork, 1920s–1930s.

Tunnel Meadow (originally South Fork Meadow; in 1930s became Tunnel Air Camp, a commercial fly-in backcountry camp): South Fork, 1880s.

21-Inch Camp: At mouth of Rattlesnake Creek, Main Fork, 1940s–1950s.

Tyndall Canyon (Creek): Shepherd Pass area, Main Fork, 1870s.

Wallace Creek: Whitney area, Main Fork, 1930s.

Whitney Creek (Volcano Creek, Golden Trout Creek) and Meadows (later called Big Whitney Meadows): Main Fork, 1870s.

Wright Creek: Below Mt. Tyndall, Main Fork, 1920s.

Kings River

Bearskin Meadow: North Fork, 1870s–early 1900s.

Bench Lake: Headwaters South Fork, early 1900s.

Big Bird Lake (originally Dollar Lake): Above Deadman Canyon, South Fork Kings, early 1900s.

Big and Little Pete Meadows: Early 1900s.

Bob Ingersoll Rock (now North Dome, Kings Canyon): South Fork, 1890s.

Bubbs Creek: South Fork, 1860s.

Bullfrog Lake (Bryanthus Lake until 1902): Bubbs Creek, South Fork, 1890s.

Burnt Corral Meadows: South Fork, 1890s.

Cedar Grove (originally Deer Park): Kings Canyon area, South Fork, 1890s.

Center Basin: Bubbs Creek, South Fork, 1910s–1930s.

Charlotte Creek: Headwaters Bubbs Creek, South Fork, 1940s.

Charlotte Lake and Meadows (originally Rhoda Lake): Bubbs Creek, South Fork, 1870s.

Cliff Bench (Camp): Wishon area, North Fork, 1930s.

Cloud (Cloudy) Canyon: Headwaters Roaring River, South Fork, early 1900s.

Colby Meadows: Evolution Valley, South Fork, 1910s.

Collin's Meadow: Middle Fork, 1890s.

Converse Mill Camp (Converse Basin): South Fork, 1870s–1890s.

Cook's Cow Camp: South Fork, 1890s.

Coolidge Meadows (now under the waters of Courtright Reservoir): North Fork, 1930s.

Copper Creek: Kings Canyon area, South Fork, 1890s.

Crown Valley (Basin): South Fork, 1880s.

Deadman Canyon (Creek): Headwaters Roaring River, South Fork, 1860s.

Deer Meadow: North Fork, 1940s.

Deer Park (Cedar Grove): Kings Canyon, South Fork, 1890s.

Devil's Punch Bowl: North Fork, early 1900s.

Devil's Wash Bowl: Middle Fork, 1930s.

Dinkey Creek: North Fork, 1870s.

Dinkey Lake: Headwaters Dinkey Creek, North Fork, 1870s.

Dougherty Corrals, Creek, Meadows (Originally a sheep camp): Middle Fork Kings, 1870s.

Dusy Basin: Bishop Pass area, Middle Fork, 1920s.

Dusy Meadows (Creek): North Fork, 1860s–1880s.

Fisk Cabin (George Fisk mining claim): Cartridge Creek, Middle Fork, early 1900s.

Fox Meadows (Fox's Camp): Kings Canyon, South Fork, 1870s–1890s.

Frypan Meadow: Lewis Creek, South Fork, early 1900s.

Gardiner Basin: Woods Creek, South Fork, 1890s.

Granite Basin, Creek (originally a sheep camp): South Fork, 1870s–1930s.

Helen Lake: Middle Fork, 1930s.

Horse Corral Meadow (originally Crescent Lawn Meadows): South Fork, 1860s.

Horseshoe Lakes. Middle Fork, 1940s.

Ionian Basin: Headwaters Goddard Creek, Middle Fork, early 1900s.

Junction Meadow: Bubbs Creek, South Fork, 1910s.

Kanawyer's Camp (became a commercial tourist camp): Kings Canyon, South Fork, 1880s–1910s.

Kearsarge Lakes (University Lakes): Bubbs Creek, South Fork, 1860s.

Kings Canyon, Upper: South Fork, 1930s.

Lake Marjorie: South Fork, 1940s.

Lake Reflection: Headwaters Bubbs Creek, South Fork, 1890s.

Le Conte Canyon, Meadows (includes Big and Little Pete Meadows): Middle Fork, early 1900s.

Marion Lake (Lake Basin): Cartridge Creek, Middle Fork, early 1900s.

Millwood, Mill Flat (originally Thomas Mill): Main Kings, 1870s–early 1900s.

Paradise Valley: Middle Fork, 1870s.

Post Corral: Meadow Creek, North Fork, 1930s.

Rae Lake (originally Wolverine Lake before 1906): North Fork, 1890s to 1940s.

Rae Lakes: South Fork Woods Creek, South Fork, early 1900s.

Ranger Lakes: Headwaters South Fork, 1940s.

Roaring River (originally Kettle Brook): South Fork, 1860s.

Scaffold Meadows (originally a sheep camp): Roaring River, South Fork, 1890s.

Sequoia Lake Lumber Camp: Mill Flat Creek, Main Kings, 1880s–early 1900s.

Shadow Creek Crossing: South Fork, 1930s.

Shadow Lake: South Fork, 1940s.

Simpson Meadow (Dougherty Meadows, originally a sheep and horse camp): Middle Fork, 1890s.

Sixty Lakes Basin: Woods Creek, South Fork, 1890s.

Sphinx Creek: Bubbs Creek, South Fork, 1890s.

Sphinx Lakes: Bubb's Creek, South Fork, 1890s.

Sugarloaf Creek and Meadow: Triple Divide area, South Fork, 1860s.

Tehipite Valley: Middle Fork, 1870s.

Tent Meadow: Middle Fork, 1930s.

Thomas Mill (became Millwood): Main Kings, 1860s–1890s.

Three Springs: Tehipite area, Middle Fork, 1900–1910s.

Twin Lakes: South Fork, 1940s.

Vidette Creek, Meadow: Bubbs Creek, South Fork, 1890s.

Vidette Lake: Headwater Bubbs Creek, South Fork, 1910s.

Wet Meadow: Tehipite area, Middle Fork, 1900–1930s.

Wildman Meadow: East Fork Grizzly Creek, South Fork, 1880s.

Williams Meadow: 1940s.

Wilsonia Camp (became a residential area in 1918): Grant Grove area, 1890s–1910s.

Wood's Corral (Copper Creek): Kings Canyon, South Fork, early 1900s.

Wood's Creek: South Fork, 1890s.

Wood's Lake: South Fork, 1870s.

Zumwalt Meadows: Kings Canyon, South Fork, 1890s.

Lee Vining Creek

Saddlebag Lake (originally Lee Vining's Lake): 1890s.

Tioga Meadows and Lake: 1870s.

Lone Pine Creek

Clyde Meadow: East side Mt. Whitney area, 1930s.

Hunter's Flat or Camp (renamed Whitney Portal in 1936: 1880s–1936.

Meysen Lakes: 1920s–1930s.

Mirror Lake: Mt. Whitney area, 1930s.

Merced River

Boothe Lake (High Sierra Camp, later moved and renamed Vogelsang): Tuolumne Meadows area, 1923.

Chain Lakes: Headwaters South Fork, 1940s.

Gaylor Lakes: West side Tioga area, Merced River, early 1900s.

Lake Bernice: 1930s.

Little Yosemite Valley: 1890s.

Long Meadow: Tenaya area, 1870s.

May Lake: Snow Creek, 1890s.

Merced Lake (originally Shadow Lake): 1870s.

Merced River, Upper: 1930s.

Moraine Meadows: South Fork, early 1900s.

Murphy Creek: Tenaya area, 1870s–1890s.

Ostrander Lake (originally Pohono Lake): 1860s.

Shadow Lake (became Merced Lake): 1870s.

Snow Flat: Glacier Brook (Snow Creek), 1860s–1930s.

Sunrise Creek, Lakes: Tenaya area, 1930s.

Tenaya Lake: 1850s.

Tuolumne Meadows: 1850s.

Vogelsang Lake: 1930s.

Wawona (Crane Flat, Clark's Station): 1850s–1880s.

Yosemite Creek: Upper Yosemite Valley, 1870s.

Pine Creek

Granite Park: 1890s.
Pine Lakes (Lower and Upper): 1890s.

Rock and Convict Creeks

Lake Dorothy: Convict Creek, 1920s.
Little Lakes Valley: Rock Creek, 1870s.

San Joaquin River

Agnew Meadow (originally Agnew's mining camp): Devil's Postpile area, Headwaters Middle Fork, 1870s.
Blayney (Blaney) Meadows (originally a sheep camp): Lost or Hidden Valley, South Fork, 1870s.
Cascade Valley (originally Peninsula Meadow): Mammoth Crest area, Fish Creek, Middle Fork, early 1900s.
Chittenden Lake: 1930s.
Corral Meadow (originally 77 Corral): North Fork, 1870s.
Coyote Lake: Big Creek area, South Fork, 1890s.
Detachment Meadow: North Fork, 1890s.
Duck Lake: Mammoth Crest area, Middle Fork, 1940s.
Ediza Lake (Mt. Ritter area): Headwaters Middle Fork, 1940s.
Evolution Lake: South Fork, 1890s.
Fish Valley (originally a sheep camp): Mono Creek, South Fork, 1880s.
Garnet Lake (originally Badger Lake): Middle Fork, 1890s.
Goddard Creek (Canyon): Headwaters South Fork, 1895.
Grouse Meadow: Palisades, South Fork, 1870s.
Humphrey's Basin: Piute Creek, South Fork, 1870s.
Hutchinson Meadows: Piute Canyon, South Fork, 1920s.
Jackass Flats, Meadow (now Jack Flat Camp): South Fork, 1870s.
Kaiser Creek: Main Fork, 1860s.
Little Jackass Meadow (became Soldier Meadow): North Fork of the Middle Fork, 1870s.
Markwood Meadow (sheep and cow camp): Shaver Lake area, 1870s–1880s.
McClure Meadow: Evolution Valley, South Fork, 1920s–1930s.
Mono Creek: South Fork, 1890s.
Mugler's Meadow: Main San Joaquin, 1850s–1890s.
Pack Saddle Lake (originally Lovejoy Lake): Humphrey's Basin, South Fork, early 1900s.
Paradise Valley: Middle Fork, 1870s.
Paradise Valley: South Fork, 1880s.
Piute Canyon: South Fork, early 1900s.
Red's Meadow (originally a sheep camp): Devil's Postpile area, Middle Fork, 1880s.

Sadlier (Sadler) Lake: Middle Fork, 1890s.
Sally (Sallie) Keyes Lakes: Florence Lake area, Middle Fork, 1930s.
77 Corrals (Corral Meadows): North Fork, 1870s–1930s.
Soldier Meadow (originally Jackass Meadow): Middle Fork, 1870s.
Vermilion Valley (now under Lake Thomas A. Edison): South Fork, 1930s–1950s.

Sawmill, Oak, and Independence Creeks
Baxter Lakes: North Fork Oak Creek, 1920s.
Camp Tamarack (in Onion Valley): Independence Creek, 1920s.
Gray's Meadows (Todd's Place): Independence Creek, 1920s–1930s.
Onion Valley: Kearsarge Pass area, Independence Creek, 1880s.
Sawmill Creek and Meadows: Sawmill Creek, 1870s–1910s.

Tule River
Bear Creek (Mountain Home, Balch Park): North Fork, 1890s.
Belknap Camp: South Fork, 1890s.
Camp Nelson: South Fork, 1890s–1920 when road was put in.
Cannell Meadow: Middle Fork, 1930s.
Dillon Mill: North Fork, 1870s–early 1900s.
Hossack Meadow (later Camp Wishon): Middle Fork, 1860s.
McIntyre Grove and Sheep Camp: Camp Nelson area, Middle Fork, 1880s.
Miner's Creek: Camp Nelson area, South Fork, 1880s.
Summit Meadow: On Dennison Trail, North Fork, 1860s.
White Meadow: Camp Nelson area, South Fork, 1900–1920s.

Tuolumne River
Ackerson Meadow (originally Wade's or Big Meadows): Yosemite Park, 1860s.
Aspen Valley: North Yosemite, 1870s.
Bagley Valley. North Yosemite, 1870s.
Budd Lake: 1890s.
Delaney Creek: North Yosemite, 1860s.
Dorothy Lake (originally Jack Main's Lake): Headwaters Fall Creek, Jack Main Canyon, 1890s.
Hetch-Hetchy Valley (now under water): North Yosemite, 1850s.
Jack Main Canyon (originally Jack Mean's sheep camp): 1870s.
Lyell Canyon: 1930s.
Mahan's Corral: Off Jack Main Canyon, 1930's.
Mather (originally Hog Ranch, base camp): Hetch-Hetchy area, 1860s.
McCabe Lakes: Early 1900s.

Miller Lake: Virginia Canyon, 1880s.
Pate Valley: Hetch-Hetchy area, 1870s.
Porcupine Flat: Hetch-Hetchy area, 1860s.
Smoky Jack Campground (originally a sheep camp): 1870s.
Statum Meadow (originally a sheep camp): Rancheria Creek, Hetch-Hetchy area, 1870s.
Virginia Canyon: 1870s.
White Wolf (base camp): Hetch-Hetchy area, 1870's.
Young Lakes: Early 1900s.

Undetermined Drainage
Biledo (Biledeaux) Meadow: Yosemite area, 1870s.
Dismal Camp: 1890s.
Dutch Flats: 1920s.
Gentian Meadow: 1890s.
Glenn Meadow: 1910s.
Gnat Meadow (later Hay Meadow): 1910s.
Green Meadow: 1940s.
House Meadow: 1890s–1910s.
Long Table: 1930s.
Loomis Creek Sheep Camp: 1870s.
Lost Meadows Camp: 1890s
Morris Lake: 1930s.
Mosquito Camp: 1890s.
Peppermint Meadows: early 1900s.
Tornado Meadow: 1870s.
2-Mutton Camp: 1890s.

Notes

INTRODUCTION

1. Oscar Lewis, *High Sierra Country* (Boston: Little Brown & Co., 1955), 111.

2. John Crowley, "A Tribute to the Mule," *The Californians,* September–October 1990, 38.

3. Johnny Jones and Dwight H. Barnes, *Following the Bells: Traveling High Sierra Wilderness Trails* (Oakhurst, Calif.: Dwight Barnes, 1994), 74.

4. John Muir, *South of Yosemite: Selected Writings of John Muir,* ed. Frederic R. Gunsky (Garden City, N.Y.: Natural History Press, 1968), 138.

5. Norman B. Livermore Jr., "A One-Man Diamond Hitch: With Suggestions on Saddling and Loading a Pack Animal," *Sierra Club Bulletin* 21, no. 1 (February 1936): 40.

OVERVIEW

6. Vada Cline, oral history, June 3, 1992, Eastern California Museum, Independence, Calif.; Norman B. Livermore Jr., "1930-1939 Trip Journal," Livermore Family Collection, San Rafael, Calif.; Ed Turner, "Turner Remembers," in *Mt. Whitney Packers and Friends: Mt. Whitney Packers Reunion Memory Book,* ed. Charles Morgan (Lone Pine, Calif.: n.p., 1995), 38. According to Turner, "When you worked for Mt. Whitney Pack Trains it was a must that you looked good. You sat straight in the saddle, you wore clean clothes—often changing before dinner. Nice shirt, nice hat, and good manners." No cussing was allowed around the customers, no bad jokes, and respect for women at all times was required.

7. Earl McKee, "Picnic-in-the-Park Program," typescript of presentation, July 14, 1996, Mineral King Preservation Society Archives.

8. William D. Fouts, "Yosemite's Pro-Packers: Part 1," *Horse and Rider* 26, no. 6 (1987): 6; William D. Fouts, "Yosemite's Pro-Packers: Part 2," *Horse and Rider* 26, no. 7 (1987): 41.

9. Murat Brunette, "Winter At Camp Nelson," *Tule River Times,* n.d. See also Joseph N. Le Conte, "My First Summer in the Kings River Sierra," *Sierra*

Club Bulletin 26, no. 1 (February 1941): 9; and Steward Edward White, *The Mountains* (1904; repr., Prescott, Ariz.: Wolfe Publishing, 1987), 18.

10. James B. Snyder (Yosemite National Park historian), interview by author, 1997. At Yosemite, equipment for mules was highly individualized. Aparejos were fitted carefully to each mule. The hot-forged shoes were made to fit perfectly to each foot. For years, a picture of each mule's shoe prints was kept on a bulletin board at the Yosemite corrals so if trouble was called in from the backcountry, the correct fitting shoe could be sent. Today, however, Yosemite cold-shoes most of its stock.

11. Steward Edward White, *The Pass* (New York: The Outing Publishing Company, 1906), 143.

12. Hank Simpson, "Horse Drive," *Preview,* June 12–13, 1986. While animals must be transported by truck on most roads now, as late as the 1980s a four-day stock drive was made annually from Big Pine winter pastures to the Mammoth Lakes Pack Outfit. Stock is still driven on portions of the Mineral King road. In areas where such drives go cross-country, a "point" rider picks out the proper trail. "Swing" riders keep the herd together, guiding loose stock away from trail hazards. "Drag" riders see that none of the stock get left behind.

13. John Crowley, unpublished memoirs, 1997, Crowley Family Collection, Visalia and Three Rivers, Calif.

14. John LeRoy Harper, "The Southern Sierra of California: A Regional Plan for Integrated Recreational Development" (PhD diss., University of Colorado, 1974), 450, 456; Robert D. Orser, "The Eastern Slope of the High Sierra as a Recreation Area," (unpublished Master's thesis, University of California, Berkeley, 1961), 66–73; "The Wilderness Home of the Golden Trout," *Sunset,* June 1959: 62. According to Bruce Jackson in an interview by the author (Shaver Lake, Calif., 1994), years ago pack animals were rented to horse riders to pack by themselves. Difficulties with care of the stock, grazing restrictions and liability concerns have now made these types of commercial trips almost nonexistent.

15. George Stewart, "Outfitting for a Mountain Trip," *Sierra Club Bulletin* 1, no. 3 (May 1903): 49–50.

16. High Sierra Packers' Association, *This Year Pack In to the Wilderness Area of the High Sierra,* brochure, ca. 1940s.

17. Norman B. Livermore Jr., "A West Side Packer on the High Trip," *Sierra Club Bulletin* 24 (June 1939): 27.

18. U.S. Department of Agriculture, Forest Service, "Wilderness Travel Tips," California map of John Muir Wilderness, Inyo and Sierra National Forests, and Sequoia and Kings Canyon National Parks, San Francisco, 1983.

19. White, *The Mountains,* 45.

20. McKee, "Picnic-in-the-Park Program."

21. Bruce Jackson, interview by author, 1994.

CHAPTER 1

22. Charles F. Lummis, quoted in Rockwell Dennis Hunt and William Sheffield Ament, *Oxcart to Airplane* (San Francisco, Calif.: Powell Publishing, 1929), 8.

23. Charles E. Hutchinson, "Juan Crespi, Diarist," *California History Nugget,* March 1938, 169.

24. Herbert Eugene Bolton, *Font's Complete Diary: A Chronicle of the Founding of San Francisco* (Berkeley, Calif: University of California Press, 1933), 391–392.

25. Elliott Coues, *On the Trail of a Spanish Pioneer,* vol. 2 (New York: Francis P. Harper, 1900), 66.

26. Ibid., 11.

27. Ibid., 249–250

CHAPTER 2

28. John Walton Caughey, *The California Gold Rush* (Berkeley, Calif.: University of California Press, 1948; First published as "Gold Is the Cornerstone" in *Chronicles of California,* 1948), 127–128; Ronald C. Larson, "Giants of the Southern Sierra: A Brief History of the Sequoia National Forest," unpublished manuscript, 1985, Sequoia National Forest Archives, Porterville, Calif. According to Hunt and Ament, "In the brief period from 1826 to 1832, as clearly pointed out by Joseph J. Hill, at least six trails were opened to California—the Smith trail, the Pattie trail, the Jackson trail, the Young trail, the Armijo trail, and the Wolfskill trail" (*Oxcart to Airplane,* 44; see also 61–62).

29. Francis Parkman, quoted in Hunt and Ament, *Oxcart to Airplane,* 44–45.

30. Jedediah Smith, "Crossing Mt. Joseph," from The Ashley-Smith Explorations and the Discovery of a Central Route to the Pacific, 1822–1829, in *A Treasury of the Sierra Nevada,* ed. Robert Reid (1983), 16.

31. John Bidwell, "Life in California before the Gold Discovery," in *Tales of California,* ed. Frank Oppel, (1890; repr., Secaucus, N.J.: Castle Books, 1989), 69.

32. Lansford Hastings, *The Emigrants' Guide to Oregon and California* (1845; repr., Bedford, Mass.: Applewood Books, 1994), 93.

33. Bil Gilbert, *Westering Man: The Life of Joseph Walker* (Norman, Okla.: University of Oklahoma Press, 1989), 80–181.

CHAPTER 3

34. J. S. Holliday, *The World Rushed In: The California Gold Rush Experience* (New York: Simon & Schuster, 1981), 303.

35. Ernest A. Wiltsee, *The Pioneer Miner and the Pack Mule Express* (San Francisco, Calif.: California Historical Society, 1931), 9.

36. Holliday, *The World Rushed In,* 303.

37. Felix Paul Wierzbicki, "California as It Is and as It Was," *The Californians* 12, no. 4 (April 1995): 36.

38. Bennet Riley, Brevet Brigadier General, to Brevet Major General R. Jones, Adjutant General, June 30, 1849, in State of California, *California Message and Correspondence, 1846–1849,* California State Library, Sacramento, Calif.

39. Holliday, *The World Rushed In,* 303.

40. Wiltsee, *The Pioneer Miner,* 9.

41. Kimball Webster, quoted in Holliday, *The World Rushed In,* 105.

42. Isaac J. Wistar, autobiography (New York: n.p., 1937), University of Nevada–Reno Special Collections, 44.

43. Wierzbicki, "California as It Is," 33–35.

44. Riley to Jones, August 30, 1849, in State of California, *California Message.*

45. James Hutchings, "Packing in the Mountains of California," *Hutchings' California Magazine* 1, no. 6 (December 1856), 247.

46. Quoted in Holliday, *The World Rushed In,* 375.

47. Mrs. D. B. Bates, "Incidents on Land and Water: Or Four Years on the Pacific Coast," in Hunt and Ament, *Oxcart to Airplane,* 30.

48. Hutchings, "Packing in the Mountains of California," 242.

49. Ibid, 245.

50. Ibid, 244.

51. Ibid, 246.

52. Bates, "Incidents on Land and Water," 30.

53. Hutchings, "Packing in the Mountains of California," 249.

54. Thomas Frederick Howard, *Sierra Crossing: First Roads to California* (Berkeley, Calif.: University of California Press, 1998). This is an excellent source for a more complete description of wagon and railroad route explorations and constructions.

55. Bennet Riley, Governor of California, proclamation, June 22, 1849, in State of California, *California Message.*

56. W. M. Maule, "Various Oblique Line Surveys between California and Nevada," *Cultural Features,* 1938, 45.

57. William H. Brewer, *Up and Down California in 1860–1864* (1930; repr., Berkeley Calif.: University of California Press, 1966), 19.

58. Ibid.

59. Ibid., 505.

CHAPTER 4

60. James B. Snyder, unpublished notes, April 19, 1999, Yosemite National Park Research Library. Regulations eventually restricted loose herding to dangerous trail condition areas only, in order to prevent excessive damage to trail sides.

61. H. W. Daly, *Manual of Pack Transportation* (Washington, D.C.: Government Printing Office, 1917), 155. In a forced march the mules were packed with a limit of two hundred pounds per pack animal. With that weight on fairly level ground, they could cover an amazing amount of ground. In one 1881 Indian campaign a pack train made a march of 85 miles in twelve hours. The next year another train made a forced march in Arizona of 280 miles in three days. And in 1892, a cavalry troop in Texas marched 108 miles with a pack train in sixteen hours with the loaded mules packed at 250 pounds.

62. Ibid., 144.

63. Ibid.

64. William Wallace, "A Night on Mt. Whitney," *Mt. Whitney Club Journal* 1, no. 1 (May 1902): 5.

65. James Snyder, unpublished notes.

66. Gabriel Sovulewski, quoted in Carl P. Russell, *100 Years in Yosemite* (Yosemite, Calif.: Yosemite Natural History Association, 1957), 160.

67. Joe Dorst to his wife, Oct. 12, 1891, Sequoia National Park Archives.

CHAPTER 5

68. James B. Snyder, James B. Murphy Jr., and Robert W. Barrett, "Wilderness Historic Resources Survey: 1988 Season Report," *Studies in Yosemite History* 1, (1989), Yosemite National Park Research Library, Yosemite, Calif.

69. John Muir, *South of Yosemite,* 64.

70. Joseph N. Le Conte, "The High Sierra of California," *Alpina Americana,* 1907, 14.

71. Emma Gilliam Crowley to Arthur Crowley, August 24, 1886. Crowley Family Collection, Visalia and Three Rivers, Calif.

72. Hubert Paul Dyer, "The Zeta Psi Camping Party: The Account of a Trip from San Francisco to Mt. Whitney, the Highest Point in the United States of America," unpublished manuscript, April 21, 1892, Eastern California Museum, Independence.

73. Ibid.

74. Ibid.; see also Le Conte, "My First Summer"; and Muir, "South of Yosemite."

75. Quoted in Junep, Herbert L. *A Chronological History of the Sequoia National Park and Vicinity* (San Francisco: National Park Service, 1976), 299.

76. White, *The Mountains*, 109.

CHAPTER 6

77. "Sequoia National Park Annual Report, 1901," 10, quoted in Larry Dil-saver and William C. Tweed, *Challenge of the Big Trees of Sequoia and Kings Canyon National Parks* (Three Rivers, Calif.: Sequoia Natural History Association, 1990), 89.

78. Inyo Sierra Guides & Packing Company, *In the High Sierras,* brochure, 1911, Eastern California Museum, Independence.

79. Shirley Sargent, *Yosemite and Its Innkeepers* (Yosemite, California: Flying Spur Press, 1989), 22. According to Sargent, "The greatest difficulty facing Mather was the old one of the proliferation of small concessionaires, none of whom he thought provided high quality services at reasonable rates. He concluded that the solution would be to create a monopoly, making one concessionaire responsible for nearly all tourist services. He hoped such a system would make it easier for officials to regulate operations in the park as well as improve the quality of service."

80. Horace Arden Albright and Marian Albright Schenck, *The Mather Mountain Party of 1915: A Full Account of the Adventures of Stephen T. Mather and His Friends in the High Sierra of California* (Three Rivers Calif.: Sequoia Natural History Association, 1990), 8.

81. Walter Smith, "Recollections," author's files.

82. White, *The Mountains*, 52.

83. Comer Robertson, oral history, interview by Ora Kay Peterson, 1988, Mineral King Preservation Society, Visalia, Calif.

84. "Dance Supplies Cash for Uncle Sam's Observatory," *Owens Valley Herald,* June 4, 1909; Roy A. Legge, "The Mount Whitney Stone Hut," unpublished manuscript, 1975, Piedmont, Calif., University of Nevada–Reno Special Collections.

85. Legge, "The Mount Whitney Stone Hut."

86. Anna Mills Johnston, "A Trip to Mt. Whitney in 1878," *Mt. Whitney Club Journal* 1, no. 1 (May 1902): 20; J.W.A. Wright, "Upper Kern Valley," *Visalia Delta,* October 7, 1881.

87. Barton W. Evermann, *The Golden Trout of the Southern High Sierras* (1905; repr., Washington, D.C.: Government Printing Office, 1906), 6, 35. Before the turn of the century, many of the southern Sierra streams were barren of fish. The Kaweah River evidently once had fish that disappeared.

88. "Report of the Committee on 1911 Outing," *Sierra Club Bulletin* 8, 1911–1912 (1912), 208.

89. "Report of Outing Committee, 1913," *Sierra Club Bulletin* 9, 1913–1915 (1915), 48, 179.

90. Andrew Ferguson, "The High Country and Related Things," unpublished manuscript, n.d., Eastern California Museum, Independence.

91. S.L.N. Ellis to Arthur Crowley, November 3, 1909, Crowley Family Collection, Visalia and Three Rivers, Calif.

92. Joe Doctor, "Hengst Tells How He Transplanted Goldens," *Farmersville Herald,* January 18, 1978; Linda Hengst, with Bill, Wilma, Bob and Golda Hengst, oral history, interview by Ora Kay Peterson, 1988, Mineral King Preservation Society, Visalia, Calif.

CHAPTER 7

93. "Report of the Outing Committee, February 1903," *Sierra Club Bulletin* 4, 1902–1903 (1903): 236.

94. William Frederic Bade, "On the Trail with the Sierra Club," *Sierra Club Bulletin* 5, 1904–1905 (1905): 54-55.

95. Orlin W. Loverin, "He Knows Mountains, Mules, Men: Mules Are the Toughest," *Fresno Bee,* n.d.

96. Marion Randall Parsons, "The Notable Mountaineering of the Sierra Club in 1902," *Sierra Club Bulletin* 5: 44. According to Yosemite National Park Historian James Snyder (unpublished notes, 1999), "These catches by the 1903 outing became one of the stories that gathered support for Barton Warren Evermann's investigation of golden trout in 1904 (supported by Teddy Roosevelt) and for their preservation."

97. Marion Randall Parsons, "The Twenty-Eighth Outing," *Sierra Club Bulletin* 15, no. 1 (February 1930): 10.

98. Josephine Colby, "Kern River Canyon: The Sierra Club's Expedition—1903," *Overland Monthly,* January 1904, 15.

99. H. Stewart Kimball, *History of the Sierra Club Outing Committee, 1901-1902,* pamphlet, Sierra Club, San Francisco, Calif., 1990. Livermore Family Collection, San Rafael, Calif.

100. Parsons, "The Twenty-Eighth Outing," 10.

CHAPTER 8

101. "Packing Industry of Three Rivers," report, ca. 1930, Sequoia National Park Library and Archives, Three Rivers, Calif.

102. Henry Olivas, oral history, interview by Bob Powers, August 19, 1972, Eastern California Museum, Independence.

103. Quoted in H. H. Simpson, "Range Management Plan, Monache Range," report, March 16, 1931, in U.S. Department of Agriculture, Forest Service, Inyo National Forest, *Grazing Atlas IV-C, 1923–1950,* Inyo National Forest Archives, Bishop, Calif. See also Simpson, "Range Management Plan, Templeton Range," report, March 19, 1931.

104. Quoted in Kimball, "Sierra Club Outing Committee, 1901-1902," 18.

105. Ibid.

106. John S. Edwards, Assistant Forest Supervisor, Sequoia National Forest, memorandum to district rangers, August 2, 1930; Bishop, Calif., Chamber of Commerce, "Fifty Years Later" (1986), 15, Livermore Family Collection; John Harper, "The Southern Sierra Nevada of California: A Regional Plan for Integrated Recreational Development," (masters thesis, University of Colorado, 1974), 450, Sequoia National Park Library. See Appendix A for listing of packers and locations.

107. T. Eugene Barrows, "Second Lake Dam," *The Album* 3, no. 2 (April 1990), 40.

108. Sam Lewis, unpublished memoirs, Oct. 14, 1968, Eastern California Museum, Independence.

109. Henry Olivas, "The Olivas Family," as told to B.C. Dawson, in *Saga of Inyo County* (Bishop, Calif.: Southern Inyo American Association of Retired Persons, 1977), 58.

110. Ethyl Olivas, "Spainhower Oral History," interviewed by Bob Powers, n.d., 29, Eastern California Museum, Independence.

111. Livermore, "1930-1939 Trip Journal," 9.

112. E. T. Scoyen, superintendent, Kings Canyon National Park, memorandums to all packers and grazing permittees, July 13, 1942, and August 11, 1942, Sequoia National Park Archives.

113. E. T. Scoyen, superintendent, Sequoia and Kings Canyon National Parks, memorandum to Region Four director, April 21, 1943, Sequoia National Park Archives.

114. H. H. Simpson, report, 1934, in U.S. Department of Agriculture, Forest Service, Inyo National Forest, *Grazing Atlas IC–C, 1929–1950,* Inyo National Forest Archives, Bishop, Calif. In 1943, the number of permits granted returned to a more typical count of twenty, with twenty-two in 1944 and 1945.

115. Hugh Trawcck, "Schedule of Basic Rates for the 1945 Season," Kings Canyon National Park, June 13, 1945, Sequoia National Park Archives; "Differences in Saddle Horse Transportation," Sequoia Kings Canyon National Park, May 1945, Sequoia National Park Archives. According to John Crowley (interview by author, April 29, 1997, Visalia, Calif.), in 1946 Mineral King Pack Station wranglers received $180 per month with "room" and board. Wranglers depended on tips as the pay was so poor. In the late 1940s, a $100 tip for a ten-day trip was not unusual.

116. Raymond Pascoe quoted in Ronald C. Larson, "Giants of the Southern Sierra," 218.

117. Claiborn Stout, interview by author, August 18, 1997.

118. Pete Olivas, oral history, 1992.

119. Bruce Jackson, interview, 1994, author's files. In 1948 Wilson Pack Trains netted $630.15 with Dick Wilson giving himself only a $1,000

salary out of the gross income of $7,753. In the same year the McKee-Maloy Pack Trains netted only $5,267.30 out of less than $18,000 total revenues with Edna McKee and Lee Maloy receiving $2,633.65 each. In Mineral King, eight shareholders had to split the $478.55 profit in 1948. The financial situation seldom improved after that.

120. White, *The Mountains,* 207.

121. Quoted in Jones and Barnes, *Following the Bells,* 39.

CHAPTER 9

122. Marc Reisner, "The End of Wilderness: The Future of Our National Forests," *Natural Resources Defense Council Newsletter* 7, no. 5 (September–December 1978), 1.

123. Richard J. Orsi et al., *Yosemite and Sequoia: A Century of California Parks* (San Francisco: California Historical Society, 1993), 34.

124. Alfred Runte, *Yosemite: The Embattled Wilderness* (Lincoln, Nebr.: University of Nebraska Press, 1990); Muir, *South of Yosemite;* and Linnie Marsh Wolfe, *Son of the Wilderness: The Life of John Muir* (1945; repr., Madison, Wisc.: University of Wisconsin Press, 1978), 190–191. Muir's first published article in the *New York Tribune* concerned Yosemite glaciers. His first article promoting government control of forests was published in the *Sacramento Union* February 5, 1876. By 1880, his stories, articles, and essays were published by several newspapers and journals, including *Harpers, Scribners,* and the *Overland Monthly.*

CHAPTER 10

125. U.S. Department of Agriculture, Forest Service, *The Use Book* (Washington, D.C.: Government Printing Office, 1906), 73.

126. John R. White, superintendent, Sequoia National Park, to T. L. Fritzen, manager, Kings River Parks Company, November 9, 1921, Sequoia National Park Archives.

127. Simpson, "Range Management Plan, Monache Range."

128. Emil F. Ernst, assistant forester, Yosemite National Park, memorandum to superintendent, November 19, 1935, Yosemite National Park Research Library.

129. Ibid.

130. Don Tressider, president, Yosemite Park & Curry Company, to Colonel C. G. Thomson, superintendent, Yosemite National Park, January 7, 1936, Yosemite National Park Research Library.

131. E. Lowell Sumner Jr., "The Biology of Wilderness Protection," *Sierra Club Bulletin* 27, no. 4 (August 16, 1942): 16.

132. E. Lowell Sumner Jr. and Richard M. Leonard, "Protecting Mountain Meadows," *Sierra Club Bulletin* 32, no. 5 (May 1947): 58.

133. E. Lowell Sumner, Jr., "The Wilderness Problem in the National Parks: Excerpt from a Special Report on a Wildlife Study of the High Sierra in Sequoia and Yosemite National Parks and Adjacent Territory," 1936, Sequoia National Park Archives.

134. Ibid.

135. Ibid.

136. "Report of the Outing Committee: Outing of 1902," *Sierra Club Bulletin* 4 (1902–1903): 236; "Report of the Outing Committee: Outing of 1903," *Sierra Club Bulletin* 5 (1904–1905): 74.

137. David R. Brower, "Are Mules Necessary?" *Sierra Club Bulletin* 33, no. 3 (March 1948): 26.

138. By 1936 the Forest Service required special-use permits for all range improvements; notification to the nearest forest offices of trip itineraries and how many animals were to be grazed on each trip; identification cards for all pack outfit employees; repair of any damage caused by the stock to roads, trails, springs, or other improvements; if considered appropriate, a bond to insure payment for all damage; and an understanding that any area could be closed to grazing at any time if deemed necessary by the forest supervisor.

139. H.H.S., P.F.R. [H.H. Simpson, Presiding Forest Ranger], to Art Frost, 1932, Inyo National Forest Archives.

140. John R. White, superintendent, Sequoia National Park, memorandum to assistant superintendent and chief ranger, November 16, 1944, Sequoia National Park Archives.

141. J. H. Wegner, chief ranger, Sequoia and Kings Canyon National Parks, memorandum to superintendent, June 6, 1944, Sequoia National Park Archives.

142. John R. White, superintendent, Sequoia National Park, to Earl McKee, October 12, 1945, Sequoia National Park Archives.

143. Earl McKee to [John R.] White, October 12, 1945, Sequoia National Park Archives.

144. E. T. Scoyen, superintendent, Sequoia and Kings Canyon National Parks, memorandum to Region Four director, November 5, 1948, Sequoia National Park Archives.

145. B. F. Gibson, chief clerk, Sequoia and Kings Canyon National Parks, memorandum to superintendent, March 7, 1949, Sequoia National Park Archives.

146. Charles Morgan and Henry Brown, oral interview by author, Springville, Calif., 1993.

CHAPTER 11

147. Stephen T. Mather, director, National Park Service, to John R. White, superintendent, Sequoia and General Grant National Parks, June 1, 1922, Sequoia National Park Archives.

148. Agreement between Yosemite Park & Curry Company and Joe Barnes, October 1, 1932, Yosemite National Park Research Library, Yosemite, Calif.

149. Bob Bright to Don Tressider, president, Yosemite Park & Curry Company, May 22, 1938, Yosemite National Park Research Library, Yosemite, Calif.

150. Don Tressider, president, Yosemite Park & Curry Company, memorandum to [Lawrence C.] Merriam [acting superintendent, Yosemite National Park], May 12, 1939, Yosemite National Park Research Library, Yosemite, Calif.

151. Committee on Pack Stock Grazing in the California National Parks, report to the board of directors of the Sierra Club, December 8, 1941, Sequoia National Park Archives.

152. U.S. Department of Agriculture, Forest Service, Inyo National Forest, packers' regulations, 1966, Inyo National Forest Archives. According to Peter Browning in "The Plague of the High Sierra" (*The Ram's Head*, Wilderness Press Newsletter, January/February 1991), by 1990 the national parks in California had cut the backcountry stock limit to twenty. Pack station operators petitioned to have the limit raised, but it remained the same with fifteen people per party. At the same time, the High Sierra Hikers Association called for total discontinuance of recreational stock use in the High Sierra, calling it "an outdated, unnecessary and harmful activity that ought to have ceased several decades ago."

153. Norman B. Livermore Jr. to John R. White, superintendent, Sequoia National Park, September 16, 1947, Sequoia National Park Archives.

154. Charles Morgan and Henry Brown, oral interview by author, Springville, Calif., 1993. See also Fouts, "Yosemite's Pro-Packers: Part 1"; and SNEP Science Team and Special Consultants, "Rangelands," in *Sierra Nevada Ecosystems Project Report,* vol. 1, no. 7 (Davis, Calif.: University of California, Davis, 1996), 1, 2.

155. Kimball, "History of the Sierra Club Outing Committee," 19–20.

156. E. Lowell Sumner Jr. and Richard M. Leonard, "Protecting Mountain Meadows," 56.

157. Charles Morgan and Henry Brown, oral interview by author, Springville, Calif., 1993.

158. Quoted in Jones and Barnes, *Following the Bells,* 37–38.

CHAPTER 12

159. Lewis, unpublished memoirs.

160. Ibid.

161. Ibid.

162. Norman B. Livermore, interview by author, August 6, 1993, Tahoma, Calif.

163. Lewis, unpublished memoirs.

164. Ibid.

165. Ibid.

166. Livermore interview. 1993.

CHAPTER 13

167. Lewis, unpublished memoirs.

168. McKee, "Picnic-in-the-Park Program."

169. Dan Farris, "A Funny Thing Happened on the Way to the Woods," *The Album* 6, no. 3 (August 1993): 39.

170. Superintendent [John R. White, Sequoia and Kings Canyon National Parks] to chief ranger [J. H. Wegner], May 15, 1945, Sequoia National Park Archives.

171. Charles Morgan, "Outfitters I Knew," in *Mt. Whitney Packers,* 24–26.

172. Claiborn Stout, interview by author, August 18, 1997.

173. Charles Morgan, interview by author, May 18, 1997.

174. Barbara and Jack Hansen to MK'ers [former Mineral King packers], Oct. 30, 1987, author's files. A majority of the young packers who worked during the 1930s and 1940s matured into highly successful businessmen. Of twenty-five wranglers associated with the Mineral King Packing Company during the Buckman years, eighteen of them were known to have become bank managers, ranch managers, veterinarians, engineers, publishers, company owners, presidents, or managers.

175. McKee, "Picnic-in-the-Park Program."

176. Earl McKee Sr., quoted in McKee "Picnic-in-the-Park Program," 5.

177. Joe Doctor, *The Man Who Could Dodge Lightning* (Visalia Calif.: Tulare County Historical Society, 1995), 2.

CHAPTER 14

178. Norman B. Livermore Jr., "Oh! For the Life of a Packer!" *Sierra Club Bulletin* 34 (June 1949): 23; Livermore, "1930–1939 Trip Journal."

179. Ibid.

180. Loverin, "He Knows Mountains."

181. McKee, "Picnic-in-the-Park Program"; "Gill Sells Fine Lot of Mules," *Exeter Sun,* July 14, 1916.

182. J. Smeaton Chase, *Yosemite Trails: Camp and Pack-Train in the Yosemite Region of the Sierra Nevada* (Boston, Mass.: Houghton Mifflin, 1911), 194.

183. Ibid.

184. Ibid., 56.

185. Ibid., 75.

186. Brewer, *Up and Down California,* 529, 531.

187. White, *The Pass,* 84–85.

188. Ibid., 85–86.

189. Andrew Ferguson, "The High Country," 85.

190. Ibid.

191. Hutchings, "Packing in the Mountains of California," 246.

CHAPTER 15

192. Francis P. Farquhar to John R. White, superintendent, Sequoia National Park, July 26, 1922, Sequoia National Park Archives.

193. John R. White, superintendent, Sequoia and Kings Canyon National Parks, memorandum, May 14, 1930, Sequoia National Park Archives.

194. O. K. Morton to John R. White, superintendent, Sequoia National Park, August 18, 1926, Sequoia National Park Archives.

195. John R. White, superintendent, Sequoia National Park, to director of National Park Service, May 5, 1926, Sequoia National Park Archives.

196. Hazen H. Hunkins, general manager, Sequoia and General Grant National Parks Company, to John R. White, superintendent, Sequoia National Park, September 9, 1926, Sequoia National Park Archives.

197. M. A. Benedict, forest supervisor, Sierra National Forest, to Ord Loverin, December 10, 1930, Sequoia National Park Archives.

198. John R. White, superintendent, Sequoia National Park, to George L. Mauger, general manager, Sequoia and General Grant National Parks Company, April 7, 1930, Sequoia National Park Archives.

199. George L. Mauger, general manager, Sequoia and General Grant National Parks Company, to Ord Loverin, April 18, 1933, Sequoia National Park Archives.

200. *Inyo Register,* October 6, 1949, Inyo National Forest Archives.

201. B. P. Bole Jr. to E. T. Scoyen, superintendent, Sequoia and Kings Canyon National Park, October 26, 1951, Sequoia National Park Archives.

202. Guy Hopping, assistant superintendent, Kings Canyon National Park, to B. P. Bole, chairman of the board of managers, Cleveland Museum of Natural History, April 30, 1941, Sequoia National Park Archives.

203. John R. White, superintendent, Sequoia and Kings Canyon National Parks, to B. P. Bole, chairman of the board of managers, Cleveland Museum of Natural History, July 1, 1942.

204. B. P. Bole, chairman of the board of managers, Cleveland Museum of Natural History, to John R. White, superintendent, Sequoia and Kings Canyon National Parks, June 20, 1947, Sequoia National Park Archives.

205. E. T. Scoyen, superintendent, Sequoia National Park, to Mrs. Richard Romaine, October 12, 1951; E. T. Scoyen to Richard H. Leonard, secretary, Sierra Club, October 1, 1951, Sequoia National Park Archives.

CHAPTER 16

206. Doctor, *The Man Who Could Dodge Lightning,* 4.

207. Ed Turner, "Turner Remembers," in *Mt. Whitney Packers and Friends,* 34.

208. Crowley, unpublished memoirs.

209. Albright and Schenck, *The Mather Mountain Party,* 36.

210. McKee, "Picnic-in-the-Park Program," 21.

211. Lillie Neal to "Anna and John," 1916, Eastern California Museum, Independence, Calif.

212. Willis Lynn Jepson, "Mt. Whitney, Whitney Creek and the Poison Meadow Trail," *Sierra Club Bulletin* 4 (1903), 213.

213. Joseph S. Dixon, "Special Report on Stock-Poisoning Plants at Goddard Canyon, Kings Canyon National Park," August 7, 1942, Sequoia National Park Archives.

214. Charles W. Kellogg, *Up to the Clouds on Muleback* (Worcester, Mass.: David Hale Fanning Trade School for Girls, 1938), 28–45. The long-standing rule of hiker and packer etiquette was clearly defined. According to "Wilderness Travel Tips" (U.S.D.A. Forest Service, 1983), "Stock users have the right-of-way on trails. For everyone's safety, hikers should stand quietly on the downhill side of the trail to allow horses and mules to pass. Do not attempt to touch the animals and don't try to hide from them. A startled string of stock can be dangerous." For stockmen, the tips advise "Ask hikers to stand on the lower side of narrow, steep trails. Standing above the trail can be dangerous to a hiker if he should slip and slide under the horses."

CHAPTER 17

215. Joe Barnes to H. Oehlmann, president, Yosemite Park & Curry Company, October 30, 1965, Yosemite National Park Research Library, Yosemite, Calif.

216. Joe Barnes to H. Oehlmann, president, Yosemite Park & Curry Company, April 7, 1964, Yosemite National Park Research Library, Yosemite, Calif.

217. Dyer, "The Zeta Psi Camping Party," vol. 2: 25.

218. By the mid-1930s, the communications were getting better with several phones in the backcountry. In 1937, there was even a post box erected on the trail out of Trout Meadows (Brown, "The Heyday of Packing," 101).

219. Lewis, unpublished memoirs.

AFTERWORD

220. Sequoia and Kings Canyon National Parks, "Stock Use and Meadow Management Plan," revised February 1986, Sequoia National Park Archives.

Glossary

aparejo (aparajo). A hardened leather covering conforming to a pack animal's back, used to support loads carried by the animal. It is made of two envelopes joined at the top with an interior framework of twenty-three to thirty green sticks. It was introduced into Spain by the Moors in the eighth century and carried to America by the Spaniards in the early sixteenth century.

bell mare. A female horse that other animals in a herd tend to follow. A bell, usually a sheep bell, is put on her so the wranglers can hear where the herd of mules and horses is grazing.

bit. A steel bar made to fit between the upper and lower jaws of an animal, with a ring at each end for the attachment of reins to control the animal. A **straight bit** has a straight bar in the mouthpiece. A **jointed snaffle bit** has a jointed steel mouthpiece with straight cheek bars. A **curb bit** has a chain or strap that passes under the animal's lower jaw and presses against it. A **half-breed bit** has a loop in the middle of the mouth bar with a small roller on it which the horse or mule tongues as it walks, a soothing occupation likened to chewing gum. A **Pelham bit** is designed to be used with two sets of reins.

blind. An eye covering used on skittish or onerous animals. Used especially during loading and shoeing operations.

blinkers. Rectangular or round leather flaps attached to a bridle to block a skittish animal's side vision.

bridle. A fitting, usually leather, made of straps around the mouth, head, and neck of a riding animal, securing a bit in the animal's mouth and allowing human control by means of reins. The headpiece passes behind the ears and joins with a headband over the forehead that connects to cheek straps running down the side of the head to the bit.

bull cook. Assistant to the pack-station cook. A bull cook helped with all food processes, including storage, preparation, serving, and cleanup.

bunch. A swollen and hardened spot on a pack animal's skin due to rubbing and poking of a packsaddle.

burro. A donkey used for packing.

cache. Food and/or equipment stashed or buried in a backcountry location to be used at a later date. Packers' term for any packed provisions.

cantle. The back part of a riding saddle, usually curved upward and high on work saddles to prevent slipping of the rider.

catch grain. Barley or other grain favored by trail stock. Used as a treat or to lure loose grazing stock.

cinch. A girth or broad canvas band passing under the belly of a riding or pack animal to secure a saddle or pack to its back.

come-along. A ten-inch chain with a snap on it that goes under an animal's chin and pinches when the animal lags. Used for pack animals that pull back on the end of a lead rope. Also called a draw chain.

commissary. Kitchen wares and food.

cut jack. A castrated donkey. Also the act of castrating a donkey.

dally up. To wrap the lead rope or lariat around the saddle horn in order to delay or slow the pack animal.

deadhead. To herd stock from base corrals to the point of departure of a pack trip (or to corrals from the point of destination).

Decker packsaddle. A packsaddle with iron loops for holding loads, slung lower than a sawbuck and higher than an aparejo.

donkey. An ass; a long-eared, often ash-colored domestic animal related to the horse.

drift fence. A fence erected to prevent the wandering of stock into any restricted backcountry area. In recent years portable wire fencing is often carried in by a pack outfit and disassembled after use.

dude. A greenhorn, or inexperienced horseman.

duffle (duffel). A customer's private gear. Also called **dunnage.** A **duffle bag,** usually made of canvas, is used to carry the gear.

dunnage trip. A pack trip on which the customer provides all provisions; these are hauled to a designated location by a packer while the customer walks, and the packer and stock may return at a specified date to haul out the gear.

firefall. Glowing embers of burning wood pushed over the edge of Yosemite's Glacier Point to provide a spectacular evening show of fire falling three thousand feet to the valley floor, near Camp Curry.

floating teeth. Grinding worn, jagged teeth, usually with a special sixteen-inch bar with a file on the end of it.

girth. A band, usually of stiff woven fiber, passed under the belly of a riding or pack animal to secure a blanket, saddle, or pack to its back. Also called a surcingle.

gravy train. A long-lasting (and profitable) pack trip.

halter rope. A rope or strap tied to a halter, used to lead an animal or to fasten it to some object.

hell-bent-for-leather. Running at top speed; in a hurry.

hitch. A series of loops and knots in a rope used to tie down a load on a pack animal. Favorites used in the Sierra were the box hitch and the diamond hitch, both tied in various ways.

hitch rail. A log or rail to which stock can be tied at rest stops.

hobble. A chain, rope, or leather or cloth strap fastened to the legs or ankles of an animal to keep it from moving far. Often used at night, usually on a bell mare to help keep a herd of pack animals together. Rope rather than leather hobbles often are preferred as they cause less rubbing and injury. A **drag hobble** is a piece of chain about three feet long that is hooked to a front leg, causing an animal that moves too quickly to step on it. A **back hobble** is a length of rope or leather tied between the two back legs to limit movement.

horn (saddle horn). A high, protruding extension, usually of leather-covered metal, on the pommel of a riding saddle. Used by wranglers to wrap lasso and lead ropes around, for inexperienced riders to hold on to, and for all to hoist themselves into the saddle.

horse rack. A hitching rail with feed bins, used at day-ride areas.

jack (jackass). A male donkey or ass.

jenny. A female donkey or ass.

kyack (kyak, kayack, kiak. In the 1800s also spelled **cuyaxes** and **cuyacks**, and in Spanish called an *alforja*). A carrier in which gear is packed, usually made of strong canvas reinforced with stiffened leather, with a rigid box or frame in the interior. Without the box it is often referred to as a **leather-end** or **pannier.** Two are used on a pack animal, one hanging on each side.

lash cinch. A cinch made of canvas or mohair with a ring in one end and a hook in the other.

lash rope. A forty- to sixty-foot rope used to lash down a pack animal's load. Manila hemp, cotton, and now Dacron or nylon are used. In California, cotton rope has been traditional.

lasso. A long rope with a running noose at one end, used for catching stock.

latigos. Long leather straps that hold the cinch or girth to the tree rings of a riding or packsaddle.

lead mule. The first mule in a pack string. The one that "...the packer leads, visits with, cusses, and in general passes the long hours on the trail with" (John Crowley). Usually the most intelligent and trusted mule in a string, although the early military manuals suggested putting a novice pack mule in the lead.

leather-end. A soft kyack without a rigid frame or interior. Also called a **pannier**.

long-term camp trip. Customers and provisions are packed to a designated camp where they stay for several days. The cook and riding stock remain at the camp while the pack stock is returned to the pack station.

loose-herding. Herding of stock not tied together, usually practiced in steep or dangerous trail areas to prevent one animal from pulling the rest with it if it falls. In early days most packers loose-herded, but with increasing traffic on deteriorating trails government regulations eventually restricted the practice. Today it is allowed only on hazardous sections.

manties. Pack covers, usually made of cotton duck or canvas with a minimum size of four to six feet, tied to the load with a lash rope. An old-fashioned term for top covers.

martingale. A strap that passes between a horse's forelegs, with one end fastened to the saddle cinch and the other to the head bridle. Used to keep a temperamental horse from throwing back its head.

mule bell. A bell put on a mule that likes to wander off from the herd, often trying to head home after it has eaten its fill. The faster the animal is moving the faster the bell rings.

nighthawk. A packer whose job it is to stay up all night watching the stock, usually on a large trip.

nosebag. A cloth or leather feed bag, with its own harness fitting over the nose and mouth of an animal, containing barley or some favored feed of the animal to be eaten out of the bag.

nose band. A band on a bridle that passes around the front of the animal's nose just above the nostrils.

outlook. View or viewpoint.

packer. A generalized term for any individual working in the stock packing industry. Name used for both a wrangler and a pack station owner or operator.

packsaddle. A saddle made with a sawbuck or other device on which to hold or hang loads. Almost all packsaddles are double rigged, i.e., designed for two cinches, fore and aft.

pack shed. A shed in which packing equipment is stored.

pannier. A pack bag most often used in pairs hung from each side of a sawbuck, and usually made of heavy canvas with leather-reinforced ends, chafes, and corners. Also called a **leather-end**.

pilgrim. A customer who is new to backcountry horse travel.

pommel. Raised front portion of a saddle.

pot boy. Cook's attendant, dishwasher, and general "swamper," or clean-up person, usually on a large backcountry trip.

push on the reins. To leave slack in the reins, not pull them tight.

rein. A long, narrow strap or thong fastened to the bridle or bit by which the rider restrains and guides the riding animal. A snaffle rein is attached to the bit bar, and a **curb rein** is attached lower, to the curb bit.

remuda. An owner's herd of horses and mules.

riata. A lariat or long-noosed rope used for catching stock.

ring bone. A bony growth on or inside a horse's or mule's hoof that usually causes lameness.

rope off. To catch an animal with a lasso.

sacking. A burlap sack used to break a horse or mule to saddle. The animal is tied to a snubbing post and a burlap sack or saddle blanket is flicked in front of it. Once it is calm with the flicking the sacking is rubbed over it, then placed on it.

saddle skirt (fender). The hanging flap of a saddle that protects each side of the riding animal from the abrasion of a rider, and the rider from the animal's sweat.

salt lick. A chunk of hard salt. Packers often carry one or two five-pound squares on a long trip for use by the stock.

sawbuck. A packsaddle, sawhorse, or movable wooden frame with two sides intersecting to form an X shape. It sits on top of a pad or blanket covering the back of the pack animal and is used as a base from which to hang kyacks and slings.

sling. A large piece of material, usually canvas, hooked over leather crosses on a sawbuck. Most often used to carry duffle bags.

snake out. Stretching out mule strings of a pack train on a trail.

snap rope. A length of rope approximately ten to fifteen feet long with a snap type clasp on one end used as a quick-connect hook to a mule's halter. Used by a packer to lead the first mule or to tie subsequent mules in a string. A snap on one end is attached to the animal's halter and the other end is attached with a bowline to the neck of the mule ahead.

spot trip. A pack trip on which the customer is taken to a designated location by horseback. The customer furnishes all provisions and equipment, which are hauled and left there by a packer. The packer and stock may return at a specified date to haul out the gear.

stirrup. A loop, ring, or other contrivance of metal, wood, or leather suspended from the saddle to support a rider's foot. The stirrup leather is a long, narrow band of leather that hangs from the skirt and is adjustable to the length of the rider's bent leg. The stirrup bar (iron) is a leather or metal bent bar on which the boot rests.

string. A group of pack animals, usually five or six, assigned to a wrangler and tied together with a lead rope for travel on the trail. Wranglers feed, shoe, pack and unpack, and take general care of the string that is their responsibility on a trip, often in cooperation with other packers.

surcingle. A leather or canvas girth or cinch passing over and keeping in place a blanket or pack, fastened by buckles.

swamping. Cleaning up and mucking out.

tack. All paraphanalia used on stock, including saddles, packing devices, and articles of harness.

taps (short for Spanish **tapaderas**). A leather casing, used most often by cattle wranglers, that prevents stirrups from snagging in brush.

tarp. A large piece of material, usually canvas, tied down by a hitch to cover and contain most of the items on a pack.

tether line. A rope attached to a stake driven into the ground to limit the pack animal's range of movement. Sometimes used by packers to keep stock contained when resting. Often called picketing.

throat latch. The part of the bridle that passes from the cheek straps under the animal's throat.

throw a hitch. To tie knots in a rope to secure the pack load on an animal.

tie up (a mule). To tie one hind leg of a mule to a post or tree when shoeing it to prevent it from kicking.

traveling trip. A trip that goes from camp to camp, with the pack crew and stock staying with the customer the entire trip. It can be an all-expense trip furnished entirely by the pack outfitter, or the customers can provide their own provisions and gear.

tree. The framework of a pack or riding saddle that fits over the animal's withers (front portion of the back).

turning or righting a pack. Retying a pack that has slipped to the side due to a loosened cinch or an unbalanced load.

unloaded. To be bucked off or fall from a riding animal.

vermifuges. Sprays or powders that kill pests such as ticks, deer flies, and other biting insects.

whip mule. The last mule in a string.

wrangler. One who tends horses and/or mules. The term comes from the original meaning of *wrangle*, to argue or make an uproar. Anyone hearing a wrangler's noisy interactions with pack animals can understand why the term is appropriate.

wreck. A situation in which one or more animals go off the trail, bog down in snow or mud, or for any other reason are in such a position that the packer has to cut lead ropes, repack, or, at worst, destroy a mule or horse.

Bibliography

Of the hundreds of primary sources and published materials consulted for this book, the following titles have been selected for this bibliography. Available books and publications that the reader may find of interest are listed here, in addition to the published sources found in the Notes. Most of the primary sources used in research for this book, however, are not listed. Letters, memorandums, notes, unpublished reports, most newspaper articles, and brochures are listed in the Notes only if they have been referenced in the text.

Albright, Horace Arden, and Marian Albright Schenck. *The Mather Mountain Party of 1915: A Full Account of the Adventures of Stephen T. Mather and His Friends in the High Sierra of California.* Three Rivers, Calif.: Sequoia Natural History Association, 1990.

Babb, Dave. "Fish Planting in the Eastern Sierra." *The Album* 2, no. 4 (1989).

Bade, William Frederic. "On the Trail with the Sierra Club." *Sierra Club Bulletin* 5 (1904–1905).

Barrett, Bob. *Yosemite: Where Mules Wear Diamonds*, 2nd ed. Oakhurst, Calif.: Ponderosa Printing, 1989.

Barrows, T. Eugene. "Second Lake Dam." *The Album* 3, no. 2 (April 1990).

Bates, Mrs. D. B. 1857. "Incidents on Land and Water: Or Four Years on the Pacific Coast." In Rockwell Dennis Hunt and William Sheffield Ament, *Oxcart to Airplane.* Los Angeles: Powell Publishing, 1929.

Bidwell, John. 1989. "Life in California before the Gold Discovery." In *Tales of California*, ed. Frank Oppel. Secaucus, N.J.: Castle Books, 1989. First published in *The Century Magazine* 41, no. 2 (December 1890).

Bolton, Herbert Eugene. *Font's Complete Diary: A Chronicle of the Founding of San Francisco*. Berkeley: University of California Press, 1933.

_____. "In the South San Joaquin Ahead of Garces." *Quarterly of the California Historical Society* 10, no. 3 (September 1931).

Boyd, William Harland. *A California Middle Border: The Kern River Country, 1772–1880*. Richardson, Tex.: Havilah Press, 1972.

Brewer, William H. *Up and Down California in 1860–1864*. Berkeley: University of California Press, 1966. First published 1930 by Yale University Press.

Brooks, George R., ed. *The Southwest Expedition of Jedediah S. Smith*. Lincoln, Neb.: University of Nebraska Press, 1989.

Brower, David R. "Are Mules Necessary?" *Sierra Club Bulletin* 33, no. 3 (March 1948).

_____. 1935. "Far from the Madding Mules: A Knapsacker's Retrospect." *Sierra Club Bulletin* 20, no. 1 (February 1935).

Brown, Barbara. *Transport through the Ages*. New York: Taplinger-Publishing, 1971.

Brown, Henry. "The Heyday of Packing." *Mineral King Country*, supplement (1989). Slightly different version appears in *The Californians* (September/October 1990).

_____. *Mineral King Country*. Fresno, Calif.: Pioneer Publishing, 1988.

Browning, Peter. *Place Names of the Sierra Nevada*. Berkeley, Calif.: Wilderness Press, 1986.

_____. "The Plague of the High Sierra." *The Ram's Head*, Wilderness Press Newsletter, January/February 1991.

Brunette, Murat. "Winter at Camp Nelson." *Tule River Times*, n.d.

Carr, Patrick, ed. *The Sierra Club: A Guide*. San Francisco: Sierra Club, 1989.

Caton, Dorothy M. "Garces the Traveler." *California History Nugget* 5, no. 5 (February 1938).

Caughey, John Walton. *The California Gold Rush*. Berkeley: University of California Press, 1948. First published as "Gold Is the Cornerstone" in *Chronicles of California*, University of California Press, 1948.

Challacombe, J. R. "Teller of Tall Tales." *Fortnight Magazine*, November 1955.

Chase, J. Smeaton. *Yosemite Trails: Camp and Pack-Train in the Yosemite Region of the Sierra Nevada*. Boston: Houghton Mifflin, 1911.

Clifford, Henry W. "Gregory's Express." *Early California Mail Bag*. Vol. 6. Los Angeles: The Book Club of California, 1960.

_____. "Pioneer Expressmen." *Early California Mail Bag* 4. Los Angeles: Book Club of California, 1960.

Colby, Josephine. "Kern River Canyon: The Sierra Club's Expedition—1903." *Overland Monthly*, January 1904.

Coues, Elliott. *On the Trail of a Spanish Pioneer*, vol. 2. New York: Francis P. Harper, 1900.

Craig, George A. "What Should Be Our Wilderness Policy?" *The Commonwealth, Part Two*. Vol. 40, no. 4. San Francisco: Commonwealth Club of California, 1964.

Crowley, John. "A Tribute to the Mule." *The Californians*, September–October 1990.

Daly, H. W. *Manual of Pack Transportation*. Washington, D.C.: Government Printing Office, 1917.

Dilsaver, Larry, and William C. Tweed. *Challenge of the Big Trees of Sequoia and Kings Canyon National Parks*. Three Rivers, Calif.: Sequoia Natural History Association, 1990.

Doctor, Joe. "Hengst Tells How He Transplanted Goldens." *Farmersville Herald*, January 18, 1978.

_____. *The Man Who Could Dodge Lightning*. Visalia, Calif.: Tulare County Historical Society, 1995.

_____. "Ray Buckman Was One of Early Packers Out of Mineral King." *Woodlake Echo*, November 7, 1990.

_____. "Spanish Exploratory Expeditions to Kaweah." *Exeter Sun*, February 28, 1987.

_____. "When the Mail Went Through On Time." *Exeter Sun*, July 14, 1982.

Eifler, Mark A. "Taming the Wilderness Within: Order and Opportunity in Gold Rush Sacramento 1849-1850." *California History* 79, no. 4 (Winter 2000/2001).

Elliott, Wallace W. *History of Tulare County California with Illustrations*. San Francisco: Wallace W. Elliott & Co., 1883.

Evermann, Barton W. *The Golden Trout of the Southern High Sierras*. Washington, D.C.: Government Printing Office, 1906. From *Bulletin of the Bureau of Fisheries* 25 (1905).

Farquhar, Francis P. "Exploration of the Sierra Nevada." *Quarterly of the California Historical Society*, March 1925.

_____. *History of the Sierra Nevada*. Berkeley: University of California Press, 1965.

_____. "Jedediah Smith and the First Crossing of the Sierra Nevada." *Sierra Club Bulletin* 28, no. 3 (June 1943).

_____. "The Story of Mt. Whitney: Part 1." *Sierra Club Bulletin* 14, no. 1 (February 1929).

_____. "The Story of Mt. Whitney: Part 2." *Sierra Club Bulletin* 20, no. 1 (February 1935).

_____. "The Story of Mt. Whitney: Part 3." *Sierra Club Bulletin* 21, no. 1 (February 1936).

Farris, Dan. "A Funny Thing Happened on the Way to the Woods." *The Album* 6, no. 3 (August 1993).

Fisher, Jane. "Packing, 50 Years Ago." *The Album* 3, no. 3 (July 1990).

Fouts, William D. "Yosemite's Pro-Packers: Part 1." *Horse and Rider* 26, no. 6 (June 1987).

_____. "Yosemite's Pro-Packers: Part 2." *Horse and Rider* 26, no. 7 (July 1987).

Fox, Stephen. *John Muir and His Legacy: The American Conservation Movement*. Boston: Little Brown, 1981.

Fryxell, Fritiof, ed. *Francois Matthes and the Marks of Time: Yosemite and the High Sierra*. San Francisco: Sierra Club Publications, 1962.

Gilbert, Bil. *Westering Man: The Life of Joseph Walker* Norman, Okla.: University of Oklahoma Press, 1989.

Hague, Harlan H. "Road to California: The Search for a Southern Overland Route to 1849." PhD diss., University of Nevada, Reno, 1973.

Halliday, Warren J., and Phyllis Skaggs. "A Packer Reminisces." *The Album* (Summer 1994).

Harper, John LeRoy. "The Southern Sierra of California: A Regional Plan for Integrated Recreational Development." PhD diss., University of Colorado, 1974.

Hastings, Lansford. *The Emigrants' Guide to Oregon and California*. Bedford, Mass.: Applewood Books, 1994. First published 1845 by George Conclin, Cincinnati.

"The History of the Sierra Forest Reserve." *The Morning Echo* (Bakersfield, Calif.), June 13, 1902.

Holliday, J. S. *The World Rushed In: The California Gold Rush Experience.* New York: Simon & Schuster, 1981.

Howard, Thomas Frederick. *Sierra Crossing: First Roads to California.* Berkeley: University of California Press, 1998.

Hunt, Rockwell Dennis, and William Sheffield Ament. *Oxcart to Airplane.* San Francisco: Powell Publishing, 1929.

Hutchings, James. "Packing in the Mountains of California." *Hutchings' California Magazine* 1, no. 6 (December 1856).

Hutchinson, Charles E. "Juan Crespi, Diarist." *California History Nugget,* March 1938.

Jackson, Louise. *Beulah: A Biography of the Mineral King Valley.* Tucson: Westernlore Publications, 1988.

Jepson, Willis Lynn. "Mt. Whitney, Whitney Creek and the Poison Meadow Trail." *Sierra Club Bulletin* 4 (1903).

_____. "Mules and Men." *Sierra Club Bulletin* 32, no. 5 (May 1947).

Johnston, Anna Mills. "A Trip to Mt. Whitney in 1878." *Mt. Whitney Club Journal* 1, no. 1 (May 1902).

Jones, Johnny and Dwight H. Barnes. *Following the Bells: Traveling High Sierra Wilderness Trails.* Oakhurst, Calif.: Dwight Barnes, 1994.

Junep, Herbert L. *A Chronological History of the Sequoia National Park and Vicinity.* San Francisco: National Park Service, 1976.

Kellogg, Charles W. *Up to the Clouds on Muleback.* Worcester, Mass.: David Hale Fanning Trade School for Girls, 1938.

Keough, Thomas. "Over Kearsarge Pass in 1864." *Sierra Club Bulletin* 10 (1918).

King, Clarence. *Mountaineering in the Sierra Nevada.* Lincoln, Nebr.: University of Nebraska Press, 1970. First published 1872 by James R. Osgood Co., Boston.

Le Conte, Joseph N. "Among the Sources of the South Fork of King's River." *Sierra Club Bulletin* 4, no. 4 (June 1903).

_____. "The High Sierra of California." *Alpina Americana,* 1907.

_____. "My First Summer in the Kings River Sierra." *Sierra Club Bulletin* 26, no. 1 (February 1941).

Lewis, Oscar. *High Sierra Country.* Boston: Little Brown & Co., 1955.

Livermore, Norman B., Jr. "Oh! For the Life of a Packer!" *Sierra Club Bulletin* 34 (June 1949).

_____. "A One-Man Diamond Hitch: With Suggestions on Saddling and Loading a Pack Animal." *Sierra Club Bulletin* 21, no. 1 (February 1936).

_____. "Sierra Packing and Wilderness Policy." *Sierra Club Bulletin* 32, no. 5 (May 1947).

_____. "Some High Sierra Recollections by William E. Colby." *Sierra Club Bulletin*, December 1964.

_____. "A West Side Packer on the High Trip." *Sierra Club Bulletin* 24 (June 1939).

Loverin, Orlin W. "He Knows Mountains, Mules, Men: Mules Are the Toughest." *Fresno Bee*, n.d.

McClure, N. F. "Explorations among the Cañons North of the Tuolumne River." *Sierra Club Bulletin* 1, no. 5 (1893–1896).

McLean, Rev. J. C. Letter to the editor. *Visalia Daily Times*, July 9, 1903.

Morgan, Charles. "Wendy Mule Goes in the River." *The Californians* 8, no. 3 (September–October 1990).

_____, ed. *Mt. Whitney Packers and Friends: Mt. Whitney Packers Reunion Memory Book*. Lone Pine, Calif., 1995.

"Mountain Trails Feud Heats Up." *Los Angeles Times*, January 5, 1999.

Muir, John. *South of Yosemite: Selected Writings of John Muir*. Ed. Frederic R. Gunsky. Garden City, N.Y.: Natural History Press, 1968.

Nathan, M. C. "Early California Local Mail." *Early California Mail Bag*. Vol. 10. Los Angeles: Book Club of California, 1960.

_____. "Wells, Fargo & Co." *Early California Mail Bag*. Vol. 9. Los Angeles: Book Club of California, 1960.

Olivas, Henry. "The Olivas Family." As told to B.C. Dawson. In *Saga of Inyo County*. Bishop, Calif.: Southern Inyo American Association of Retired Persons, 1977.

Oppel, Frank, ed. *Tales of California*. Secaucus, N.J.: Castle Books, 1989. First published 1890.

Orsi, Richard J., Alfred Runte, and Marlene Smith-Baranzini. *Yosemite and Sequoia: A Century of California Parks*. San Francisco: California Historical Society, 1993.

Otter, Floyd L. *The Men of Mammoth Forest: A Hundred-Year History of a Sequoia Forest and Its People in Tulare County, California.* Visalia, Calif.: Tulare County Historical Society, 2003. First published 1963.

Parsons, Marion Randall. "The Notable Mountaineering of the Sierra Club in 1902." *Sierra Club Bulletin* 5.

———. "The Twenty-Eighth Outing." *Sierra Club Bulletin* 15, no. 1 (February 1930).

Pearce, Bill C. "Overland Mail." *Early California Mail Bag.* Vol. 8. Los Angeles: Book Club of California, 1960.

Powers, Bob. *North Fork Country.* Spokane, Wash.: Arthur H. Clark Company, 1989.

———. *South Fork Country.* Los Angeles: Westernlore Press, 1980.

Randall, Marion. "Some Aspects of a Sierra Club Outing." *Sierra Club Bulletin* 5 (1904–1905).

———. "The Second Kings River Outing." *Sierra Club Bulletin* 6 (1906–1908).

Rawls, James J., and Richard J. Orsi, eds. *A Golden State: Mining and Economic Development in Gold Rush California.* Berkeley: University of California Press, for the California Historical Society, 1999.

Redinger, David H. *The Story of Big Creek.* Glendale, Calif.: Trans-Anglo Books, 1987. First published 1949.

Reid, Robert L., ed. *A Treasury of the Sierra Nevada.* Berkeley, Calif.: Wilderness Press, 1983.

Reisner, Marc. "The End of Wilderness: The Future of Our National Forests." *Natural Resources Defense Council Newsletter* 7, no. 5 (September–December 1978).

Rose, Gene. *Sierra Centennial: 100 Years of Pioneering in the Sierra National Forest.* Auberry, Calif.: Three Forests Interpretive Association, 1994.

Runte, Alfred. National Parks: *The American Experience.* Lincoln, Nebr.: University of Nebraska Press, 1979.

———. *Yosemite: The Embattled Wilderness.* Lincoln, Nebr.: University of Nebraska Press, 1990.

Russell, Carl P. *100 Years in Yosemite.* Yosemite, Calif.: Yosemite Natural History Association, 1957.

Sanderson, Charlotte. "With the Sierra Club in King's River Canyon." *Sierra Club Bulletin* 4 (1902–1903).

Savage, Milton. "Early Days Recalled at BCHC [Back Country Horsemen of California] Rendezvous." *The Kaweah Commonwealth*, March 21, 1997.

Simpson, Hank. "Horse Drive." *Preview*, June 12–13, 1986.

Small, Kathleen Edwards. *History of Tulare County, California*, Vol. 1. Chicago: S. J. Clark, 1926.

Smith, Jedediah. "Crossing Mt. Joseph." In *A Treasury of the Sierra Nevada*, ed. Robert Reid. Berkeley, Calif.: Wilderness Press, 1983.

SNEP Science Team and Special Consultants. *Sierra Nevada Ecosystems Project Report*. Addendum. Davis, Calif.: University of California, Davis, 1997.

SNEP Science Team and Special Consultants. *Sierra Nevada Ecosystems Project Report*. Summary report. Davis, Calif.: University of California, Davis, 1996.

SNEP Science Team and Special Consultants. *Sierra Nevada Ecosystems Project Report*. Vol. 1–3. Davis, Calif.: University of California, Davis, 1996.

Snyder, James B., and Walter C. Castle Jr. "Draft Mules on the Trail in Yosemite National Park." *The Draft Horse Journal*, Summer 1978.

Stamm, Henry E., IV. "Forgotten Legacy: U.S. Army Environmentalists at Yosemite." *Journal of the West* 38, no. 1 (January 1999).

Starr, Kevin, and Richard J. Orsi, eds. *Rooted in Barbarous Soil: People, Culture, and Community in Gold Rush California*. Berkeley: University of California Press, for the California Historical Society, 2000.

Starr, Walter A., Jr. "From Yosemite to Kings River Canyon, 1896." *Sierra Club Bulletin* 20, no. 1 (February 1935).

Steen, Harold K. *The U.S. Forest Service: A History*. Seattle: University of Washington Press, 1976.

Stewart, George. "Outfitting for a Mountain Trip." *Sierra Club Bulletin* 1, no. 3 (May 1903).

Sullivan, Maurice S., ed. *The Travels of Jedediah Smith: A Documentary Outline Including the Journal of the Great Pathfinder*. Santa Ana, Calif.: Fine Arts Press, 1934.

Sumner, E. Lowell, Jr. "The Biology of Wilderness Protection." *Sierra Club Bulletin* 27, no. 4 (August 1942).

Sumner, E. Lowell, Jr., and Richard M. Leonard. "Protecting Mountain Meadows." *Sierra Club Bulletin* 32, no. 5 (May 1947).

Swain, William. "Diary of William Swain." In *The World Rushed In: The California Gold Rush Experience*, ed. J. S. Holliday. New York: Simon & Schuster, 1981. First published 1849.

"Travel Slow and Tedious in Early Days of Porterville." *Porterville Recorder*, November 6, 1953.

Turner, Ed. "Turner Remembers." In *Mt. Whitney Packers and Friends: Mt. Whitney Packers Reunion Memory Book*, ed. Charles Morgan, 32-38. Lone Pine, Calif.: n.p., 1995.

U.S. Department of Agriculture. Forest Service. *The Use Book*. Washington, D.C.: Government Printing Office, 1906. Revised 1918, 1936.

Vallejo, Guadalupe. "Ranch and Mission Days in Alta California." In *Tales of California*, ed. Frank Oppel. Secaucus, N.J.: Castle Books, 1989. First published 1890.

Walker, Dale L. *Bear Flag Rising*. New York: Tom Doherty Associates, 1999.

Wallace, William. "A Night on Mt. Whitney." *Mt. Whitney Club Journal* 1, no. 1 (May 1902).

Walton, John. *Western Times and Water Wars*. Berkeley: University of California Press, 1992.

Webster, Beverly. "The Whitney Survey Party in the Sierra Nevada." *The Album*, 1993 annual edition.

White, Steward Edward. *The Mountains*. Prescott, Ariz.: Wolfe Publishing, 1987. First published 1904.

_____. *The Pass*. New York: The Outing Publishing Company, 1906.

Wierzbicki, Felix Paul. "California as It Is and as It Was." *The Californians* 12, no. 4 (April 1995). First published 1894.

"The Wilderness Home of the Golden Trout." *Sunset*, June 1959.

Wilke, Philip J., and Harry W. Lawton. *The Expedition of Capt. J. W. Davidson from Fort Tejon to the Owens Valley in 1859*. Vol. 8 of *Publications in Archeology, Ethnology and History*. Socorro, N. M.: Ballena Press, 1976.

Wiltsee, Ernest A. *The Pioneer Miner and the Pack Mule Express*. San Francisco: California Historical Society, 1931.

Wolfe, Linnie Marsh. *Son of the Wilderness: The Life of John Muir*. Madison, Wisc.: University of Wisconsin Press, 1978. First published 1945.

Woods, Robert J. "Early Staging." In *Early Transportation in Southern California*. Los Angeles: Book Club of California, 1954.

Public Libraries and Collections

Bancroft Library, Berkeley, Calif.

Beale Library, Kern County, Bakersfield, Calif.

California State Library, Sacramento, Calif.

California State University, Fresno, Henry Madden Library, Fresno, Calif.

Eastern California Museum, Independence, Calif.

Fresno County Library, Fresno, Calif.

Huntington Library, San Marino, Calif.

Inyo County Library, Independence and Bishop, Calif.

Inyo National Forest Archives, Bishop, Calif.

Laws Library, Craib Collection, Bishop, Calif.

Maturango Museum and Historical Archives, Ridgecrest, Calif.

Sequoia National Forest Archives, Porterville, Calif.

Sequoia National Park Library and Archives, Three Rivers, Calif.

Sierra National Forest Archives, Clovis, Calif.

Three Rivers Historical Society Archives, Three Rivers, Calif.

Tulare County Library, Newspaper collections and History Room, Visalia, Calif.

University of Nevada, Reno, Special Collections, Reno, Nev.

Washoe County Library, Reno, Nev.

Yosemite National Park Research Library, Yosemite, Calif.

Private Collections

Ardis Walker Library, Kernville, Calif.

Buckman Family Collection, Fresno Calif.

Charles Morgan Collection, Springville, Calif.

Crowley Family Collection, Visalia and Three Rivers, Calif.

Livermore Family Collection, San Rafael, Calif.

Loverin Family Collection, Three Rivers, Calif.

Mineral King Preservation Society Archives, Visalia, Calif.

Pogue Family Collection, Exeter, Calif.

Sweet Family Collection, Visalia, Calif.

Acknowledgments

The list of those who have contributed to this history are too numerous to relate here. Of those many who have given of their time, interest, information, tales, memories, photographs, and general support, the following people, libraries, and institutional archives deserve special mention.

My thanks go to Norman B. "Ike" Livermore Jr., wrangler, pack station owner, environmentalist, former Sierra Club director, and secretary for resources for the State of California. This 1936 Olympian has been active in the lumbering industry and an activist for wilderness and redwoods preservation. I am grateful for his unflagging support, encouragement, and extensive editorial help as well as his contribution of photographs, materials, and many wonderful tales.

I would also like to express my gratitude to the late Charles Morgan, a pack operator for many years as well as an environmentalist, conservationist, writer, and editor, who died in the fall of 1999 in a pack-station accident. His interest, stories, photographs, materials, and the time he took to carefully edit early drafts added greatly to the book.

I also thank Earl McKee Jr. for his stories; pack operators Tim Loverin and Don Bedell for their input; and wranglers John Crowley and Bruce Jackson for their photographs, contributions, and editing.

I am extremely grateful to Cathy Lean and Barbara Buckman Hansen for their Mineral King photographs; Pat and Clay Stout, who provided two hours of invaluable stories and information beside a Sierra campfire on a cold fall day; writer-historian Sophie Britten, for materials and photographs of Ord Loverin; and Jock and Ora Kay Peterson, who opened the Mineral King Preservation Society files to disclose priceless photographs and oral history tapes.

Special people working in various archives also deserve my thanks for their invaluable assistance: several employees at the Bancroft, Huntington, and Beale Libraries have helped me over a period of five years; Melanie Reusch, Maureen Weeke, Ward Eldredge, and Tom

Burge of Sequoia National Park and the Sequoia Natural History Association; Jan Cutts and Linda Reynolds of Inyo National Forest; the late Mary Anne Terstegge of the Annie Mitchell History Room at the Tulare County Library in Visalia; Bill Michaels, Kathy Barnes, and Beth Porter at the Eastern California Museum in Independence; Keith Pringle, caretaker of the Ardis Walker Library in Kernville; Linda Eade of Yosemite National Park and the Yosemite Natural History Association; and Jim Snyder, Yosemite National Park historian, trails expert, and long-time wilderness traveler, for his dedicated and extensive editing, corrections of factual material, and help on final drafts.

Finally, my gratitude extends to independent editors and the staff of Mountain Press, most importantly Gwen McKenna for her wonderful help in organizing the material and making it far more readable.

And to all who have made High Sierra packing a unique and memorable part of our American heritage, thank you.

Resources

Back Country Horsemen of California, (888) 302-2242; www.bchc.
com

California State Parks, (800) 777-0369 or (916) 653-6995; www.
parks.ca.gov/default.asp

Devils Postpile National Monument, (760) 934-2289; www.nps.gov/
depo/index.htm

Eldorado National Forest, (530) 644-6048; www.fs.fed.us/r5/eldo-
rado/

High Sierra Packers Association, Western: www.highsierrapackers.
org; Eastern: (760) 873-8405

Humboldt-Toiyabe National Forest, (775) 331-6444; www.fs.fed.
us/htnf/

Inyo National Forest, (760) 873-2400; www.fs.fed.us/r5/inyo/

Kern Valley Museum, (760) 376-6683; www.kernvalley.com/news/
museum/htm

Lassen National Forest, (530) 257-2151; www.fs.fed.us/r5/lassen/

Lassen Volcanic National Park, (530) 595-4444; www.nps.gov/lavo/
index.htm

Maturango Museum, (760) 375-6900; www.maturango.org

Plumas National Forest, (530) 283-2050; www.fs.fed.us/r5/plumas/

Sequoia National Forest, (559) 784-1500; www.fs.fed.us/r5/se-
quoia/

Sequoia/Kings Canyon National Park, (559) 565-3341; www.nps.
gov/seki/

Sequoia Natural History Association, (559) 565-3728; www.sequoi-
ahistory.org

Sierra National Forest, (559) 297-0706; www.fs.fed.us/r5/sierra/

Stanislaus National Forest, (209) 532-3671; www.fs.fed.us/r5/stanislaus/

Tahoe National Forest, (530) 265-4531; www.fs.fed.us/r5/tahoe/

Three Rivers Historical Society Museum, (559) 561-2707; www.threerivers.com/trhs.htm

Yosemite Association, (599) 379-2646; www.yosemite.org

Yosemite National Park, (209) 372-0200; www.nps.gov/yose/

Index

military, responsibilities of, 58–61; and mules, relationship with, 50, 152–57; personalities of, 3, 147–51; stories told by, 151, 171, 173–74; wages of, 13, 98, 104–5. *See also* packing, commercial; packing, recreational; packing companies; wranglers

packing, commercial: and government (*see* government); during Great Depression, 101–5; and movies, 104; during World War II, 105–6, 107–8, 125. *See also* packers; packing, recreational; packing companies

packing, military. *See* military; packers, military: responsibilities of; packing expeditions, military; pack trains: military use of. *See also* surveys

packing, recreational: early, 65–71, 75–78; environmental impact of, 107, 116–19, 120–24, 131–32, 133, 134; and fish stocking, 82–86, 101; future of, 182–83; and grazing rights, 116–17, 118–20, 123, 124–27; Park Service contracts with, 163–68; prices charged by, 47, 49, 88, 97, 98, 183; self-regulation in, 128–36; and show-business style, 108, 110. *See also* individual packer names; packers; packing companies; pack trips, recreational; Sierra Club

packing companies, 75–77, 87–88, 93–95, 141; number of, 98–99. *See also* individual packing company names; packers, packing, commercial; packing, recreational

packing equipment. *See* equipment: packing

packing expeditions, military: 40, 43–44, 57–64; difficulties of, 61–62; preparations for, 62–64.

See also military; pack trains; pack trips; surveys

pack trains, *14, 26, 66, 69, 81, 102, 121, 122, 183*; difficulties of moving, 28–29, 38, 41, 46–47, 48, 70; and emigrants, 42–44; during gold rush, 46–52; and mountain men, 41–42; military use of, 43–44; 46–47, 57–64; schedules of, 51–52, 58; size of, 38, 39, 41, 42, 44, 52, 60–61; and Spanish exploration, 37–40; and surveys (*see* surveys). *See also* packing expeditions, military; pack trips

pack trips, recreational: camping on, 27–28, 30, 32–34; difficulties on, 28–29, 67, 77, 156–57, 158–62; 174–76; early, 65–71, 76–78 (*see also* Sierra Club High Trips); food on, 14, 23–24, 26, 32–34, 67–68, 90, 92–93; preparations for, 22–24, 26, (*see also* equipment; supplies); Sierra Club High Trips, 11, 12, 22, 76, 87–95, 98, 123, 132–33, 144, 155; supplies for, *see* supplies; *See also* packing, recreational; packing expeditions, military; pack trains

Parish, Helen ("Toady"), 149

Parker, James, 70

parks, national: creation of, 61–64, 70, 72, 114–15, 116; fish stocking in, 82; lack of funding for, 182–83; military operation of, 76–77; number of visitors to, 71; trail construction in, 80. *See also* Forest Service; government; individual parks; Park Service

Park Service, 75, 96, 103, 120, 128, 130–32; relationship wtih packing companies, 163–68; and the Three-Corner-Round Pack Outfit, 169–70. *See also* government; parks, national

Parsons, Marion, 90, 95

Louise A. Jackson hails from a California pioneer family of miners, preachers, hunters, packers, ranchers, businessmen and women, politicians, teachers, public servants, road builders, and soldiers. She spent her childhood summers in Mineral King, a remote cabin community in the Sierra Nevada. While there, she spent many hours at the pack station learning packing techniques and lingo and absorbing stories.

Over the years, her occupations have included business management, elementary-school teaching, historical research, writing, and painting.

Her published works include the book *Beulah: A Biography of the Mineral King Valley*; a weekly column entitled "Educating Your Child"; numerous history articles; and poetry. After living for thirty-two years in the northern Sierra Nevada, Ms Jackson recently returned to the southern Sierra and resides in a one hundred-year-old adobe home in the foothill community of Three Rivers, near the entrance to Sequoia National Park.

In addition to *The Mule Men: A History of Stock Packing in the Sierra Nevada,* Mountain Press Publishing Company publishes a series of Roadside Geology guides, Roadside History guides, full-color plant and bird guides, outdoor guides, horse books, and a wide selection of western Americana titles, as well as The Tumbleweed Series—reprints of classic cowboy short stories and novels by the famed artist and storyteller Will James.

For more information about our books, please give us a call at 800-234-5308 or mail us your address and we will happily send you a catalog. If you have a friend who would like to receive our catalog, simply include his or her name and address. Thank you for your interest in our titles and for supporting an independent press devoted to providing high-quality books to readers interested in the world around them.

Name _____

Address_____

City _____

State_____ Zip_____

MOUNTAIN PRESS PUBLISHING COMPANY
P.O. Box 2399 / Missoula, Montana 59806
Phone: 406-728-1900 / Fax: 406-728-1635
TOLL FREE: 1-800-234-5308
E-mail: info@mtnpress.com
Web site: www.mountain-press.com